They Call Me Panda

Co-authored by

Bob "Peterman" Hunt

&

Matt "Firestarter" Hunt

ISBN: 97810966549819

DISCLAIMER

Although this book is non-fiction, names and identifying details have been changed to protect the privacy of individuals and businesses, except those giving us releases. We have tried to recreate events, locales and conversations from our memories of them. In order to maintain their anonymity in some instances we have changed the names of individuals and places, we may have also changed some identifying characteristics and details such as physical properties, occupations and places of residence and as such any resemblance to actual persons, living or dead, or actual events or places is purely coincidental.

A majority of people, in fact a vast majority of people, never finish the Appalachian Trail. Most never make it out of the state of Georgia with the starting number being almost halved by the time you reach Virginia, and by the time you reach the halfway point in West Virginia, you're down to less than one-quarter of those who set out from Springer Mountain. The reasons a person may not make it all the way are as varied as the reasons people decide to undertake the trip in the first place. Some people are just in way over their heads with no resolve, I fall comfortably into this category, my father on the other hand is a category of his own. He is stubborn and won't give up no matter what the cost.

Some people fall victim to the trail itself, for the trail takes no prisoners, rocks, roots, spider webs, puddles, mud, streams, wild animals, etc. That's just on the trail, lest we forget the ups and downs and ups and downs and ups and downs and ups and downs, well I think you get the point, the mountains. It can and does become overwhelming.

Now we come to the weather. I could tell you every day was sunshine and rainbows as father and son strolled through the woods together, but that would be a lie and I am no liar. I think in our time on the Appalachian Trail we saw it all, except thankfully, no major accumulation of snow. There was a snow shower on one bald, and one morning we woke up to an inch of snow on the ground, but all in all it was nothing. North bounders, on the other hand, who leave Georgia in the early spring do often encounter snow, but that's extra gear you must carry, and we were not about to do that.

While you are physically hiking there is no such thing as good weather, sure when you stop and set up camp it may seem nice then, but even then, the bugs make sure you are never truly comfortable. You are working and sweating so much that a crisp spring day may as well be a Vietnamese jungle and a hot dry day may as well be the inside of Satan's asshole, because there is no relief. You may think the wind is harmless enough, that is until you are one thousand feet up on a trail two feet wide that is completely unstable and carrying forty pounds on your back. The wind at your back though can be a welcomed friend, a boost up the trail or a natural bug deterrent. You learn to sleep through the whipping winds at night, but of all things out there, the wind is the easiest to deal with. The hardest thing to deal with and the bane of my entire existence is the rain.

The God damn rain. I will say for the most part we got lucky and overall it rained mostly at night except for Georgia. That's not to say we didn't get our fair share during the day. The storms we encountered seem to be biblical in proportion considering our elevation, causing us at times to seek shelter or separate for fear of lightning strikes. We've encountered parts of the trail that became running rivers themselves as the water drains from up high on the mountain. You have rain gear but it's all crap. And all this rain leads us to two things, two of my most hated things, humidity and the wet.

The God damn wet. You get used to the wet, to a degree, from the fact you sweat nonstop, but something special happens when it rains, your boots get wet. Once the boots are wet its game over man. There is nothing more uncomfortable than waking up in the morning and having to put on wet socks and slide them into wet boots, then your wet clothes, it's much like putting on a wet bathing suit. It's the very definition of cruel and unusual punishment, and because of my stupid idea all this was self-inflicted. However, so as not to completely dissuade you from continuing to read this book, there were pleasant aspects to the rain, and it was welcomed at times. There were quick showers in the middle of the day that give you a blissful cool down which didn't soak your boots, and gentle rains at night whose methodical rhythm on the shelter or tent help lull you to sleep.

Another big draw to the Appalachian Trail is the chance to spot some wildlife that's not splattered on the side of a highway or in a cage. We've sat and had lunch four feet from a doe and her fawn eating berries on the other side of a bush and we've had to run from pissed off wild hogs that got a little too close. The trail is full of wildlife and most of us don't get the chance to interact in this type of environment, let's say there is a reason the phrase, "don't poke the bear," is a thing. Animals you may have hated at home you learn to love, snakes for example. Where there are snakes there are no mice. We've come across wild hogs, wild dogs, deer, bears, even a turtle on top of a five-thousand-foot mountain. In Virginia we came across wild horses, one of which took quite a salacious liking to my father. This includes people here as well, not in a sense of coming on to my father, but rather grouped in with animals.

The people on and around the trail are amazing. As can be expected when one embarks on a journey such as this, there are quite the variety of personalities and personality disorders. There are people who hiked because "Hey, God told me to do it," yeah, okay, sure. People who hiked naked on the summer solstice. People who earn nicknames like "Buns of Steel" and "Psycho," however they may have not known that these were their nicknames. There were people who had done it before and just wanted to beat their time or inversely take their time. People trying to lose weight or maybe just got laid off and are planning the next step in life. Then there are assholes like me who say, "Hey Dad wouldn't it be cool if...." Assholes who think they made a comment in passing and end up spending their summer in the woods.

Then there is the green. Everything is green. Everything. Let that sink in. You may think, "Oh you're out in the woods, it's so colorful," well let me shut that shit down for you right now. There is mainly one color and it is green. The grass, the endless sea of trees on all sides, the bush and thickets, hell, even most the snakes I saw were green, and while your body is adjusting to your new health and diet most of your crap is green. There is no escape, and what isn't green is brown. Step after step, foot after foot, for 2,190 miles.

We'll talk about some of the places we passed through. The town that hung an elephant, a town that took us four minutes and sixteen seconds to walk through, hostels, motels, and other places, some historic sites, some haunted, and some right out of the damn Twilight Zone. The trail itself is an enigma, a different adventure for anyone who hikes it, be it a day or months.

Ideally you need to be a masochist to attempt this. You need to like pain. Everyday it's something new, a new unforeseen pain. Rolled ankles, sprains, bruises, falls, and blisters. The God damn blisters. My blisters even had blisters, so much so that we had to wrap my feet in duct tape just to make walking bearable. Hell, even your eyebrows and your fingernails will ache. It doesn't end, but it does get easier as your body adjusts, or so they told me, but my body never actually adjusted, so that's just bullshit.

Ultimately, I think we had a father and son team starting this trail believing that life is about experience. It's about doing things that a sane person would not do, and one upping the other. Neither one of us could live with the other holding this over their head. And so, for that reason it had to be done. Like I said at the start, to hell with your lofty ideals and sense of wonder. My father has chronicled our story in the coming pages. The good, the bad, and the funny. He draws mostly from journals we kept while traveling but also quite a bit on drunken recall. Remembering and telling our stories over, let's say "a glass of wine." He is an excellent storyteller with a great memory for details, or as some have called him, "a true bullshit artist." Either way, we hiked this trail and she is a cruel mistress to be sure, but you'll hear our tales, and some that we have heard, and in the end draw your own conclusions, but it is all true, so strap yourself in, here is our   story.

Chapter 1
What the Hell Was I Thinking?

What the hell was I thinking? I mean seriously, What? When I finished the trail, everyone, and I mean everyone who talked to me about the trail, the first question they asked me was, "Where did you get the idea from?" The second question is inevitably, "Why?" I must blame my mentally deficient son Matthew; believe me he was promptly written out of my will. The idea was his, at first.

The Appalachian Trail is one of those things almost everyone knows about. I don't know how we all know about it, but we do. It's part of the American Lore, especially on the East Coast and the states the trail runs through. Every now and then you see a news story pop up about a local man who hiked the trail or maybe about volunteers maintaining the trail. You see it but you don't really notice. You think, "Hmm, that was interesting," and go about your day, you never say to yourself, that's something I could see myself doing.

Like I said, I always knew about the trail, but it was two years from when the seed was planted in my mind before I took my first step on the Appalachian Trail. Originally, my son made a slight mention of the trail thinking it might be a good thing for us to do when he graduated from college. He gave me an article about the trail, an excerpt from Bill Bryson's bestselling book, "A Walk in the Woods." It was the first time I ever thought I could actually see myself doing this. Around Christmas time that year, this less than wonderful male seed of my loins asked for a subscription to Backpacker magazine, which in my mind is the Bible for those who seriously love to hike, camp, and live in the Great Outdoors. I looked into it and read the magazine. At the time they were running a two for one deal, so wham, I was now a subscriber and Matt got his only Christmas present of the year.

We had both read about "THE TRAIL," the other trails, all the different adventures to be accomplished in the outdoors, but our discussion always came back to the AT, as it is affectionately known. Imagine, as I did, stupidly, a two-thousand-one-hundred-eighty-nine mile walk from Springer Mountain in Georgia to Katahdin in Maine. No sweat, right? I thought what a wonderful experience, we could be spending the summer bonding, just father and son. We'd be living in the wilderness, depending on each other, surviving on our wit, our instincts, and forming an eternally memorable trip. Something we would have between us forever. Well the memories I pictured were a bit different from what reality dished out.

I could not stop reading about the mountains, the rivers, shelters, towns, and the people around the AT. It all seemed to lure us to the wild. One waitress we met before we left on the trip described the trail experience as, "glorious an amazing," well, she's an idiot. She had hiked part of it, but not its entirety, and some of that's true, especially the way you read about the trail in the magazines and newspapers. Bryson made the trail look like a walk through Central Park, although a walk through Central Park maybe much more dangerous. It's precisely because the AT had such a certain seduction factor that Matt and I decided we had to conquer the beast. If it were ever going to happen plans had to be made for this marvelous adventure to take place, but when? I started looking into it, why the hell not, I was retiring the next year anyway, let's do it.

I guess I should tell you a little bit about myself. I was a middle child, who growing up thought my first name for the first ten or so years was Jackass. "Hey Jackass, get this," "Hey Jackass, do that," you get the drift. But as I got older things got better, it changed to, "Hey, what's your name," and then finally my parents started remembering who I was and started calling me by my given name. There was very little attention paid to me growing up, I ran away once and they didn't notice for three days. They didn't really come looking for me, just checked to make sure I was okay.

Growing up I was told things such as, "Sorry Bob, the music on the ice cream truck means they are out of ice cream." That's the life I lived, no ice cream for Bob. When the family was functional, summer vacations were spent camping since there were six of us and Dad was cheap, camping was cheaper. We traveled all over New England early on and eventually we settled at a seasonal campsite in New Hampshire at a place called Shawtown on Danforth Pond. I grew a love for the outdoors and outdoor sports. We spent our time swimming, water skiing, and the now extinct sport of discing. We would sneak out at night and steal canoes and drink beer or have bonfires out in the woods. These were memories that would stay with me when I began to think about the AT.

Then I graduated high school and started college part time. Well, I loved cars, was a good mechanic and worked for several dealerships, but my father wanted me to do more with my life. Why do what you like? He was vice president of a large insurance company in New York City which was a forty-five-minute commute on the Long Island Railroad. Real fun. One day he took me to work with him and brought me into Human Resources at his company to apply for a job. I did the applicant testing and then an interview with a gentleman that went something like this;

"So, how did I do on the testing?"

"Well, Mr. Hunt, we can start you as an auto insurance salesman working in this building."

"Hmm, is that a supervisory position?"

"No, of course not, you will start as an apprentice and work your way up."

"What about medical benefits, pension, time off, overtime, promotions? Do I get a secretary?"

He scoffed at me. "Are you for real? I can't tell if you're being serious right now."

Then I dropped the bomb. "Do you know who my Dad is?"

Unsurprisingly, he did not take kindly to that question. I think at that point he began to realize I wasn't exactly taking him seriously. "Yes, I know who your father is. That's why we are making you this offer."

"Nepotism, I love it. Okay, then let's talk cash. How much?"

"Roughly eleven thousand."

I scoffed at him this time. "I'll get back to you on that one. Thank you for your time."

I spoke with my Dad on the train ride home, explaining how I enjoyed the mechanical jobs better. I liked to work with my hands and couldn't stand the thought of life chained behind a desk. He agreed, but then again, it's mostly because he had spoken with the human resources guy and found out how the interview went. We talked about it at length and decided we would look at other options.

He knew that many of my friends were police officers and being around cops kept me out of trouble and possibly prison. So, at the insistence of my father, I took several police tests. I got called by one Police Department with a decent starting salary and not too far from home, but still I was currently making much more as a mechanic at a Mazda dealership. Again, at his insistence, I took the police job, as he said any dealership would take me back as a mechanic if I did not like police work. Well, as they say, I hit the ground running and never looked back. I spent thirty years on the job and I loved every minute of it. I have no regrets about taking it. My father always knew what was best, just like I keep telling Matthew, his father knows best.

After the thirty years on the job, a divorce, and raising two kids and marrying my second wife, Patti, I retired and moved to a golfing community on the shore of North Carolina. A retired cop's dream. I could golf several times a week, the wife was close to the beach and the clubhouse bar was in the neighborhood. What else could a man want? Besides, I thought walking the AT couldn't be so bad, I spent half my time in the woods when I golfed anyway. That's when fate intervened.

In the summer of 2006, the golf course owners decided they were going to close the golf course from May until September to redo all the greens and tee boxes. This was it, this was the window I was looking for. Matt finished college early in May, so that gave me a time frame to plan our pilgrimage. Chris Columbus, Magellan, Lewis and Clark be damned, two out of the three got lost anyway. In my mind I would join the ranks of these great explorers. So, the call went out to Matthew.

Matthew was, let's just call it a surprise, not just the fact that he was born, but was the fastest swimmer in the bunch of two million. Eight years after his sister was born, I drank a fateful case of Coors Light at a barbecue, and the rest is history. Matthew's mother and I amicably split when he was six, so he spent his weekends and summers with me. When my daughter Kathy graduated high school, he moved from New York down to Georgia with his mother. Still I made my trips down to Atlanta and he would spend his summers in New York with Patti and myself. He graduated high school and went to college at the University of Tennessee in Knoxville, which is only about 40 miles from the AT. Perhaps it was spending all that time in the hills of east Tennessee that sparked the idea.

I had a habit of calling him on Friday nights after I'd watch the television show "Joan of Arcadia" and had maybe a few too many glasses of wine. For those who don't know, the show is about a young girl that God speaks to through different people and helps Joan learn life lessons, and as Matthew would say, blah blah blah. I would call him when the show ended, before his night would even begin and share God's lesson for the week. I did it because I know in my heart he treasured these calls, he would be waiting on the edge of his seat every Friday. That is how I broke the news to him.

So, sticking to my schedule I called him and he answered. "Yeah, yeah, so what did God teach Joan this week?"

"What son. No hello for your father?"

"I think we both know where this is going and I'm up next in Beer Pong."

"It's good to see your tuition paying for itself. The lesson this week is "all who wander are not lost," and actually, it's a great segue for the next part of our conversation, anything you need to tell me before we get started?"

I loved doing that to him, using my interrogation skills to get him to admit to things he might have done before I found out about them through other channels, but he's wised up to it over the years.

"No Dad, nothing to admit, I'm good."

"Well they're shutting down the golf course for the summer to redo the greens."

"I'm sorry to hear that, sounds like it will be really tough on you."

"Tough on us son, tough on us." All I heard on the line were crickets as I'm sure a million scenarios played through his mind as to how the golf course closing would be hard on him.

He could only answer, "Uh, okay, how's that now?"

"We're going to hike the AT."

Now this being Friday night his response was not unreasonable. "Dad, have you been drinking?"

"It's Friday night and Joan of Arcadia is on, of course I've been drinking, but I think we should do this anyway. It's not like you have a job and you're missing out on anything."

I think in his mind he began to realize I was serious and that all his romanticizing over hiking the Appalachian Trail may have been an error in judgement.

"Gee Dad, I don't really have the money to lay out for a trip like this."

"Don't worry about that son, I can add it to the hundred-twenty-thousand you owe me for school. Or are we even for the school t-shirt you bought me at the gift shop?"

"Well, it is a nice shirt…"

"Yeah, I don't think so. What do you think? Let's do it."

"Free has always been the right price. I guess so."

I didn't waste any time as there was much to do. Research needed to be done, equipment purchased, maps assessed, first aid kits put together, food, accommodations made, mail drops needed to be packaged and prearranged. So much planning was required it boggles the imagination. This was, after all, an epic undertaking of immense proportions which needed to be well thought out and properly executed. Months in the woods with life and death situations loomed in the future for us, we needed to be prepared. I spent hours upon hours laboring over the computer, other resources, contacts, and previous hikers. Since Matthew was in school this was not done by father and son together but done by father alone. We wouldn't want to interrupt the frat parties, beer pong and over the hump Wednesdays. I don't mean to sound like a martyr, but he would have died without me and all the research I did, the equipment I bought, all the planning was mine. The scheduling? All me. Mail drops? Me again. Everything.

I had all the maps with elevation charts delivered to my home in North Carolina. I cut out of these maps the elevation tables and trail profiles, which gave elevation, water sources, shelters, and other landmarks along the way. By doing this we could always tell roughly how far we were from the nearest water supply, but perhaps most importantly we knew how far to the next shelter and how many peaks we would have to climb that day. We could see just how steep our climb would be or if we would be on a ridgeline for most the day. These maps were vital for planning how far you would hike each day. I scoured the annual AT Hiking Companion, which really is a necessity on the trail, and found the best places to have mail drops delivered. I spent my time grocery shopping to plan an entire summer's worth of meals for two, boxing them up, and planning timetables so my wife could send them as we were approaching the next town. I studied all the

Backpacker Magazine reviews on backpacks, boots, clothing, water filtration systems, and everything else you think you need. It's a learning process and most importantly you learn that you don't need half the shit you think you do. I would practice setting up my tent in the yard and would walk the loop in my community with a backpack loaded with forty pounds of bricks. I would be prepared if nothing else, or so I thought.

2,189 miles to go.

Chapter 2
The Start

I t was a sunny crisp spring day, the kind of day you would expect in the mountains of North Georgia in May. It was not unlike the hundreds of others I've experienced, but this unassuming spring day was different, it was D-Day and we were storming the beaches. A slight breeze hung in the air, there were birds chirping, children playing, barbecues, church socials, pickle ball courts in full swing, not that anyone knows what pickle ball is, but all was right in the world. Suddenly and without warning, veering off an old cracked asphalt highway onto a country dirt road, a bronze colored Mazda 626 sped spewing dust and stones into the air as it navigated the rapidly rising mountain in front of it. As the driver I should have seen this road as a clear and obvious foreshadowing of what was to come with all the sharp turns, potholes, and steep uphill climbs.

Yes, this is the beginning of the story.

The trail doesn't just start on the side of the road somewhere, no that would be too easy. There is no parking lot where you just pull up and go on your merry little way. The trail begins eight or so miles up on Springer Mountain. For those who do get dropped off on the side of the mountain there is the approach trail. Many hikers choose to hike up the Appalachian approach trail from nearby Amicalola Falls State Park, it's a steep uphill climb and a brutal introduction to the AT, but well-traveled to say the least.

It is the only way in for those who don't happen to live in Georgia and have rides readily available. Those that chose this route would shelter their first night on the top of Springer Mountain and officially start the trail the next day. It's not even part of the AT so those miles didn't count. Freakin' amateurs.

Had they done the research I did, they would have found a dirt road that is one-tenth a mile from the starting point. So, my son, my family, and I parked on the edge of the road where it crosses the trail. Matt and I headed the one-tenth of a mile to the starting point, which was marked by a simple bronze plaque in the ground. We spent an hour taking pictures and what would be our first of many photo ops. In retrospect, walked doesn't fit the way we headed toward that plaque, rather we strutted that one-tenth mile, then had our pictures taken by attending and adoring family members, who are also very possibly the heirs to my estate should I perish on this trek. We made our mark in the log at the first shelter atop Springer Mountain. It housed those who took the suckers route. We made our mark knowing that book would be worth a fortune one day. After countless poses and holding smiles like idiots for the camera we headed back to the lot and returned to the motel. That night we sat down to what might be our last decent meal for some time to come.

Now mind you we were in the middle of nowhere Georgia, there wasn't exactly a Longhorns on the corner, but we would come to find that was part of Appalachia's charm. The clerk at our hotel recommended a small Mom and Pop restaurant that was close to where we were staying, with, and I quote, "the best gizzards in the county." We forwent "the best gizzards in the county" and settled on the classic American meal instead. Dinner was of course a nice medium rare steak, baked potato with lots of butter, vegetables, and an ice cream sundae for dessert. The dinner conversation was fast and furious.

While eating dinner I turned to my beloved wife Patti, who was graciously allowing me to leave her alone for months on end while I walked in the woods and I asked her, "Gee Honey, you going to miss me?"

Without missing a beat, and I personally believe she rehearsed her answer, she said, "You just go ahead and take as long as you need to finish the trail dear." She didn't even bother looking up from her plate.

"But your Stud Muffin will be gone for months."

"I'll manage somehow Stud Muffin. Watch out for bears and snakes. I'd hate to have to collect on that two and a half million-dollar insurance policy."

Stud Muffin didn't know if she was kidding or not. When Patti finally did glance up the look on her face was terrifying, like the twisted smile you'd see on the Joker's face as he's fleeing after beating Batman, laughing maniacally the whole time. I felt like telling her I changed the beneficiaries, but she has power of attorney and would have changed them back. Anyway, I would have put down my son and daughter, and if I should kick the bucket out here, Matt was going with me, or before me in all likelihood.

After dinner wrapped up, we headed back to our humble country motel. It was important that we got a good night sleep because in the morning there was no looking back. That night I wasn't exactly a bundle of nerves, but sleep wasn't what I hoped it would be. Here I was thinking of a night of fully satisfying sex with the wife, but her idea was to have the girls in one room and the boys in the other. Just great. Matthew was fast asleep in the bed besides mine. To make matters worse, he was dreaming and whimpering in his sleep, thrashing about like a helpless puppy. Fantastic, I'm sharing a tent with him. I couldn't help but think ahead imagining what tomorrow would bring, what each day would be like, and the endless combinations of fatal accidents awaiting us.

The morning finally broke. There was a nervous excitement buzzing around us. If Matthew was worried, he wasn't showing it, but I knew he was. I also knew that I would be twice as stoic as him because he would pounce the first chance he got if I showed the slightest hint of nerves. We got our packs in order, donned the clothes we would wear for the next several days, and headed to the local diner in town. With barely taking a breath we ate a quick hearty breakfast, slammed black cup of Joe, and piled back into the Mazda to make our way back up to the top of Springer Mountain for the final time.

God, I remember that day like it was yesterday. We eventually decided that we were, in fact, ecstatic and the nerves began to melt away. We were starting on a life altering experience, one in which few ever endeavor, and it would also provide us with an ample source of braggadocio in the future. We were all smiles. The family had once again come to see us off, or should I say drop us off. Matthew and I posed for our last few pictures at the trailhead before we started into the woods. It was a typical scene that you would witness at an airport drop off, there were hugs, kisses, and well-wishing as we prepared to take those fated first steps. Nobody shed any tears, which now that I think about it was very disappointing. I mean I didn't expect my son-in-law to shed a tear, but my daughter, my own flesh and blood, hearing a "Gosh, I'll miss you Dad," would have been nice, and my wife, well she was showing her true colors. She was smiling as though she had just won the lottery and she kept that shit eating grin on her face. I wasn't feeling the love in this particular moment. Daylight was wasting as they say, so I left an opening for her to wish us luck, but just silence.

"Well, I guess Matt and I should get going then, we gotta do thirteen miles today. Any last words for us?" As I asked this I was staring directly at Patti, hoping she would get the hint and play the distraught wife. In my mind I wanted to see her as an old sailor's wife on the widow's walk, staring longingly out at the sea, awaiting the return of her mate. I realized later in her mind she saw herself as burning her bra and singing "Freedom Hallelujah" over and over. So much for that fantasy. I was beginning to think she didn't believe we would do it.

Eventually she said, "Sure, I'll see you two in a few days after one of you pushes the other off a cliff. If I don't see you in a few days, it's because you two idiots are probably lost in the wilderness."

"You won't be seeing me for a while Hon, Matt might punk out but I'm made of steel and you will be seeing me in Maine on top of Katahdin." I didn't believe a word of it, but it needed to be said. Inflection and tone are important.

"Right, go ahead and be stubborn to prove a point. Either way I win."

"What does that mean?"

"It means I love you. Okay ladies, and you too Noel, everybody back in the car, Lewis and Clarke here need to be on their way."

And so it was.

I wholeheartedly believed I was ready for those first few steps. I had been mentally preparing myself for over a year and physically preparing for months. Matthew prepared by running to the liquor store every day, eating and drinking every beer and taco in town before spending his summer in the woods with his father and leaving his friends behind. Imagine the horror. Only we didn't have to

23

imagine it, our bodies lived it and Matthew would soon come to learn what "toughing it out" was really like.

I would walk everyday around the three-mile circle in my neighborhood to ensure I was in shape and to break in my boots. These three miles had no bearing whatsoever on being "trail ready" as we would call it. I did manage to break in my boots which would be of great comfort to me. Matthew though? Not so much. I even took extra steps of precaution. Over the course of my research, I found some people use products like "Tough Feet" or "Rhino Feet." It was this red solution that I would cover the heels and soles of my feet with. They use it on horses to toughen their hooves. I should have just drank it and ended this whole thing before it got off the ground. For you chemistry majors, it's basically an acid that eats the skin on your feet and in turn toughens them up like leather. I didn't know if it would work or not and what kind of effect it would have, but luckily, I had Matthew to use as my control group in this experiment. Not knowing if the sole hardening solution worked or not made it easy to save a little bit of cash and skip buying Matt his own bottle. Oops. Talk about hindsight and all of that.

We strapped on our backpacks, tied our bandanas tight, and checked the laces on our boots one last time. Now realize, these backpacks were our lifeline, so to speak. These huge vinyl sacks held almost everything we needed for the next few months. I tried to go light with all I ordered, but I soon learned with every day that I hiked, I could have gone lighter

Throughout our hike certain equipment was lost in favor of lighter equipment and some was just plain old lost. Matt had a knack for losing headlamps, which is rather remarkable if you think about it, since you know, they are strapped to your head and all. The backpack we carried, and this is just some of this stuff, not all; a sleeping bag, blow up mattress, tent, food, water, rope, fuel, first aid, stove, rain gear, extra clothes, and so on and so forth. This forty-pound Quasimodo type hump on your back was strapped over your shoulders and around your waist with straps that seldom felt comfortable. And for people who were not, as we called it, in "trail shape," this meant the straps digging into your fleshier parts. Then there was a myriad of smaller straps to adjust load, tension, and God knows what else. I could get in and out of a suit of armor quicker than I could my backpack. I think most hikers understood quickly that the weight of your backpack is important.

Day three on the trail gets you to Neels Gap. The people at the outdoor store in the gap will rummage through your pack and start dumping things onto the floor to be discarded or sent home, the whole time laughing at you behind your back, and sometimes to your face. I saw them take a blow dryer out of a woman's backpack. Like everything else on the trail your backpack is a learning experience. What worked at the beginning of the trail may not necessarily work for you in the middle or the end.

So back to the story.

It was a left turn into the woods from where we stood on that dirt logging road. Now I'm not what you would call a praying kind of man, but I said a quick little prayer to any or all the gods that would listen.

"God please don't let me look like an asshole in front of my son. Keep my body from falling apart before his and I swear I'll finish this damned trail. Buddhist God, if I die on this trail, do not reincarcerate me, I don't want to do this shit again. Thanks."

We ducked into the woods and began our new normal. When all was said and done, we believed we

25

would return after this trip as heroes to those who knew us. An awakening was on the horizon for both of us. A maelstrom. Pandemonium. What a difference a day makes, that is so true. Hell, it's only five million steps. 4,999,999 to go.

Still 2,189 miles to go.

Chapter 3
Lessons Learned

As we've established several times already Springer Mountain is in Georgia. That's the start of the Appalachian Trail, so we bore left and ventured forth. It was early May, and at our elevation and location in the north Georgia mountains it was still quite cold. We wore sweatshirts to start our days in the beginning and would peel them off as we warmed up. Matthew, of course, had not thought this far ahead, to him May equals warm. Luckily, I brought an extra sweater for him, it was white with giant red letters that said, "Bob's Sweater." He was close to having Bob as his trail name. Instead though, his sister beat everyone to the punch. When Matthew was younger, he was a big fan of Lord of the Rings, and if you don't know what that is then you need to get out from underneath your rock and join us here in the real world. My daughter noted his more Hobbit like qualities and just like that he was "Frodo." He didn't like the name, but I didn't care. Myself, besides being cynical and sarcastic, I bore a resemblance to the character "Peterman" on an old Seinfeld episode. That nickname had been given to me at work, so I kept it as a trail name. One can only imagine what some others may have chosen to call me.

Survival note: Start the trail with your own trail name, don't let others name you for various reasons.

For our first day we planned to do thirteen miles, it should have been a realistic look at what we could expect going forward. All the books said to start easy, and hey, easy is my lifestyle. It was nine o'clock in the morning when we finally set out. In four quick hours we should have been at the shelter, doing three miles an hour, a nice relaxing stroll. From what we could see of the sky it looked like storms were brewing, but this is the mountains and that happens here all the time, so we weren't worried. By four o'clock my thoughts had changed drastically. This was by far the most grueling walk I have ever undertaken in my life. I am walking in a dense green fog of trees, pollen, and bushes that eternally go up to windy mountain tops and then down into stifling valleys where there was absolutely no air movement whatsoever. The father/son bonding didn't start out well either. We talked very little that first day, mostly because neither of us could catch our breath. What little talking we did was only on the downhills, it's easier on your lungs, but not your knees, they will start to ache beyond imagination.

I believe for the average person there is truly no way you can prepare physically for this trail. Sure, you can try to get in shape, we tried, but forty pounds on your back while clambering uphill and downhill is something to experience. You can train for that, but in reality you are stepping on unseen rocks and roots, rolling your ankles, testing the strength of your tendons and muscles, and testing your fortitude. Even your toes will be tested like never before, our first night I spent a solid twenty minutes wiggling my toes in my sleeping bag, and I know Matt was doing the same since his feet were right next to my face. The only true way to prepare for this hike is to hike and even then a long-distance trail like the AT is a monster all its own.

You learn quickly that your only scenery is nothing more than the trail immediately in front of you. It was said to me by a hiking buddy, and I believe it to be true, that a herd of giraffe could be ten feet off the trail to your left or right and you would not see them. To prove this point, there was a section of the trail in New York as you come around a bend, and if you're busy watching every foot placement, you will not see the twenty some odd plastic pink Flamingo statues on the hillside approximately thirty feet from the trail. I missed them till I heard a startling, "Hey!"

Now you need to understand that you are "in the zone" while hiking and hearing any loud noise, let alone a shout is quite startling. You become use to the sound of your breathing and easily get lost in your thoughts. It's a sort of an autopilot, your mind becomes programmed to scan for the two R's, roots and rocks. You become "The Terminator."

So naturally a loud noise stopped me dead in my tracks. A fellow hiker and I had been hiking a few miles apart that day and he should have been well past this section, but I thought perhaps he had hurt himself and was lying on the ground helpless. You know, all the things a concerned fellow hiker would think. Instead I looked over and saw an old guy sitting in a lounge chair laughing at me. "Don't worry young fella," he laughed, "you're the fifth one through today and no one has seen them yet."

While I was relieved it was pink Flamingos and an old man, it still seems a strange sight to chance upon in the woods.

"What's with the pink Flamingos?" I asked.

"Hiked the trail years back, missed a lot of scenery and realized why."

"Why's that?" I couldn't wait to hear his words of wisdom.

"Hiked too fast, didn't see much so now I do this to bring awareness to you hikers. No better way to spend a day, drinking a few beers and laughing as you all walk by."

It's not often that you can grab a beer while hiking, so I asked if he had an extra beer. "Sure, and an extra chair, take a seat." We sat and chatted for some time, but no other hikers came through. I had pounded down a few beers and told him I had to be on my way, I needed to catch up to my fellow hiker. I described him to the old gentleman, he mentioned he had seen him go by, but the hiker had not noticed the flamingos.

While on the subject of watching almost every footstep, never try to look right or left while walking, other than a quick glance, or you will end up hurting yourself. Stop. Then look. Another lesson I learned over and over.

For our first night we camped on top of Sassafras Mountain, out of the thirteen miles we planned on we ended up doing eleven, so although we didn't hit our target, we were still pretty proud of ourselves. At this point we didn't realize the difference between staying in a shelter and doing what was called "stealth camping." There are definite benefits going shelter to shelter and for the most part they are spaced at reasonable distances. We did not understand that yet, we were rookies, but like everything else that first day offered, our first night would be a learning experience too. We came across a tent site that was just a few feet off the trail. It was overgrown, we were novices, sleeping in a small double tent. Like I said before "stealth camping," it was a stone's throw from the trail and invisible to someone hiking past. It seemed so primitive that it had to be right.

The sky was growing darker and like any survival situation our first concern was shelter. We had run this drill a dozen times in preparation for this exact moment. We were ready this time, we could get this tent up in a minute flat. We had practiced at home, in a cleared out living room, in perfect conditions and only had to order a few extra poles in a friendly environment, so we should be fine here, right?

It's hard to believe these poles bend like that without snapping, but there comes a point where they do snap. It happened several times, chalk it up to just another learning experience. Put the right pole in the right spot. Well it doesn't always go that easily. We manned our stations, Matt spread the tent apart while I snapped all the poles into place. Once we had done that Matt would hold up the tent so I could easily slide the poles through their assigned slots, and just like that we had a tent. And that's exactly how we would do it after about a week of trying. The rain was starting to come in at this point and we ended up with a comedy of errors rather than a quick assembly of our tent. First, I put the wrong poles in the wrong slots and when correcting the problem the wind picked up so Matt couldn't hold the tent properly without it whipping around him. Then another lesson we learned, never take your frustration out on your equipment. I jammed one of the poles into its loop to create a base to work from and I ended up ripping through the loop. Cheap piece of shit tent, luckily nothing some duct tape couldn't fix later. It took longer than expected but we got that damn tent up.

Fortunately, we did get it up just before it started raining in earnest. Unfortunately, that's all we got done before the torrential downpour came. This we would find to be another benefit of staying in shelters. There is not much to do at four-thirty in the afternoon when it's raining and you only have a tent for shelter. One can get a bit stir crazy. It was still raining when we finally decided it was dinner time at four-thirty-five. We didn't want to sit in the rain and cook something then have all the clean up afterwards, so we ate cold cereal. I don't recall this in any of the books I read, but I knew not to light the stove in the tent, I guess all these survivalists assume we have common sense.

Additionally, due to the haste in which the rain came nothing else had been set up in the tent. Here we are, two full size men, I call my son a man here in size only, not mental capacity, in this little six by four by three cubicle with our two very full backpacks. Now we had to blow up our mattresses, roll out our sleeping bags, all this without hurting ourselves or each other. Man do I wish I had a video of that one. It had to look hysterical if you could have peeled the top open and watched. We would blow up our mattresses, which took about a hundred breaths, then tried to get them under us without popping them, and we were constantly in each other's way. This was more of a Laurel and Hardy routine than a Greek comedy. A lot of crawling, cursing, and bumping heads. Finally, mission accomplished, the sleeping bags were rolled out, but now we realized the backpacks would not fit in the tent with us, as we ourselves barely fit. Since I had read all the books, I remembered one said to always carry a fifty-gallon trash bag, because like duct tape, it would have many uses. Its first job was keeping our packs dry as we placed them in the green bag, tied them shut and placed them outside the tent. We realized, somewhat to our dismay, on this rainy night that we could only fit and sleep in the tent with my head facing his feet and vice versa. So, like small children do, we slept head to toe.

It was still early, too early to crash and go to sleep, so we talked about our accomplishments of the day.

"Okay, so we're through day one Matt, and we're both still alive and unhurt."

"Better than that we're still talking to each other. I hope every day isn't going to be like this."

"We need to get better at setting up the tent. This could have been a miserable night if we got soaked. Good thing we stopped when we did."

"What do we do now? It's only five-thirty. How about Gin Rummy?"

We played for a time then I decided to study the topography maps and the Thru Hikers Guide. For the next hour or so I strapped on my headlamp and scrutinized the material hoping the route would look easier the more I studied it. Not so. Matt did some journal writing and then was fast asleep. I wish I could fall asleep like he does.

The rain, I thought would help me sleep with the sweet light pitter patter of falling drops on the tent's waterproof cover. Let me tell you this, if you set your tent up under a tree, there is no rhythmic pattern to the rain. Some light rain hits the cover, but when the wind gusts there are huge crashes of what seems like a whole bucket of water coming off the tree leaves, yet another lesson learned. Are you still having trouble catching on to the theme of this chapter yet?

Matt had fallen asleep at about seven PM, poor little guy was tuckered out. There is something magical about watching your children sleep, just not when they are twenty, sleeping an inch away from you while snoring and farting all night. Earplugs became a must sleeping with Matt, and I made a mental note to pick up some for myself. He must have allergies or a deviated septum to make those unholy noises.

Another mental note; have Matt see an allergist when we get home, nothing about these noises is what I would refer to as normal. I slept from eleven PM to four AM. Matt also woke up in the early hours of the morning. It was raining and dark, so what else can you do but lay there and wait for the sun. Good first day my ass.

Morning finally broke and freed us from our nylon prison. Neither one of us slept well. Don't get me wrong, we both slept hard for a few hours each, but not well. Our bodies demanded at least a few hours comatose. Once it is light out and someone starts stirring in the tent there is no going back to sleep. The sound of the zipper on the tent became the alarm clock. This was mostly true for Matt, as I was usually the first one up. That first morning was also a mess, there was no rhythm to our routine, but it wasn't quite as bad as the night before.

We emerged from our tent to be greeted by a damp wet cold world. I was hoping for a magical Disney type sunny morning. I imagined Mister Bluebird on my shoulder and a bouncing, smiling sun in the sky. Instead everything was wet from the past night's rain. I'd be damned if I was starting this day cold and wet without a hot breakfast. I pulled the trash bag off our backpacks and used Matt's bandana to squeegee the water off the bags, I doubt he'd notice. I dug out our MSR stove, screwed in the gas tank that Matt was carrying in his bag, gave it a few pumps, and behold, I have created fire and heat. Matt was still barely moving but he was showing signs of life. He perked up considerably when he heard the mild roar of the small stove.

"Oh, so your father cooking breakfast is enough to get you moving?" Matt kicked off his sleeping bag and unzipped the screen from the tent.

"Well breakfast in bed is preferable, but I've been on earth long enough to know that is probably a pipe dream."

He was right on that one. "Okay, I'll make you a deal," I told him. "You go deflate our air mattresses and roll them up, oh, and our sleeping bags too and I'll cook breakfast." I think he was more shocked that I would make such an offer and he didn't really have the time to think about it.

"Sure, that will take two minutes. You go ahead and get started on my breakfast chump."

I think he believed he was getting the better of me, but all I was doing was sitting and boiling water while he was putting my things away. Idiot kid.

While we ate our breakfast, we watched other hikers start passing us by. We looked at each other puzzled, where the hell did they come from? How the hell did they get up so early? We would find out in the future that they were the normal ones, getting up at normal times. But we had survived day one, so, whatever. We obviously had not figured out the division of labor when it came to our chores in those first few days, but we eventually set up a system.

We were now staring down the barrel of another twelve-mile day and we didn't even finish our first twelve-mile day. As we took our first few steps Matt threw his bandana on his head, "Jesus, this thing is sopping wet and freezing. What did you use it for? To dry our bags?"

I kept a straight face, as any good father should in this teachable moment. "No son, you must have left it out overnight, I'll bet you won't make that mistake again." I laughed inside as I saw him racking his brain trying to remember if he had left it out or not.

The second day was nothing but up and down mountains that to us were unbelievable. The guidebook called them hills, but that's a bunch of horse shit.

Fun Fact: Hiking the entire Appalachian Trail is equal to climbing up and down Mt. Everest sixteen times from sea level, a total of 464,500 feet in elevation changes. Something I am glad I found out later, that might have been a deal breaker.

2,168.4 miles to go.

Chapter 4
Rainy Days in Georgia

It's funny how routine every day becomes yet each day is completely different from the one before it. The terrain may be similar, but each step is a new opportunity to break the routine and your ankle while you're at it. That second day we began forming a routine which included a stop every half hour to hydrate. However, at this point neither one of us was flexible enough to reach back and grab our own water bottle from our side pouches. Matt would get my bottle, I would get his, and I'm sure we looked ridiculous, but it worked for us.

After every two hours we would have an extended stop to snack and shed our packs for a minute. Sometimes we munched on salted peanuts and other times it was homemade jerky Patti had prepared for us. Lunch for the next few months on the trail would basically consist of tuna in a foil packet with packets of mayo squirted into it, eaten with our sporks, and we learned to love it. You pick up on what other people are doing out here as well. We came across a guy eating tuna in oil rather than water, which we were accustomed to. We found tuna with oil was much better than tuna with water, it's tastier, with a much more palatable consistency, and most importantly it contained more calories.

With our scheduled stops now in place we set out to conquer Georgia. Georgia is by no means the toughest part of the AT. It only seems that way because you are going up and down extreme elevation changes in relatively short distances. Blood Mountain, for instance was a fifteen-hundred-foot climb and you do not have your hiker legs yet. That takes about two weeks if you survive. The gasping and heavy breathing are all part of starting the trail and for most people that is in Georgia. So, the math adds up, most people quit in the first few days, which still puts them in Georgia. They are tired, out of breath, injured, or have had their romantic image of hiking the trail shattered in those first few days. It's really no wonder that Georgia carries a reputation.

We decided that we would give the shelters a try after our experience that first night. Shelters along the trail are basically wooden boxes that can sleep six to fourteen people. A floor, three sides, and a roof. The sizes and shapes of these shelters, also known as lean-tos, vary as much as the camp sites they were built on. You could stop for the night at a shelter on the top of a mountain at four-thousand feet, be down in a valley, or nestled on the side of a mountain. Some are right on the trail, others a bit of a hike down a side trail. Some seem to be a few sticks of wood nailed together and others are a gazillion years old. I swear we stayed at a shelter in South Carolina that probably housed Revolutionary War soldiers. I'm pretty sure I saw at Francis Marion's name carved into the back wall. And on that note, they are also covered with hikers' names carved into the wood, or sometimes just plain graffiti, or stupid hiking limericks.

Most of these places you accept as naturally a bit grungy. They are, after all, miles deep into the woods. You'll usually find a broken broom head and a dustpan in one of the corners so you can sweep them out, but really who wants to do that after hiking all day. However, there are a few of these things I wouldn't mind living in. They are clean and luxurious. In one of the shelters up north there is even a shower and pizza delivery service, which you bet your ass we were going to take advantage of.

We will discuss that one of the main problems we experienced in the shelters occurred when the guidebook said it sleeps six, there is usually a seventh asshole trying to squeeze in. It gets tight fast when you are cramming bodies together. I hated those people. They were late arrivals banging around after dark when everyone else has gone to sleep. Occasionally, there were smokers in the shelter, it's not common but it does happen. I never got that one, hike twelve or so miles and then light up a cigarette, but then again, I would have killed for a cold beer.

Rather than pitching our tent again we decided to quarter at Gooch Mountain Shelter, our hiking prowess was not impressive yet, we only did five miles that day. The next shelter was twelve miles past Gooch, and that was not going to happen.

I had a way of turning things around so it would seem like I wanted to go for it, but Matt didn't. "Well Matt, the next shelter is twelve miles, it's a bit early to call it quits, so lets rest up and make for the next shelter." I knew there was no way he would want to do that, he wasn't a complainer, but I knew he was a bit lazy.

"I don't know Dad, you know it's already the middle of the afternoon and we aren't really ready for that kind of day, and we don't want to overdo it, and this shelter is the nicest one we've seen yet. Look there is already firewood cut up…." The excuses just poured out of him. I agreed with him entirely but couldn't let him know that.

"But we've only seen two so far," I hated to agree with him, but this shelter was pretty nice. "Oh, come on, we can do it, I'm sure the next shelter is nice too. Besides, I think I'm starting to get the hang of this."

He looked at me about to give in and call my bluff. I couldn't let that happen. "But I guess this would give me time to catch up on our journal."

Matt breathed a huge sigh of relief and unclasped his pack. We could always make up the mileage later. Sure, Gooch was a new shelter and in extremely great shape compared to what we would see later, in fact it was even a double-decker, but it was our first shelter experience.

The water source nearby was a spring and it had a privy, which is an outdoor toilet, and they all varied, but this was the first one I'd seen. Since it was early we could get our chores done quickly. Out came our water filter, a cartridge with a hose that had a small filter on the end of it that you throw in the water source and start pumping. It really wasn't a one-man job either, one person had to pump while the other held that line and collapsible water pouch we used. In coming weeks this piece of crap constantly needed cleaning, weighed about a pound, and we determined it to be useless. After observing what other hikers used to acquire water, we decided it would be replaced by two tiny little squeeze bottles called Aqua-Mira. The Aqua-Mira weighed next to nothing and killed almost all bacteria and viruses, or so the label said. The only trouble with Aqua-Mira was it did not filter the water per say, it left sediment and coloring in the water. There were times we drank brownish water from some of the faster flowing water sources. It was always interesting adding our Gatorade packs to the brackish water, the colors were less than appetizing.

For the most part your water sources are springs straight from this side of the mountains, which is the ultimate filter. Some of the best and obviously freshest water I've ever tasted was on the trail. However, everyone was afraid of catching Giardia, a bacterium in some water, which would cause a case of the Hershey squirts for two or three weeks, thus the reason for filtering. You needed to keep hydrated if this happened, and sometimes water was hard to find, plus the more you hydrated the more you squirted. At any rate, you needed to carry extra water which was weight on your back and extra toilet paper, known commonly as "trail dollars." Basically, Giardia sucked and might cause you to step off the trail for a week or more.

Mind you this is still early in our adventure. We had yet to figure out which foods were easiest to make and clean up after. You don't want the scent of food lingering in or near your campsite. We made a hot dinner at Gooch, macaroni and cheese. I probably can't say what brand we ate but you'd recognize that cheesy goo sauce from the commercials. It also happens to rhyme with schmell schmeeta. What a bitch it is to clean up that stuff in the wilderness. That cheese could be used as glue in an emergency. It stuck to everything. It was delicious though, after a long day hiking everything was delicious. We would always say as we ate our dinners, "PFG", meaning "pretty fucking good."

Setting up in a shelter is much easier than a tent. They are first come, first served, with the exception of a few places in National Parks where thru hikers are supposed to have priority. As soon as you get to the shelter you throw your backpack on the spot you are claiming for sleeping. Some shelters can get crowded, then you will have to tent or "cowboy camp," sleeping under the stars. You also learn that some spots are better than others to sleep in. If you take a corner, critters in the shelter that come out at night tend to run, or slither, along the walls. Many was the time I could feel a mouse run over my hand, and on occasions over my face. If you slept in the middle you never knew who would be coming in and crashing next to you, so you take your chances with that. I preferred to take my chances with the critters and usually set up shop in corners. Besides, in my mind I pictured the bear snatching someone from the middle of the shelter where it could get a better angle. Matt was a good buffer for that too.

After all is said and done, and you are finished with dinner and you are ready to sleep, you then hang your food bag. This is mostly because of bears, but raccoons are pretty clever animals as well and are smart enough to undo several different knots. The food bags I got for Matt and myself were made from a Kevlar blend, the same stuff bulletproof vests are made from. This is supposed to make them bear proof. I never wanted to find out.

Gooch had food hoisting cables which made this an easier process. You also hang your backpack, you don't want to leave it on the ground, the critters will get in. I hung my pack on a wooden peg that was drilled into the wall of the shelter. Matt hung his pack on a rope dangling from the roof. On the end of the hanging rope was an old tuna can that was pierced in the center to allow the rope through it, and had a stick tied on the end. I didn't understand the practical use of hanging your backpack like this yet, but I would.

Hikers midnight is at dark, usually around eight at night in the woods. Once the sun goes down there is really no reason to stay up. This isn't an ordinary camping trip where you stay up singing songs and roasting weenies over the fire. You sleep and rest from a hard day. This evening I blew up my air mattress and this time it only took ninety-six breaths, I must be getting my wind. As I laid down to sleep every muscle in my body was aching and sore. I thought that I may have neurologically damaged myself.

Still on the top of my list are those damn earplugs, Matt is already sound asleep and snoring.

The next morning we awoke to rain. God damn mountains, weather changes all the time on you. Two days out and two days of rain. We found it much easier operating under the roof of the shelter than cramped in our tent. Plus, shelters don't hold in the scent of stale farts quite like the tent did. We started breaking down our equipment and to my pleasant surprise I found that mice had gotten into my backpack. I don't know how the little bastards got in there, the wood walls seemed flush. The only thing I can imagine are kamikaze mice diving from the rafters for my bag. It's the only thing that makes sense. Unless these mice have been breeding with spiders and just crawl up walls, that's a world I don't want to live in. They must have spent some time in there because holes were chewed in my shirt and socks. What stupid creatures. Why chew up socks and a shirt? The answer in short is the salt from your sweat. Deer have been known to chew on shirts left hanging to dry by hikers for the same reason. One of the other hikers in the shelter had his backpack attacked also, but he found a nest in the bottom of his pack made from our shredded clothes, with three newborn mice. What a mess. I don't think I'd be able to put that pack on again.

Survival Note: Hang your backpack from ropes in shelters, not the pegs on walls.

The rain had stopped so we took the opportunity to start our day off dry, but much to our surprise, the cosmic joke that is Bob's struck, and the rain fell again. At least my socks drained well, they had holes in them from the mice. We were heading to Blood Mountain Shelter, cool name. It was thirteen miles, and we were determined to get there so we could roll into Neel's Gap the next day.

Blood Mountain is the second worst climb and the highest mountain the trail crosses in Georgia. The shelter was at four-thousand feet and had no water source so a north bounder, which we were, had to pick up and carry water about a mile before the shelter. You may or may not know, water weighs approximately eight pounds per gallon. Weight we did not want to carry uphill.

Blood Mountain is also one of the shelters that is more a cabin than shelter as it crowns the top of its namesake mountain. It is one of the more well-known shelters due to the proximity to the trail, so it's easy access for overnight hikers and weekend warriors. It is an old stone cabin that once housed the Civilian Conservation Group after it was built in 1937. The shelter was a barren two room stone building, cold and damp as I remember, there are a few of these on the trail. Oh, there were also thunderstorms in the area, we made it through the night without any problems, so once again our confidence was building.

Fun Fact: "The Thru-Hikers Guide," a guide published by the Appalachian Trail Conservancy, tells us that it was named Blood Mountain because two Indian tribes had fought on the slopes of the mountain and there were such numerous loses the ground turned red.

The walk into Neels Gap the next day was only three miles. It took us a little under two hours, and we arrived in the mid-morning. We ate, God did we eat, and food that's not good for you, but who cares. This was our fourth day hiking, when you say that out loud it doesn't seem like much, like a long weekend of camping. The reality is by the fourth day Matt already had the thousand-yard stare and I was feeling pretty beat up myself. A quick command decision was made to spend the night in a nearby rental cabin, where there were soft beds and a shower. Matt did not resist the idea, in fact he embraced it joyfully. If I recall correctly, he called it one of the "best decisions you ever made." Who would have thought?

There was also a hostel at Neels Gap where you can shower and bunk in a large room with others for a much smaller fee, but I'm retired and spending Matt's inheritance anyway, so we upgraded to a private place of our own.

We watched with great interest and awe as the salespeople at the Gap went through the other hikers' bags. This was a service they provided for free so that you might lighten your backpack and get rid of unneeded items. We did not have the people at the Gap go through our bags, deciding that instead of the embarrassment, we would watch and learn. After all, we were smarter than everyone else and knew what we needed.

Hikers were sending crap home via the Postal Service in droves. We decided we had a few things we could send home and started to pull out those items. Into the Postal box we packed gaiters, a Leatherman, pot scrubber, liquid soap, most of our first aid kit, deodorant rock, vitamins, gloves, candles and bugspray. We kept some things, like the pillows we had, but they were twelve inches by eight inches, and you could stuff them into themselves making them half their original size. Essentially a glorified airplane pillow.

This stay at the Gap was to be what hikers call a "nero" day. On the trail every five to seven days, you take a "zero" day, for us sometimes more often. It is a day where you stay in town for the entire day, restock, do laundry, drink a few beers, enjoy and relax. A "nero" day is when you get into some place early, stay, and do the things that need to be done, and the next day instead of chilling you hit the trail again. We had yet to learn the importance of taking a "zero." Later in the hike we had some "nero" days next to a "zero" day, essentially creating a weekend for ourselves. These were the days Matt's spirits were highest. I've never seen him so eager to start a morning's hike when it meant he wouldn't have to hike for two days. His pace was incredible too, he'd practically bolt down the trail when he knew a town was nearby. He could smell it. I didn't mind so much either, but he was hard to keep up with.

We decided we would head back out the next morning. This was the first time, and it became the norm, that Matt would get into the shower before me and spend an hour or so in it. This was a problem when we hit some fleabag motels, no hot water for me

We did another exorbitant dinner that night, since the cabins we were staying in were mostly for couples and the only delivery food was from a restaurant twenty miles away, but it was that or Ramen noodles, and this time it was me who objected. Matt being a college student had an unnatural fondness for those freeze-dried salt noodles, probably because they only took three minutes to cook, but I wasn't eating them if I had better options. This thru hike was starting to become expensive. After dinner we popped on some stupid movie that was left in the cabin and relaxed.

We slept like babies in a rustic, but clean cabin. I remember this cabin particularly due to the worst taxidermy job I've ever seen. There was a beaver mounted on the wall that was barely recognizable. The teeth gave it away, otherwise I would assume it was a giant hamster. This night Matt would have his own room, which is great for Bob, however it seems the walls of this place are as thin as the tent lining. I still need to get earplugs.

Another phenomenon we encountered in Neels Gap was what they refer to as hiker boxes. These are boxes where hikers dump things they don't want any longer, such as extra food, books, clothes, snacks, almost anything and everything can be found in these boxes. I saw an electric coffee maker in one box, what the hell were they thinking? Unfortunately, it's mostly stuff you don't need, after all there's a good reason it was left behind.

Every now and then though, you strike gold. Our first foray into the hiker box landed us our first Mountain House meal. Bacon and eggs. There is always room for improvement even for people who are as prepared and perfect as we were, which also led us to our first trail purchase at Neels Gap.

We first realized as other hikers zoomed past us that hiking poles were a necessity, for uphill, downhill, hell, even for just standing, but they were also expensive. I thought about just getting a set for myself, but Matts sulky little face made that difficult, if not impossible. I do have a soft spot for him. I also knew I would never hear the end of it, so this was just as much a preservation move. The second item we purchased were Crocs, you've seen them around, the rubber moccasins that come in all shades and colors except normal ones. We saw them strapped to the back of almost everyone's pack. These were also a necessity, as it is the greatest pleasure a man can imagine after hiking numerous miles, to take those damn boots off, let your feet breathe, and put on soft shoes. That was money well spent.

We did end up eating Ramen for breakfast that next morning, we figured it would be better to continue with a nice hot meal in us instead of the cereal with powdered milk that we had been eating. We also took a dose of Tylenol, commonly called "Trail Skittles," because we saw people pop them as if they were candy. One fellow we hiked with for a short time took so many they caused a hole in his stomach wall. He got off the trail, was hospitalized for a week, and never came back.

We walked down the side of the highway until we made it back to Neels Gap where the trail was ever waiting. With our bodies cabin rested we had a good stride that morning, knowing we were passing a major AT milestone. A majority of thru hikers quit at Neels Gap three to four days in. There is a bit of a business to be had there for some locals who shuttle these hikers between Atlanta, the closest city, and Neels Gap. With that stumbling block out of the way we continued to push on into greatness.

That afternoon after setting up at a shelter we continued our time killing tradition of a continually running game of Rummy. We would keep a running score throughout our hike and see who won at the end. Things get heated in our family when we play games for "fun." So, we were at are our best when three twenty-something year old girls sauntered in.

"Matt, you're adding your points wrong."

"No, I'm not! Shut up. I know how to add. You're the one cheating if anything, you God damn cheat."

"Well I learned from the best in the family, you know who that is," I told him.

"Oh, so Aunt Barbara is the biggest cheat in the family?"

I couldn't help but laugh at that, he was right. I informed him, "I don't cheat, I creatively interpret the rules."

We could now hear the girls approaching and from the looks on their faces they had been hearing us much longer. They were walking at a snail's pace surveying the shelter we currently occupied and the rest of the campsite, all the time mumbling between themselves.

I couldn't help myself. "Hey girls, the shelter is empty except for us, plenty of wood to lay on!"

Matt's look was hard to describe, he seemed to be between horrified and bemused by my playfully suggestive invitation to share the shelter, but he kept his composure. The girls apparently did not share the same sense of humor we did.

One of the girls piped up, "No thanks, we'll camp up the hill a bit and tent it for the night."

"Okay," I said, "but it is supposed to rain tonight."

She gave me a half puzzled, half defiant look and informed me they would "chance it."

They were unsociable to say the least. The girls headed up the hill to the shelter's tenting spots. Most shelters have several spots nearby that you can set your tent in. They were flatter areas tamped down by repeated use. I didn't think we looked that disheveled, so I don't know why anyone would choose to tent it when there are empty spots in a shelter. Only took us two days to learn that lesson. Guess some people are faster learners.

"Nice going Dad, you scared them off. That was my chance to sleep with three girls."

Now I audibly laughed at him. I knew what he meant but you still have to take your shots when you get your chances. "I think you mean sleep next to three girls. You wouldn't know what to do with yourself. You'd be too scared to get out of your sleeping bag."

He mustered a short "whatever" and we continued our card game, as well as the arguing.

We finished our dinner that night and set about doing our designated chores. We were getting more efficient with each passing night. It was nice to see progress. Our dinner was "PFG," as I've said, pretty much everything you eat after a day of hiking is. Matt and I were alone in the shelter and the girls were all settled in up the hill in their tents. Then the rains came. Again. Another night of high winds and driving rain. Sure glad we weren't in a tent.

We had decided on the freeze-dried bacon and eggs for breakfast the following morning. We quickly discovered why these were left for the next unsuspecting fools. They were awful, but this would not be our experience with almost every other Mountain House Meal, but I don't think that even the wildlife would have come out for these.

The problem was that doing this for breakfast required taking out your stove, priming it, boiling the water, mixing it all up, sealing it, and then waiting ten minutes until it's ready. That's a lot for the first thing in the morning when you've got mileage to cover. Now for the dinners, they were the absolute best. No clean up, no mess, you eat right out of the pouch and you're done. Not to mention the dinners were quite hardy compared to the tuna and powdered cereal.

We knew we were heading to Tray Mountain the next day. We had to start slowing down as Matt's feet were really starting to blister. The wet socks and constant friction can have this effect. No hiker escapes without them. We stopped often that day, every few hours so Matt could dry his feet, change socks, and hang the used ones off the back of his bag so they could dry in what little sun there was.

Finally, we stopped and used duct tape on the blistered areas. I don't know why everyone recommends duct tape, I guess it keeps the friction off the blister so there is no more rubbing. It didn't matter, we had lots of duct tape and the more we used the less we carried. Around three in the afternoon, Mother Nature took a shit on us again and blessed us with another bout of liquid sunshine and thunderstorms. I just love this weather. I couldn't be more miserable, but I can never admit it to Matt or anyone else. It was hard to hike in weather like that and sometimes you need a little push. Something else of consequent happened that rainy afternoon. I needed to have a little push of my own. I had to crap. It would be my first "shit in the woods" moment. A normal person would not dedicate so much time to crapping in the woods, but I am not normal, so I wrote an entire chapter dedicated to the subject. You're welcome.

P. S. I sent a picture of my first crap in the woods to my wife.

2,133.7 miles to go.

Chapter 5
The Art of Crapping Outdoors

How proud I was of my first outdoor crap. As I said, I even took a picture to send home to my wife. My first was in the woods, I could not wait for a "privy," "privies" being the outdoor toilets. I got lucky at the cabin where we had indoor plumbing, nothing like sitting over water as they say, so I had yet to experience this more ancestral form of relieving oneself. Privies are found at most shelters, and are in themselves a piece of art, a necessary part or the trail, and sometimes a welcome sight. Some are built in wooden closets and some are nothing more than a toilet seat set over a deep hole. Some are on mountain tops with windows, you have a magnificent view while taking care of business. Other privies were out in the open with just a piece of plywood as the wall between you and the shelter. This plywood was set up high enough so that if you saw someone's feet, then the privy was occupied. There was one privy that was just set up one hundred yards from the shelter, no walls, nothing, just a raised platform over a hole in the middle of the woods.

At one point In the Great Smoky Mountains we came across a single porcelain toilet, like the one you have in your house, right next to the side of the trail. One has to wonder how it got there, we were at least a mile from any roads, and this was not an old homestead. Someone had to have carried it there. There were no shelters around, nothing, just an actual toilet. You'd have to be ballsy to use that one and I did not look in it to find out.

No matter the exterior, never look into the hole, you don't want to see what's down there. Perhaps more importantly, what's down there doesn't want to see you. These closets are full of bugs, spiders, and various wildlife. You never need reading material, you can watch spiders weave webs, bugs scurry back forth, and pray that anything bigger does not enter while you are in there. These are not the refuges we seek at home for a few minutes of relaxation. Out here this was a race to the finish. You could always find words of wisdom on the walls, the names and dates of hikers gone by. I never got that, why would you write your name and the date you took a crap, is that your legacy?

I found I became master of the thirty second crap, never even having to touch this seat. I now have more respect for the ladies using public restrooms. Aside from purely sanitary reason there was a more sinister reason for my coveted hover technique. From time to time we'd come to more popular shelters, maybe near highways, they are easy to get to for families, in popular state or national parks, either way there was always more, let's say volume. On a normal day at home I'm pretty proud when I can stack my shit and break water, but in these places, my God. People would manage to stack crap above the seat of the privy. I'd tell you to let that sink in, but I don't want you or anyone else to have that sink in. Turd piled high enough to poke through the toilet seat. However, for kicks, I'll give you a visual. That's a pit that dug four feet deep filled with enough crap and toilet paper and God knows what else to reach ground level. Add another two feet to reach the raised seat of the privy. A proverbial mountain of shit. I'll never complain about a gas station bathroom again.

Privies at least give you the illusion of modernity. Crapping in the woods was a whole different ordeal. There are several different ways to accomplish this fine art in the wilderness without the benefit of a privy. I spent an enormous amount of time on my trek studying this art. Being a cop, I was trained to be aware and use my surroundings to my advantage. This was true when shitting in the woods, be aware of and use your surroundings. I tested several of the more common methods and I developed a few of my own. I heard other hikers talk of their methods and compiled a short list in my mental bank.

All methods assume you have dug the mandated six-inch hole for your waste product to nestle in. This, by itself, is a chore and one you don't always have the time for. If you didn't bring your plastic trowel, which most were a bright orange plastic, then the heel of your boot pounding into the hopefully soft ground would accomplish this. When we started our hike, we brought one of these orange trowels, it was largely ineffective and basically a Bat Signal that you were going to shit. We sent it home, less weight.

Survivor Note: Do not use the method of digging your heel into the ground if you have blisters on your heel. This method tends to aggravate your blisters.

Some hikers use a stick to dig a hole, but snakes and sticks look a lot alike. If you pick up a stick that moves in your hand, drop it. At this point you will not have to worry about crapping, you will have already done it in your pants, I know.

I suggest you dig a hole that is oversized, unless you have the aiming skill of a bombardier, because you will find yourself rolling turds that missed back into the hole. As always, you cover the hole when done. It's not always pretty but it serves a purpose, I'm not sure what that purpose is but that's what "they" say. I don't see how a basic human function is unnatural, but whatever.

The other problem you can run into crapping in the wilderness is other hikers. For me, this isn't really a problem, I'll let it fly anywhere. When my sister, the aforementioned family cheat, trail named Hiker Babe, joined the hike for ten days to do a little section hike, she had with her two hundred feet of kite string. I had to ask, "Now what the hell is the kite string for? If you haven't noticed there aren't many meadows about for kite flying."

She told me, "You tie the string to a tree when you need to go, and that way you can always find your way back". It's nice in theory but not practical, she continued, "You know I read fifty percent of hikers get lost while going off for a private moment."

I took the string and threw it out. Less weight. If you think you'll get lost when you need to have a private moment do it twenty feet off the trail.

She continued to argue with me. "All the books say two hundred feet. I don't want anybody seeing me."

"Look I've seen all sorts of actual shit on the trail, bear scat, deer scat, even human on occasions, I think you'll survive twenty feet into the woods. Do you really think anyone wants to watch?"

Just one more thought for those of you who may develop diarrhea. Ejections are much more forceful and can cover quite a bit of distance. A splashing effect can occur. For this condition, this is assuming you have the time to dig a hole and follow directions, I recommend the tree hugger position, ass pointed downhill or sitting positions. Never the looker position.

Method #1-The Tree Hugger

On a difficulty level of 1-5, this is a 1. This is a widely used method of the novice hiker. This is evident, as you will see, because the other methods described each require some skill or proficiency in some area. First, the tree cannot be too thick, you should be able to interlock your fingers, and if need be, hold onto the tree with one hand, this is a necessity if you need to adjust your shorts, swat bugs, or wave on other hikers. You should be on the downhill side of the tree, so if you miss the intended hole the round ones don't roll under your feet and onto your shorts. Also, very important, make sure you are leaning far enough out with your ass that any droppings clear your shorts which are now around your ankles. That can make for a potentially embarrassing mistake.

Method #2-The Cossack
On a difficulty level of 1-5, this is a 4.
The trick here is to find a clean log, no ants or bugs crawling on it. As I said before, this is part of being aware of your surroundings. If there are bugs on the log they will scamper across your hands during your business, and there could be disastrous results if you are a bug hater. Once you have found the proper log, you place both hands on it as if you were going to sit on the log, but your bare butt never touches it as you walk your feet out and away from the log, supporting your weight on your hands and positioning your ejection port several inches past the edge of the log and over your preconstructed hole. You will look like a Russian Cossack doing his dance, all the while building a strong core while crapping.

Method # 3-The Squatter
On a difficulty level of 1-5, this is a 3.
The most basic of all positions, it requires some dexterity, so many people have trouble squatting

unsupported. Important in this position is to make sure the bombs drop well clear of your shorts. Make sure you have disposed of all your payload before standing up or any hangers will be forced to drop as you stand, missing your primary target, and landing in your clothing. Murphy's law.

Method #4-The Three Point Stance
On a difficulty level of 1-5, this is a 2
Favored by college jocks hiking the trail, this style allows more stability than the squat, but experienced hikers prefer the squat over this, as your hands remain clean (hopefully.) You enter a squat position and place one hand on the ground to balance yourself. Then you push your ass out to allow clearance over your clothing, yell hike, and drop the Browns off at the Super Bowl.

Method #5-The Sitter
On a difficulty level of 1-5 this is a 1
A safe and efficient position if you can find the right log or stone. Again, as with the Cossack, most people want a clean bug free log or stone. If you are lucky enough to find one, it cannot be too wide, as you need your discharge port to be hanging over the object and clear of all obstructions. This style allows your clothing freedom from any type of aiming errors or mishaps.

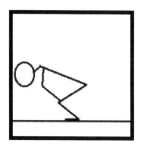

Method #6-The Looker
On a difficulty level of 1-5, who would want to do this?
This is an advanced and truly perverted stance. It is a knock off of the squat, but the truly flexible hiker

can now bend over far enough and has developed an uncanny sense of balance from weeks of hiking, that he can actually see his bomb doors. He is capable of watching the drop and making sure all the payload has been dropped off before cleaning up, preventing a mess.

Method #7-The Nudist

It makes no sense at all to do a stick figure for this method. Who could tell? The nudist is just that, period. This was Matthew's favorite, though you are only afforded the chance in certain situations. It was also Matt's preferred method throughout most of his life so why not bring it into the woods with him? He called it "going full Costanza," after a Seinfeld episode. We usually slept in our underwear in our tents, so if you woke at night and had to do your business, why not get as primal as you can. This method may be best suited for use under cover of darkness, for obvious reasons. Strip off those undies an let fly in your birthday suit. There are some benefits to this method, no worry of pissing into your shorts or getting any on you. You are unrestricted in your stance since there is nothing down around your ankles confining you. This is for those who are truly free. The downside is if someone stumbles across you, I don't believe there needs to be an explanation.

There are other variations, these being the most common. After you finish your duty (get it?), cleanup is most important. Try to have toilet paper with you and some hand cleaner. Purell works fine. If you must use leaves, dead ones are good if you don't know what Poison Ivy looks like. If you do, green ones are better, they hold together. If you eat properly, you'll have a lot of what I called no-wipers, but I always wipe twice, because I am the suspicious type. I just don't believe that the paper remains white. If you have a no-wiper, do not save and reuse the paper. Make sure everything is clean, swamp ass is bad enough, but being unclean while having swamp ass and hiking all day, well we will leave that as it's not very pleasant.

Still 2,133.7 miles to go, but now I am not afraid to crap in the woods.

Chapter 6
Georgia On My Mind

Well now that "that shit" is over with, back to Georgia. We arrived at Blue Mountain to a different experience than we've had before. The shelter at Blue Mountain was packed. By the time we got there, most of the spots in the shelter had been claimed. We were a touch more confident in our abilities to raise our tent, so we said to hell with cramming into the shelter, we're adventurous, we'll rough it. It turned out it was not the night for "roughing it." One of the more outright reasons we didn't squeeze in was there was a Boy Scout troop there.

Now they didn't spend the night, in fact they were packing up to move on when we got there. However, and this was disappointing to see from an organization as prestigious as theirs, they were leaving trash everywhere in the shelter. Candy wrappers and stray gummy bears meant the people sleeping there were going to be eaten alive by bears. End of story. At the very least it attracts the mice and ants, two things you don't want crawling all over you at night. There are rules on the trail, what you "pack in" you "pack out." We brought gallon zip lock bags so we could carry our trash out with us. Believe me when you're eating bag tuna for lunch every day it gets unpleasant, but you carry it out, always.

At times on the trail there are occurrences which amaze and leave you awestruck. This night was one of them. Blue Mountain's elevation is about four thousand feet. The site the shelter sat on was sparsely treed, but what trees there were appeared to be very tall. We tried to set up our tent away from the trees, a lesson we learned after our first night setting up under a tree. There was also an incident a few days back where a limb had broken off a tree and just missed the college girl's tent. We had found that one out over breakfast the next morning. I wanted to make another joke about there being plenty of wood to lay on, but something told me it wouldn't be appreciated.

Just after dinner the thunderstorms rolled in, and I mean rolled in. The thunder and lightning were coming in bursts, one after another. It was brighter and louder than I had ever seen or experienced in my life. And since this is all about honesty, it was truly fear inducing. The raw exposure to the elements with nothing but a thin line of plastic protecting you is unnerving. It's hard to describe in words, the booms and bright flashes, I imagine it's a less terrifying version of being in the trenches during the war. Mother Nature may be a bitch, but she's also beautiful and mesmerizing. As the storm rolled through it continued to rain all night.

We packed up a wet tent again, I don't think it ever had a chance to completely dry since day one. Tray Mountain was the next day's destination, but again, thunderstorms rolled in about noon time. Those were rainy days in Georgia, almost like the song. It's commonly agreed upon that the proper protocol when hiking in a thunderstorm is to find a gully and maintain a squat position till the lightning passes, or if hiking keep forty feet between you and the closest hiker. They also tell you to stay away from trees, we are in a forest for God's sake. I mean, seriously? Where the hell are you supposed to go? We kept hiking in the storm, the lightning seemed to be cloud-to-cloud, we didn't see any land strikes, so on we went. The downpour finally let up after about two hours, the trail itself was a river, and needless to say, we again looked like two drowned puppies.

We have been traveling in a group so to speak. The same three girls were shadowing us, but still won't stay in the shelter with us, they seem to prefer tenting. What they really prefer is avoiding us. After a time they started warming up to us and would sit and eat dinner with us. There were also a few others that we always seem to run into at the shelters. At least we weren't the only ones crawling all the way down the trail. As we became more friendly with these girls and the interchangeable others that would keep pace with us, we began to share more trail life experiences with each other. We would share with one another the best practices and equipment and what worked for us and what worked for them. Some of my best practices that I shared all correlated directly to the previous chapter.

You may or may not have noticed but there was no mention of Matthew and him crapping in the woods. He had not crapped for eight days. EIGHT DAYS! I may have at one point mentioned this around day four or five to the girls shadowing us. Matthew didn't appreciate the gossip, but it worked to his advantage. All of a sudden he was like a wounded animal. All the girls wanted to look after him and help him. All because he hadn't shit. I don't get it. They were offering remedies and feeding him prunes. He loved the attention but not for the reasons behind it. Each day when the girls pulled into camp they would immediately ask for a progress report. Did it happen today? Did you go? Matt would look away with sad eyes and whisper "no."

Blue Mountain was where the magic happened. Blue Mountain is where my son pleased three college girls at once. We were sitting during our nightly Rummy game and he just perked up, eyes wide, and grinning from ear to ear. Out of all the places for him to finally go, Blue Mountain was about as good as it gets. Their privy was on the side of the mountain with breathtaking views.

He was gone a short while and then walked back to the shelter all smiles. The girls by their tents all stood and began cheering and clapping their hands like he just won the World Series. A great weight had been lifted off all of us, especially Matt. I was a proud father that day. My son had shit.

The next night was a repeat of the previous night and pretty much all others since we started. Thunder and lightning again, but this time it was far worse. We cowered in the back of the shelter, as did everyone who was tenting, even the three girls. The lightning strikes were consistent and all over our area. We witnessed one bolt hit a tree maybe one hundred feet from the shelter, shredding the bark on the tree it hit. You could feel the burst of air, it blinded you for a few seconds and the crack was deafening. After the strikes the air had a sulfurous smell to it. There was just something so primal about it. At the time we didn't think so, but in hindsight it had been one of the coolest things that had happened to us on the trail. We sheltered the next night also and then proceeded into Hiawassee.

2,114.6 miles to go.

Chapter 7
Bare Encounter

It was in Hiawassee that Matt needed to treat his blisters. They were getting bad, even other hikers were shocked at the state of his feet. It wasn't just one blister either, he had one on each toe, the balls of his feet, and his heels. I wondered how he could even fit his feet into his shoes. That's when Frodo officially died, and a new trail name would rise from the blistered ashes of his feet. I worked on a few new names for the taped-up lad. I went back and forth on names for him since at this point every toe and half his foot was covered in silver duct tape. I decided between the two favorite choices that being "Tin Man" or "Silvertoes." Matt didn't care for either name but agreed if he had to have some asshole name anything was better than Frodo. He went with Silvertoes, I guess in his mind that sounded better than Tin Man. I think it was very generous of me to give him a choice in the first place. I am proving to be a benevolent father; besides it would change again.

Hiawassee was the largest town in Georgia that the trail comes close to. It was eleven miles down the road, our legs were getting stronger, but eleven miles is basically a day's hike for us, so our thumbs went out. Hitchhiking is an interesting subject on the AT. While it is generally frowned upon in most of America, out here it can be a necessity at times. It's easy to understand why there is an inherent distrust when it comes to hitching, but along the trail it's a common sight. Still one must be vigilant. I saw one hiker later on down the trail grab a ride from a pickup truck and when he threw his bag in the back, the truck took off without him. It was funny and sad at the same time. Matthew and I grabbed a ride in a Jeep that pulled over for us, the driver told us hikers are common here and most people will give them a ride to town as a courtesy, plus hikers spend money in town.

We were dropped off in the middle of town. There was a town map in my Hikers Guide. We were hungry and chose a Hardee's to eat at. I think our eyes were bigger than our stomachs, we both ordered the largest burger they had, the two-third-pound burger with bacon and cheese, large fries and a milkshake. Neither one of us could finish it. Hardee's won that round. We picked up some snacks in the local grocery store and went trucking down the street to find a motel.

We had planned on staying in a fleabag motel in Hiawassee but by the time we got into town there were no rooms available. Instead we had to stay at the only place in town we could find, the Holiday Inn. This was much nicer, and more expensive than we had planned but we were glad for it after more than a week in the woods. The second we got to our room Matt dropped everything and beelined for the shower, so of course, I had to wait an hour or so for my turn. Now that we were smelling socially acceptable, we ventured down to the laundry room in the motel to do our laundry. We'd donned our rain suits so we could wash all our hiking gear, then back to the room while it was being washed so we could relax. Although I'd like to say you relax, the only thing you can wear is your rain suit while washing your clothes, it's less than comfortable, you try freeballin' in plastic pants.

That night we ate at a $6.95 all you can eat buffet, and we ate, though the old adage is true, you get what you pay for. I spent the rest of that evening "processing" what I ate, but like a good friend once said, "never pass up a chance to shit over water." We restocked by picking up our mail drop package at the post office and got our gear in order. Early to bed, we took another "nero" day. We slept in and took our time the next morning and left early, sometime before lunch. We were going to Muskrat Creek that day which meant we would have knocked off our first state, leaving Georgia in the dust and heading to a shelter in beautiful North Carolina.

We managed to hitch a ride back to the trailhead that early afternoon. Hitching as I said seems to be very easy down South. Coming from New York I wouldn't pick up anyone, I imagine each person hitchhiking is a serial killer. I don't care if the hitcher is a twenty-one-year-old female with the body of a Greek goddess clad in a mini dress and tank top with no bra, I fear she is going to make me a eunuch using some rusty old knife. Imagination, like Mother Nature, can be a bitch. I think Matt would have chanced castration for the above scenario.

We had been hoping to see a bear or two since we started, especially Silvertoes, and for that reason he would often take the lead while we were hiking. Now being lead man can be quite bothersome. If you are the first hiker out of a shelter in the morning you will be knocking down spider webs that were constructed overnight on the trail. The width of the trail makes it ideal for spiders to set their traps, although they're usually catching someone's face. Some you can see as the dew moistened silk is lit by sunlight, others you end up eating or wiping off your face. Matt being a little shorter than I was would miss some of the higher webs which would then be at perfect height for my eyes. Just lovely.

As we headed out this afternoon Matt was leading once again, but since he had opened up the sphincter floodgates there was now no holding him back. He had to do a Chapter 5 in the woods. Whenever this would happen to one of us the other would continue down the trail at a slower pace, which is hard to believe that we could go slower than our usual pace. Matt went about a dozen yards or so uphill off the trail to pop a squat. I kept going and rounded a corner ahead. I heard some noises in the woods to the right of me. It was too soon for it to be Matt, besides he knew better than to leave the trail. I looked in that direction and saw a black bear stand up and look at me. Now it wasn't the largest bear on earth, but on its hind legs it seemed it was a good foot taller than I was. It was only twenty-five yards away and believe me, that was plenty close enough.

Let me tell you, your first bear encounter is as exciting as it is nerve wracking. You are in awe, but in the back of your mind you fear it is going to charge you and maul the living shit out of you. I always figured I'd go out in a blaze of glory, not as bear shit. I stood quietly hoping he would stay there so Matt could see him, (or her, I wasn't that close). A few seconds of checking each other out and the bear bolted off. I figured the bear smelled my less than perfect hygiene and couldn't take the stink. It took a few seconds for me to realize the bear bolted precisely in the direction of my crapping son.

Now this is a situation that straddles the line between hilarious and dangerous. A startled bear running from perceived danger coming across another person is not an ideal situation. Then I heard Matt yelling for help. I turned and started running back around the bend where Matthew had scurried up into the woods to find him scrambling down the hill while yanking his drawers up, but his shorts were still around his ankles. He couldn't run full stride because of his shorts, and he was running like a penguin walks. Funny as all hell. I was tearing up, not because he was alive, but because the sight was hysterical.

The bear had come within ten feet of him while he was finishing up. The sight of the bear caused him to fall backwards, narrowly missing his pile of Chapter 5. He finally saw a bear, only it was the ass end while he was knocked on his ass end. He told me he yanked up his drawers and started running, forgetting he still had to pull up his shorts. I asked if he had wiped, and he told me that task still awaited. At this point I was free to continue laughing hysterically. If someone had to be the punching bag of this trek, well, better him than me. Right? What's the saying? "The bear went over the mountain to see what he could see," well, all he saw was some damn mountains and Matt's ass.

Besides seeing our first bear this was a monumental day anyway, we were now in North Carolina. Seventy-nine miles under our belts. It didn't come with fanfare or people cheering, instead it was a bunch of steep climbs over three mountains in four miles and stifling heat. We stayed in a shelter that night. On this section of the trail they have what they call Nantahala style shelters, consisting of an extended roof over an eating area, usually with a table and shelf for cooking on. When it rained this was a dream come true.

2,110.1 miles to go.

Chapter 8
North Carolina and Psycho

The next few days hiking in North Carolina were hell. Rain and thunderstorms were intermittent every day, some lasting for hours. We were becoming well versed in thunderstorms, but they never became enjoyable. We were now able to "read and smell the sky," and knew when they were coming. Those first few days in North Carolina we were introduced to thousand-foot climbs, some peeking at over five thousand feet. Georgia had some steep climbs and a noticeable lack of switchbacks, but the mountains themselves weren't as tall.

North Carolina threw another curveball at us, we met Psycho. Now Psycho didn't know he was Psycho, well he didn't know he was "a" psycho, but his code name was Psycho. It was the name Matt and I called him between ourselves, and for good reason. We did this with quite a few hikers. Some of their trail names should not have been what they called themselves by, they were being delusional. It almost made it easier for us to talk about someone without them knowing.

Each state is its own chapter along the AT journey and as I said North Carolina is where we met Psycho. It was as though he was waiting for us. The first night we sheltered in North Carolina he was there. There were two shelters at that site, a brand new one and an older one. Everyone else was setting up shop in the new shelter so Matt and I figured we'd get away and stay in the old one. Along comes this scraggly old nut job throwing his gear besides ours. He was skinny and ragged looking, the exact kind of guy you wouldn't pick up hitching on the side of the road, thinking he was homeless. At first he didn't say much, just a series of disgruntled looks and a few mumbled words designed to move us out of the way.

Right away my police instinct kicked in, this was the kind of guy I would do a stop on. Matt was getting that vibe as well and said as much. "Dad, is it just me or is there something really off about this guy?"

"I don't know Matt. Kinda scary looking. Let's keep an eye on him."

"Maybe we should go to the other shelter?"

I looked over to the other shelter and it was pretty much full. "It's full, but they're close enough to hear our screams during the night if something happens." This did not reassure the lad much, his expression said it all.

There was something off with him, in fact it turned out there was quite a lot wrong with him. Psycho was a Vietnam vet and Purple Heart recipient. Of course we didn't know this at the time, but he had sustained serious injuries, both physically and psychologically. The trail was one of the few places he felt "sane." He thought the only place he could survive among other people was on the trail. Now this was not his first time doing the trail, he had done the whole trail of few years prior but never got up Katahdin. It was closed when he got there in mid-October. It's hard to believe they can "close" a mountain, but you'd be stupid and probably dead if you went up Katahdin when it was "closed." He never went back to do it. I think in hindsight if he finished Katahdin he would be done with the trail and not hike it anymore, then what would he do six months out of the year?

The first night with him we were going about our chores when he showed up. Like myself, Psycho had a thing for the corners, so he took all my gear and slid it over so he could have the corner. Ballsy move, I didn't say anything. When he went down to fill up his water bottles, I told Matt to be alert around him, I just couldn't put my finger on what was bothering me. The spring was a quick walk past our shelter down a little hill and Matt went down to fill up our water bags. Psycho was down there crouching besides the spring, as though about to leap and attack, as if Matt were his prey, after all he was tender and supple. He spoke to Matt, never turning to look at him.

"Hey, watch your step, it's muddy and slick." All I could hear was intermittent cursing and an old raspy laugh. Psycho came walking around the corner smiling. "That guy you're with is an idiot."

I agreed but was a bit taken back by this. "That idiot is my son."

"Well that makes sense," Psycho said to me. "I warned him, he didn't listen."

Matt came around the corner covered in mud from the waist down. He had slipped going down the hill and landed on his ass. Being covered in mud is bad enough but being covered in mud and knowing you're a week away from a shower, well that can put you in a mood.

Survival Note: Don't wear Crocs on muddy downhill terrain.

Matt was being a bit pissy due to his disregard for Psycho's warning. Naturally this was a window for me to pick on the lad a bit, and I do like picking on the lad. After a few minutes of our usual back and forth banter Psycho jumped in blasting Matt with jokes. For some unknown reason, he took a liking to Matt and me. That's when it hit me, the reason I was uneasy around him, the thing I couldn't put my finger on. He was just like us, damaged goods. My years on the force gave me a dark sense of humor which was passed to my son and struck a chord with this lunatic. He saw us as allies against the normal liberal hippie bullshit assholes, as he would often describe people who usually hiked the AT with their guitars and weed.

We still did our best to avoid him, but he was like a gnat constantly buzzing at our ears. We pushed ourselves to make up extra miles and sure enough, he'd come wheezing into the shelter, "Hey Bob, Matt you guys hike fast. I didn't think I'd catch up." Then while coughing he lit up a cigarette or two.

Shelter after shelter he would inevitably come wheezing in and we gave him names like "Huff and Puff," due to his smoking and "Sergeant Bilko," all of which he found hilarious. He was loud, cantankerous, and argumentative.

We slept that night with one eye open, as we had heard about weirdos that hike the trail. In fact, the next few nights we slept with one eye open. Psycho would cozy up to Matt and me, telling us about his past little by little. In those few days we learned he was a hard time reformed alcoholic and drug user, in and out of asylums and rehab centers for years being treated for things we never knew existed. He went as far as to tell us he has his own suite at one asylum, gold name plate and all. It had been named after him when his friends took him out for the day, but returned after curfew, so he decided to sneak in. As he describes it, he was banging on the fire exit doors for one of the inmates to open, but they were just doing the zombie walk around the room from being over-medicated. He decided to break the glass so he could open the door, and in doing so the alarm went off, the guards poured in, and he was put in a padded room. As he says, to date, he is the only person to try to break in and not out of an asylum.

A few days into North Carolina I had a food drop set up at a campground that was right on the trail. We got to the campground only to find out that it had been closed for a year. The package had been returned to my wife, but she somehow forgot to mention it during our communications. She probably thought we would never get this far when the package was returned.

Let me step aside to talk about communicating with home while hiking the trail. Almost all hikers had cell phones, which are great, but service sucked in most spots. Mountain tops were best for signal, but not so much down in the gaps, and most shelters happened to be in the gaps. There were several service providers, and as such, some of us would get signal while others would not. We would share phones if batteries were good so hikers could quickly communicate with home if needed. To save your battery you would hike with the phones off, so they made lousy cameras.

In this comedy of errors, I had loaned my phone to a young girl who was homesick a few days prior to us arriving at this now defunct campground, and she returned it to me telling me that my phone was dead. No shit, she was on it for over an hour, so for this reason my wife could not relay to me that the food drop was returned. Matt and I were out of food, but we were by a popular hiking mountain with decent traffic. The plan that we concocted was Matt would stay at the parking lot with our bags and I would hitch into town to get enough food till the next drop. The nearest town was Franklin, some twenty miles away, but still our only hope of not suffering from malnutrition. You cannot hike without food or your body "bonks" and shuts down. Plans made, I was stepping out to the road to start hitching when I heard, "Yo, Peterman, where you going?"

It was Psycho coming into the parking lot. "Got to get food for me and Matt, the campground we sent our food drop to is closed."

"Poor planning Peterman. I need to get cigarettes, I'll go with you. Matt can watch my pack too."

Just God damn great, this psychopathic nutjob is hitching twenty miles for cigarettes. "Long ride for just cigarettes, maybe you should wait till next town. I would, but we are out of food." I also resented the poor planning remark.

"Nah, no problem, need some down time. Matt watch my bag, will ya?"

We got lucky and got a ride directly to the local supermarket. I spent some time shopping for resupplies, a Subway was nearby so I grabbed four sandwiches, two for lunch and two for dinner. I was going to load Matt's with jalapenos, but he already had enough anal noises and gaseous releases as it was. Plain tuna for him. He wasn't happy, as that's what we had for lunch everyday anyway. I got myself two roast beef with the works. This was also the first time I learned Psycho did not carry a lot of cash. I graciously loaned him money so he could purchase sandwiches.

We needed a ride back and I realized this would be a little more difficult than the ride to town. We asked a few people in the parking lot but got nowhere with that. Psycho suggest that we should split a cab. I thought about it for a moment and laughed.

"What's so funny Peterman?"

"How are you splitting a cab when you borrowed money from me for your food?"

"You loan me money for the cab, you think I'm not good for it?"

"Wow, that sounds like a great deal. How could I go wrong giving somebody I don't know more money and trusting him to pay me back? You live in the woods, we only see you at shelters, and I should trust you?"

"So, we're good to go then?"

We needed to lose this guy and fast. I got on the phone to call a cab company when a hunter came out of the market and asked if we needed a ride back to the trail. I jumped at the chance and told him where we needed to be dropped off. It wasn't far out of his way and I threw him a few bucks for gas. Cheaper than and more reliable than Psychos IOUs.

This mountain, and it was not a big one, had two parking areas, one on each side of the mountain. With my never-ending luck, he took us to the lot on the wrong side and dropped us off there. It was hardly his fault, it's not like I knew where I was, but when Psycho and I hopped out the hunter sped off. It was about a second after he pulled away I realized we were in the wrong place. The biggest clue was the lack of an adoring son thanking the Gods for his father's safe return. Or more realistically, the lack of a hungry annoyed son asking for his lunch.

"Peterman, you believe that asshole dropped us on the wrong side of the fuckin' mountain?" Yes, I believed it. Psycho continued lighting up a cigarette, "Looks like it's up and over, unless you think you could bring my backpack with you and I'll wait here."

Now Psycho is the type of guy that has seen an "I'll kill you" look a time or two, but the look in my eyes snapped him out of that thought. "Easy, Peterman, easy. I was just kidding. Besides who would you talk to while you walked? What if something happened to you on the way, what would I tell Matt? Sorry kid, your Pops was abducted or something, he said he doesn't want you anymore, see ya?"

I think if I went missing Matt would know exactly who to start with. The only thing to do was to hike the three or so miles over the mountain to the other parking lot where Matt was waiting, probably agonizing and missing his dad I'm sure. Psycho's hands were empty except for his two packs of cigarettes, he chuckled as he lit one up and walked past me toward the white blazed opening in the woods. I, on the other hand, had my hands full. I carried the grocery bags from town, which included the sandwich I loaned him. I could see why this guy didn't make many friends.

Meanwhile, Matt was left sitting on the side of the road with our backpacks waiting for us to turn up. It's hard to imagine in today's world of smartphones and tablets, just sitting and waiting for someone. Imagine the horror. He knew we'd be gone for a while, but it could have been any number of hours before we showed up again. What if we couldn't get a ride back? There was that distinct possibility that we could have had to walk.

Instead Matt found himself lounging on the side of the road when another group of hikers came out of the woods. Out of the three guys one had a severe limp from a fall the day before. They were weekend warriors whose plans were ruined on day one of their hike. They threw their bags down near Matt and waited for their ride to pick them up. Since they would not be camping that night, they broke out the bottle of Scotch and decided to drink it while awaiting their rescue. Matt, having already sat around by himself for an hour, was not about to let this opportunity pass him by. When Psycho and I returned we found him sitting in a circle passing the bottle around. I could hardly blame him, it seemed like a great idea in the short term, but it would not make the rest of his day hiking pleasant. Some days I wonder what the hell my life is all about.

The next two days at the end of each torturous hike Psycho kept coming into shelters we were staying in. We just couldn't lose this guy. He reminded me of the scene from the Steven Segal movie "On Deadly Ground," when one guy talking about Segal says, "he's the kind of guy who would drink a gallon of gasoline so he could piss in your campfire. You could drop him off at the Arctic Circle wearing a pair of bikini underwear, without his toothbrush, and tomorrow afternoon he's going to show up at your poolside with a million-dollar smile and a fistful of pesos." That's Psycho.

One of the shelters we stayed in the next few days was such a shithole the mice didn't even live here. Like I said before, most shelters are maintained by volunteers, and for the most part decent, they do a good job. Hikers should keep them clean when they pack out, taking their trash, but there are some who just don't bother. This place was the worst we had seen to date, paper stuffed in holes in the walls, crap all over the ground, the fire pit full of trash, garbage in the shelter, the surrounding area look like a shit bomb had gone off.

We had hiked enough that day, so we decided to stay there. I was wrong about the mice. That night, and what we could only assume was a coordinated attack, a pack of voracious mice pounced on us. We could hear the nonstop scurrying across the floors and feeling them run over our sleeping bags. Worst of all, they were jumping onto our backpacks and falling off, hitting the ground with a thud and squeak than scurrying off again into the night. In the middle of the night we set the tent up outside the shelter for fear that if the tent was in the shelter the mice would chew through it. Psycho slept through it all.

2,058 miles to go.

Chapter 9
Nantahala

Most of my conversations with Matt while hiking were about Psycho. We talked of how we could lose him, or how he might butcher us in our sleep, or who he is going to piss off at the next shelter. It was a surprisingly great way to pass the time in the flatter areas where we had enough breath to speak. We took a small break from the Psycho daydreams when we heard some rustling and whimpering coming from up ahead. It had, at that point, become instinct to smack our walking sticks together and shout in case that rustling was in fact a bear. Instead of a bear a skinny chocolate lab burst through the bushes to our left. It scared the ever-living crap out of both Matthew and me. Luckily Matt was in front of me, so he didn't see me nearly soil myself, but I saw him.

"Jesus Christ!" Matthew shouted at the top of his lungs as this little mocha colored dog licked at his shins. The dog was friendly, and its tail was moving too fast for the rest of its body to keep up with. Matt was bent over still recovering from the shock. That was my opening.

"Aww, what's the matter, you afraid of puppies now? Did the big mean puppy scare you?"

He was calmed and petting the dog. "Damn right, this little stinker almost made me drop a stinker."

The dog was very skinny and looked just on the side of malnourished. Matt took off his pack and dug out his bowl and poured in some water from his bottle. The dog lapped it up and grabbed his bowl and started trotting off. Matt trotted off after the mutt as another hiker was jogging quickly toward us and the dog from the opposite direction we were hiking. The dog went straight for the other hiker, so we thought it was his dog. "Hey, your dog stole my bowl!"

"Sorry man, actually it's not my dog. Believe it or not I just found him further up. Someone left him tied to a tree. I came across him and I was looking for his owner. He slipped away from me, I figured I had to at least attempt to find him."

I could see this was making Matt visibly angry. I, by no means cared for it, but as a cop I'm no longer surprised by the sick shit people can do. "What kind of asshole leaves a dog tied to a tree?"

It wasn't hard to piece together. We were about half a mile or so from the road and the Nantahala Outdoor Center. "Well, if I had to guess I'd say someone came here last night and tied that dog up knowing that some hikers would be through and help." At least I hoped that was the case. The other hiker handed Matt his bowl back.

"I'm headed down into the N.O.C. for the night, I'm gonna bring him there and see if they know anything about it." That was really the only thing you could do. The three of us and our new four-legged friend continued down into the gorge.

Between two mountains runs the Nantahala River and on its shores is the N.O.C. The Nantahala Outdoor Center is a campground, has some cabins, a restaurant, and a general store which had everything a hiker might need. We went into the general store to check in for the night. We had planned on taking a "zero" day here anyway since they offered white water rafting and the boy was yearning to prove himself a man once again.

We gave the dog to the owner of the N.O.C. and explained how we came up on it. She fell in love with it from the start and told us if no one claimed it she would let it live at the center. Later and further down the trail we learned from some "flip-floppers" that the dog had been kept at the lodge as a pet. For those not savvy on the terms of the trail, a "flip-flopper" is a hiker that starts late, gets to a certain point, usually Harpers Ferry in West Virginia, because it is accessible to major transportation, then goes to the end of the trail in Maine and hikes back to Harpers Ferry, usually to avoid the cold weather.

We thought we might lose Psycho in the Nantahala River Gorge. We hoped he would hike right on through; he surely didn't have any money to stay and besides there were way too many people around. Psycho doesn't like people. Well, it turns out Psycho doesn't mind being around people when he's got us around. When we were around, he could say whatever he wanted to us without getting himself in trouble. Weren't we the lucky ones?

While I was checking in Nantahala, Matt and I decided to take a cabin instead of staying in the hostel. It's nice to have an option that isn't communal living, which we would come to find is mostly smelly and dirty. In walked Psycho and it was then I actually think I heard God laugh.

"Yo, Peterman, you and Matt staying here? That cabin got three beds?"

"Sorry, small cabin and two beds, the next shelter is only a few miles, you can make it."

"Think I'll stay at the hostel. You guys going to "zero?"

"Yeah, we think so, not sure yet. How are you staying at the hostel, I thought you were tapped out financially? You had me buy your sandwiches."

"Well if I paid for the sandwiches, I wouldn't have money for the hostel."

Can't argue with his logic on that one.

"Peterman, I want to have you and Matt for dinner." What did he mean by that? Silence of the Lambs and Hannibal Lecter flashed through my mind. "The restaurant here is cheap. Is it a date?"

I felt relief that we would be eating in public. I figured it would be best if Matt and I ate with Psycho and not have him terrorize some other diners. "Yeah, sure, we would love to. See you about six."

The cabin wasn't so much a cabin as it was a lodge with multiple rooms inside. It was across the river on the northern riverbank opposite from the general store. We made our way over to the cabin and Matt made a beeline to the bathroom, number one to do a number two, and number two, to get in the shower. I could have set a timer from the second he closed that door. One hour…. ready, go.

I knew I had some time before I would have a turn in the shower, so I strolled over to the general store and got a six pack of Corona beer. Here's what I learned from hiking and getting into a town, nothing tastes better than an ice-cold Corona. It was like mothers' milk. I was in heaven. I put on my rain gear, because it is only good for wearing while you do your laundry but do so before you shower because you will sweat your balls off in those rubberized suits. Laundry done, I headed back to take my shower only to find Matt sitting outside the cabin with his feet up on the rail chugging down my leftover Coronas. Kids got some nerve.

"Showers open, man it was great."

"Enjoying my beer? Hope you're not being stressed or anything."

"Nah, I'm good. You got that laundry under control? Anything I can do?"

"Yeah, go and get more beer, here's some cash, and watch out for Psycho, I saw him lurking around out there. And don't give him any money."

Dinner was no different than expected. Psycho didn't mean he was buying, he just wanted to have dinner with us. We ate at a little place next to the general store with a nice porch outside. As always on the trail, the food was "PFG". Matt and I sat sipping some beers while we learned more about Psycho during dinner. He told us about his time in Vietnam, what he remembered of his life after the war, (drugs and booze do affect the memory), his time living in Alaska, and by the way, he claims he held the record for the longest naked run in Alaska during the month of January. He did have some funny stories, but it also confirmed how screwed up he was.

The following morning was the best kind of morning, a "zero" day. We had blinds in our room, a luxury that nature does not afford. We slept in the next day, which means only sleeping till nine, but still, it seemed luxurious. When you stay at the NOC you don't stay in bed all day. We ate our breakfast and signed up for whitewater kayaking. It started with a class teaching how to survive should you end up in the river.

Basically, you want to be on your back with your legs pointed downstream and try to make your way towards the closest shore. If you should run into something your legs absorb the impact, so when you're swept up by the rapids you can continue downstream with broken legs. It's also important to remember not to try to stand up. Your foot could get jammed under a rock and the current keeps pushing you forward and under the water. Not a good place to find yourself.

I could see the apprehension in the boy's face. He had never gone whitewater rafting before, and he didn't want to do anything that involved paddling, or for that matter anything that was physical in nature. I had done this before, years back, so I knew what to expect. These were Class III rapids at their peak which meant this was mostly a leisurely trip. We rented one-man inflatable kayaks known as "duckies," I wish they had a better name for them, but that's what they were called. They drove us eight miles upstream and dropped us off so we could shoot the rapids back to the NOC. On the way to our drop point we shared the van with another family, a mother, father, and younger son, maybe ten years old. The whole ride there Matt tried to deflect his anxiety by joking about the adventure we were about to experience. He kept saying things like, "this is it man, this is how I die," and "I'm as good as dead," over and over. This young family behind us found it amusing and joined in laughing as Matt describe all the different ways in which he would meet his end on the river. One scenario involved man eating beavers.

The van eventually pulled over to the side of the road and we launched our kayaks. There were dark clouds gathering overhead when we pushed off, so in his mind it was another sign that he was doomed due to the inclement weather. He added flash flooding, lightning strikes, and tidal waves to his scenarios now. It didn't help when the driver of the van told him his "duckie" was named Titanic. We made it back to the general store about two and one-half hours later just before the rain really started coming down. We returned our equipment and made our way back to our room. Psycho was not staying the night, but we were. He was doing a "nero" and was getting ready to move on.

"Yo, Peterman how was the rafting?" Psycho inquired.

"Well, I just drifted down the river till we got to the whitewater, but the young lad here had to practice with the kayak paddles a bit. When we got to the whitewater, I saw he was frozen with fear, so as his father I knew I had to talk him through it. I knew I would have to guide him down the narrow churning channel of raging foamy ice water. As I shot through the steep slot nature had formed, I hollered commands to him, beckoning him to follow my lead. I know I led him to safety and back to the calm waters of the Nantahala River. We got back to the center and beached our kayaks. Matt was unsteady on his feet, his adrenaline still coursing through him. I sat him on a log at the beach and carried the two kayaks back to the resort. It was in this moment I realized I had taught him not to fear the white-water monster and that he was now becoming more of a man. It seems the little tyke is growing up right in front of my eyes." I tussled his hair just to add emphasis.

"Okay Matt, we've heard from you father, but something tells me he is full of shit. Now what really happened?"

"It was fun."

"Okay, great talk. Well boys, I have to live off V.A. money so I'm being evicted from here. I'll walk slow so you guys can catch me up the trail."

"Yeah, you do that. We'll walk even slower."

"You guys are always breakin' my balls. I love it." If only he knew we were being truthful. I thought when he said he was getting evicted they probably caught him in the hostel without paying. Who knows?

The next day we left the comfort and safety of our cabin after breakfast and headed out of the Nantahala. We had a food drop at the general store, now we were fully loaded again meaning forty-five pounds on our back climbing out of the gorge. Three-thousand feet in just six miles. We were only going to the next shelter, but a "zero" day has such a soothing effect on the body and mind that it's hard to get going again. Coming out of the NOC means climbing out of the river gorge. The hike up was not all switchbacks. To think we were complaining about how long it took to get to the bottom a few days before, especially when we could see it just down below. Boy was that short sighted.

The climb to the ridgeline was pure unadulterated torture, like it would be a challenge in a SAW movie, it was a nearly vertical climb. Imagine climbing the Empire State Building, which brings me to my next point.

I have a theory about the designers of the trail. They are, purely and simply, masochists and sadists. What in the name of all things big and small in God's heaven above are these people thinking? Really? They have you climb every mountain, no matter what the height, so when you get to the peak you can easily see the next mountain they want you to ascend, with no thought about how you might feel about it. Then they send you back down the mountain so you can repeat this process several times in one day. Idea. Why can't you go around the mountain? I'm sure the early settlers did not clamber up every mountain, I'm pretty sure they went around them. But these AT blazing assholes think this is such God damn fun. I was later told down the trail that some of the original designers of the trail were from the Pennsylvania Mountain Climbing Club, or some such organization, which explains why all we do is go up and down peaks. But I digress, you must vent every now and then.

To make things better, leaving Nantahala, only an hour into our climb, the sky opened up and we had thunderstorms for hours on end. Again, we hiked uphill in a torrent pouring down the mountain side which mirrored the river below.

2,040.2 miles to go.

Chapter 10
We Forge On

We forged on. It was hard to remember a time before Psycho. He had dominated our thoughts so much it seemed like he was with us from the beginning. Now we are free, but as it's said, the past is the past, so we hoped. We now hiked with the ghost of Psycho, he was still very much a part of our conversations and jokes. Matt and I would ask each other questions, "what do you think Psycho would do if..." and "who do you think Psycho is terrorizing now?" We did this day after day.

Now I don't want to sound repetitive, but I hate the damn mountains. It's a general theme for this story. Each night I would study my maps and the topography and all I see is ups and downs. I hate uphill and I hate downhill. I do like sleeping. I do like towns and drinking. Why can't they make a trail that ends in a town each night with nice featherbeds and food that isn't feet freeze-dried, even though it is "PFG." Maybe a Tilted Kilt or a Hooters restaurant.

To make the uphills seem quicker and simpler, I have started singing 100 Bottles of Beer on the Wall to myself. I'm getting it down to a science how many bottles it will take depending on the elevation of the climb. Matt just goes on ahead in silence and misery. His suffering is sometimes my joy. My friend Carl who I spoke with before this hike was right in hindsight, I should have started in Maine and hiked south, it's all downhill according to him. There's some rationale for you.

The hiking and all the routines that are the trail are now becoming much easier at this point. We have learned to "camel up," drinking a quart of water before we would leave the shelter, we didn't have need to carry as much water. We never really had to stop and suck wind anymore, though that doesn't mean these climbs still didn't kick our collective asses. Every now and then, like when leaving the NOC, we experienced a climb that would keep us humble. Setting up camp was now a methodical process, I would cook and hang our bear bags, which usually involved throwing a rope with a carabiner at the end over a tree branch. Matthew tried a few times but would get them tangled in the branches and we would need to cut the rope. We went through a fair bit of rope and carabiners. Matt would get the water, sweep out the shelter, and get a fire going. He would have burned down the forest just to get away from the bugs.

One night on our way to Fontana Dam we were the only two in a shelter. It got dark and when we realized no one else was coming in, we decided to set up our tent in the shelter. I'm surprised it took us this long to do that. With the tent pitched in the shelter there were no mice to worry about running over your face and no bugs buzzing around your ears. You would also be amazed how easy it is to convince yourself that this thin nylon layer of tent is an extra layer of defense from a bear. I've seen videos of bears peeling car doors open like I would peel an orange. Still, we continued to do this whenever we were alone in shelters. Something about it was a bit snugger and more protective, almost reassuring, like being in a cocoon

It wasn't a long trek into Fontana Dam from the NOC, maybe thirty miles, a two or three-day hike at the most. We trudged into Fontana Dam in the middle of the afternoon, looking at back to back "nero" days. We didn't get to take another "zero" day, but staying the night here allowed a brief respite from another night of sleeping on wooden boards. It also said in my AT Hikers Guide that this was a solid place for getting laundry done.

Fontana Village Resort is an interesting attraction by the dam. There is a main lodge that has a nice restaurant and surrounding that, smaller cabins. There was a general store with a laundromat in it and a marina on the dammed-up lake. It seemed like a pleasant place to spend the weekend.

Fun fact: It is said Fontana dam at 480 feet is the highest in the eastern United States.

You don't actually cross the dam until you leave heading north so that would have to wait for the following day. We headed to the lodge, instead of going the extra mile to the next wooden three-sided shelter, our collective thoughts being its insanity to walk past a nice comfy room so you can sleep outdoors on a dirty wooden floor. At least I couldn't make any sense of it. The registration building was just past the general store, so we headed up the hill in that direction. Now I don't know if it was the universe sending me a warning, but just then I got goosebumps that tingled up my spine and the hair on the back of my neck went up. This was familiar to me from being on the job that my mind sensed danger. From the front of the general store a shout broke the relative silence of that gray morning. "Hey, yo Matt, Peterman, what's up?"

Looking to our right, there was Psycho sitting on the general store porch in an old wooden rocking chair talking with some old geezer. This was unbelievable, inconceivable. We thought he had no money and he was staying at Fontana Dam. There was no escape now, he had seen us and locked on us like a SCUD missile. We turned and walked up to the general store, if Psycho was going be here, we needed a six pack, maybe two, and grabbing a sixer had become somewhat of a staple when we were able to do it. It made unpacking your entire bag, cleaning everything, and reloading everything somewhat more enjoyable. That and I needed something to do while Matt was showering ad infinitum.

"What's going on, what the hell are you doing here? I thought you were moving on?" I definitely thought he was out of our lives.

"Miss you and Matt, Peterman. The other people I met were as boring as hell compared to you jokers. I was finishing up some laundry and trading war stories with my buddy here. I was gonna pull out of here after that but since you guys came along I can hang around a bit. Whatcha' doing for dinner?"

Great. No serenity now.

"Don't really know. We still need to check in and clean up. We'll probably eat in the restaurant. Seems like the only option cause I'm sure as shit not eating Ramen noodles at this place."

"Too expensive for me Peterman. I'll be here a while, the laundry is next door. I'll wait here for you guys while you check in and come back with your laundry."

You can't imagine how disturbing this was to my frightened child and myself. This guy is a stalker, he has to be. We took our sweet time showering, that shouldn't come as a surprise to anyone by now, and we headed back over to the laundromat about an hour or so later. True to his word, Psycho was still rocking away and chain smoking his cigarettes. Matt and I were in our rain gear, doing our laundry, sitting in rockers on the porch with Psycho.

We sat with him drinking a few beers while waiting for the auspicious buzz of the washing machine. Psycho, being a recovered alcoholic, was telling us what booze can do to you. This usually led him to telling us some rather hilarious stories about going on benders, being banned from certain states or countries. I didn't need that, all I wanted to do was relax and enjoy my beer. But no, not for Bob. Bob gets no peace in this valley. "Hey Peterman, you know what that shit does to you?"

"Yes, that's why I'm drinking it."

"Funny, you know I did a lot of crazy shit on booze, man. Have I told you ab-?"

"I don't know, I don't care. I just want to enjoy my beer on this porch. I swear to God the more you lecture me the faster I'll drink. I'll even make the boy drink faster."

Well the last part is probably not true since I had to pay for his beer, but either way that shut him up for the moment. "Wow, Peterman, where did that come from? The hike getting to you?"

In my head, where I keep the really cruel remarks in silence, I thought, "no, not the hiking, it's you."

An hour or so later, with our laundry done we headed back to our room, but realized we needed another shower since we were drenched after sweating in our rain gear for the last hour.

Psycho wound up having dinner with us after all. I don't know where this newfound windfall came from, but I made a mental note not to lend any more money to him. Matt and I ordered a Caprese Salad which was honestly the best part of the meal. Fresh mozzarella cheese on a sliced tomato the size of a softball. We had to sit and listen to Psycho rant as to why this was not a proper salad and that anyone who thought it was a salad was an idiot. The two idiots eating it didn't seem to mind much. We followed that up with a full rib dinner, a comfortable bed, and sound asleep by eight. TV did not seem to matter much to either of us at this point, staying up to watch a show was precious time wasted that could be better spent sleeping in a natural bed.

The next morning was a "nero" day, so we ate breakfast and shuffled on out of the Fontana Dam Village and back into the mountains. Psycho was nowhere to be found as we made our way across the dam, praise the Lord. When you crossed the dam and head north on the trail you officially enter the Great Smoky Mountains National Park.

I've touched on this before, but national parks, and to a lesser degree, state parks, are different from other parts of the trail. The trails are much more traveled, generally better maintained, but what's unique to the Smokies are the bear cages. Several of their shelters at one time or another had a pseudo-front made of chain link. A reverse zoo, if you will. You are inside, caged in like an animal. All this did was cause hikers to feed the bears through the fence, taking pictures. The Parks Service decided to start putting an end to this, taking down the fences a few at a time. We stayed at a few shelters like these, but never had a bear encounter at one. Just imagine being in one of those shelters and there is a bear outside. It's pawing at the chain link and the handle on the door starts jiggling. I know I would do a Chapter 5 on the spot.

It should also be noted that the Park Service did not believe in privies by these shelters, so they had designated waste areas with supplied shovels if needed. A master of all positions by now, no shovel was needed by us.

Fun Fact: Another lesser known fact about the Smokies and the trail is that they allow horses to share some parts of the trail and even some shelters. Horses are skittish creatures, so all night long you hear them making noises.

Survival Note: The presence of horses tipped us off to another discovery, always get your water upstream

from the animals. I don't believe that needs any further explanation.

The first shelter into the Smokies is Molly's Ridge Shelter. This is one of a handful of "haunted" shelters, which we'll delve into later. The story goes it is still haunted by a Cherokee Indian maiden that died from exposure while looking for a missing hunter. It's said she is still seen sometimes in the early morning mists.

The Ranger report for the area was high bear activity, but alas it seems our first bear encounter remained the only one to this point. Matt must still have the stink on him. Our first day in the Smokies had us feeling pretty good about ourselves. We celebrated every milestone we reached. However, it would have been asking a bit too much to think Psycho left us and had pushed past Molly's Ridge.

Everyone's favorite nut job waltzed into the shelter about seven PM. A ravenous bear would have been more welcomed. He greeted us with his trademark, "Yo Matt, Peterman, what's up?" while lighting up a cigarette. "You guys won't believe the day I had."

He preceded to tell us about his perilous day. "They detained me man."

"Who detained you?" I asked, not wholly surprised by the statement.

"Fuckin Feds man, Homeland Security, or cops, hell, probably all of them."

Matt chimed in with a joke, "Oh, so they finally caught Sgt. Bilko Huff and Puff, yeah? Please tell me that's your skin and you're not wearing some poor victims."

"Nah, I'm telling you guys. I was at the Dam's Visitor Center minding my own business and the lady that runs the place just starts hassling me, can you belive it?"

"Yes, yes, I can believe that," Matt guffawed at him. So could I.

"So, we start arguing. I can't really remember the details of the conversation. A lot of blah blah blah and I said, "look lady, get out of my face or I'll blow this fucking dam up and you with it." Turns out this bitch can't take a joke. She's not like us Peterman."

Like us? I was like him? Jesus, maybe I should be nicer to people. Rethink my entire life. "What do mean people like us? Don't lump me in with what's going on in your head."

"Ah, come on Peterman, we're both sick and you know it."

I didn't have much of a dog in that fight. Most people who know me would agree with him. More and more people seem to tell me that they think there's something wrong with me. Matt wasn't having much luck containing himself at Psycho's story and demanded to hear the end.

"Alright Sarge, now get to the rest of it. You said you were detained. Let me guess, a full body cavity search?"

"Nah, man. I ate a snack outside the visitor center and then started to cross the dam, I got about half-way and the cops blocked off both sides. They came at me with guns drawn, yelling at me the whole time. Luckily, I've been in some similar situations, so I knew to drop to my knees with my hands behind my head. Man, I'll tell you, these guys were eyeballing the hell out of my backpack thinking it'll blow any second. They searched my bag pretty good, not even a firecracker in there. I told them I was traveling with a Lieutenant Colonel from the NSA and that he was waiting for me at the next shelter since we got separated. I even gave them your name, but they never heard of you. Imagine that. They let me go but told me to never come back unless I wanted to end up in jail. Like that's a threat. Fuckin' cops."

I cleared my throat at that remark, Psycho smiled at me and so Matt asked another poignant question. "So, what's that bring your total to? Of places you've been banned?"

"Too many." Psycho was smirking and lit up another cigarette. "Too many, man."

I truly never know when to believe him or not.

2,007.4 miles to go.

Chapter 11
Bambi vs. Peterman

Another common theme aside from my undying hatred of the mountains, is the rain. The next few days it continued to rain. If anyone told me there was a drought in the east, I would have strangled them. One day it rained the entire time we were hiking from start to finish. Try to imagine that, slogging through the mountains in a downpour all day. Imagine you had to work an entire eight-hour shift while someone continually poured water on your head. That would still be better than this. There is nothing worse than leaving a dry shelter to hike in the rain. It's hard to muster motivation when you wake up and you realize you'll be drenched before your done taking a piss. God forbid you need to do a Chapter 5. You ever try wiping with wet TP? The problem was, although we were used to walking in the rain, a cold front had moved in chilling the air and rain. That was just more good news. Of course, nature used this as a teachable moment for us.

Matt and I decided to forgo our afternoon snack; the weather was such crap we agreed to just book it to the next shelter. That was a mistake, it's easy to understand why people make poor decisions in bad weather. We made it to the shelter but both of us suffered for it. Severe cramps, headaches, low blood sugar, and dehydration to name a few of our ailments. One of the best things we did was carry powdered Gatorade with us. It was a good recovery drink while setting up camp. This time it came especially in handy. That was the last time we skipped a meal while on the trail.

Fun Fact: Clingman's Dome is the highest mountain on the Appalachian Trail at 6643 feet.

We came upon Clingman's Dome. As the highest peak it certainly and thankfully didn't feel like it on the trek up. The climb up to Clingman's Dome was relatively easy when considering some of the places we had been. After trudging to the peak through the dense forest you come out on a paved road leading to an observation tower with a huge parking lot. Just wonderful. We opted to continue to the shelter rather than climb up the observation tower. There wouldn't be much of a view unless you could see through the clouds. We could have hitched up to the Dome, but that would have been a highly frowned upon practice known as "yellow blazing."

The Appalachian Trail is marked in regular intervals on trees, rocks, signs, guardrails, etc., with "white blazes," paint strokes about two inches by six inches, and by observing them you know you are on the trail. Now if you are hiking for twenty minutes and don't see a blaze, turn around and go back, you are off the trail. You may even be lost. It happens to the best of us. Lost is not good.

When you choose to catch rides and skip parts of the trail, because the highway is marked with yellow lines, it is called "yellow blazing" by the thru hikers. There are also those called "purists," who when picked up on one side of the road to go into town, upon being dropped off they will go back to the side of the road where they were picked up and walk those extra twenty or so steps across the road to cover every inch of the trail. I would think only a psycho would do that, but I know a Psycho and there's no way he would do that.

However, I would have preferred going around the Dome instead of up and down it, which is basically what we did. It always got my goat when I would look at the maps and see them sending us up a mountain to come back down it not far from where we started up it. Why can't the mountain be cut out and the trail blazed across to where we would have come down? Would it shorten the route? Is that a problem? Not for me.

I thought we might have bear trouble in this section. As I said, the Ranger reported that sightings were high. Honestly, I wouldn't mind going out that way, just Man vs. Bear. Man vs. the Wild. I would fight valiantly to give my son time to escape so he may pass on our family name and tell stories to his children about his heroic father. Once again, that would not be Bob's fate. Instead it seemed I might meet my untimely demise at the hands, or rather the hooves, of a frenzied deer.

Matt and I had stopped for lunch at a shelter. It was a beautiful day and that is not something you hear me say often. We ate lunch and were resting and lounging around. Next to the shelter was a nice little meadow, the grass was only about ankle high, perfect for sunbathing. I pulled out one of my garbage bags and laid it down in the field. I was on my back for maybe ten minutes or so when I heard rustling behind me. On the edge of the woods was this little deer with budding antlers growling at me, or whatever it is deer do.

I don't know if I was on his turf or what, but this damn deer was stomping the ground and gnashing its teeth at me. This naturally startled me. I won't go as far as to say I was scared of this deer, but flight or fight kicked in and my blood was pumping. Now I always thought deer were meek, mild, fearful, nervous animals. Not so for this little critter. I took a few quick steps toward it expecting him to bolt off. As I got closer the dumb deer started setting into what I can only describe as an attack stance. I've seen enough of those dopey animal channels to know what elk and caribou do when they are ready to attack. They broaden their stance, snort, the head goes down, and they charge. This was happening in front of me and this was a first for me. It wasn't in any of the survival books I read on how to survive a deer attack. What should I do? I was at a loss.

My son, however, showed no signs of concern for his suddenly endangered father. He was sitting on top of the shelter's picnic table reading. It was good of him to put his book down and take the time to laugh at this upcoming wrestling match. "Matt, this stupid deer won't move."

"It's probably rabid, you're a dead man."

"That's funny, real funny, how about getting off your ass and helping me over here?"

"You need help in a staring contest with Bambi? Fine, but I can't promise I won't tell your friends about this."

"Right, so if it bites me I'll be the first asshole to die of deer rabies. No thanks. Throw a rock at it or something."

"I got this Dad, relax." Matt jumped off the table and headed toward their showdown. My son was coming to the aid of his father. My heart swelled with pride. It had me thinking that trail truly is a character-building experience.

"Hey little fella," Matt started, "I don't know if you heard the story of Bambi. Bambi's mom was being an asshole like you are, so all of a sudden the guy she was pissing off took out his .380 laser scoped Remington rifle, pointed that little red dot on Vixens head, and BLAM, that semi jacketed hollow point bullet hit her furry little head and it was blown to kingdom come. She now hangs in some lodge over a fireplace. Want that to be you little guy?"

Damn if that deer's eyes didn't widen with fear for a second, then suddenly it bolted into the woods. Matt grabbed his backpack and threw it on. "You're welcome tough guy," he said laughing as he slapped my shoulder.

"Whatever, I would have kicked that deer's ass." It wasn't my best come back. I pulled on my backpack and continued down the trail.

Survival note: Not all deer are timid, but the Bambi story sure as hell works.

Just like clockwork, later that evening, into the shelter rolls Psycho, followed by two of the reddest rednecks I have ever seen. "Hey yo, Matt, Peterman, what's up? I made a couple of friends here."

I couldn't understand a damn word those two guys were saying. Matt had lived in the south longer than I had, I thought maybe he could translate. I turned to Matt and asked, "Is that even English they're speaking?"

He just rolled his eyes and shrugged. He's always so helpful. Following behind them a few minutes later were their four young kids, and all of them had twelve-inch Bowie knives strapped on their sides. I don't know what these people were expecting to happen out here, but swords aren't really a necessity on the trail. Perhaps it could have helped against the killer dear.

We thought this might not be good with Psycho here, we hadn't yet had the chance to see Psycho interact with children, but to our pleasant surprise he just ignored them. Maybe there is hope for him, or maybe he knew better than to mess with redneck kids. All those horror movies about southern redneck cannibals went flashing through my mind. These are the nights when sleep eludes you, for many reasons. First, cannibal rednecks, second, Psycho, and third, four guys come stumbling in at midnight and woke us all up. As I mentioned earlier, when you don't

101

see white blazes for a while you are lost, and to get lost in the dark is far worse. What asswipes.

1994 miles to go.

Chapter 12
Never Get a Deep Tissue Massage on the Trail

To our delight we eventually came to Newfound Gap. It's a popular tourist stop in the Great Smoky Mountain National Park, right off HWY 441 in the Pigeon Forge/Gatlinburg area. The gap was also a rest stop off the highway. It split the park, it offered great views, and had a large parking lot for tourists. Of course, its proximity to Gatlinburg made it easily accessible as well. Hikers are a common sight there, but thru hikers still managed to look out of place.

At this point on the trail you've started to lose weight and for men the beards are getting a bit scraggly. It could have been the defeated look in my eyes, or it could have been my smell. Who knows? Tourists gave us a wide berth either way.

We had planned from the onset of this excursion that my wife Patti would meet us in Gatlinburg if we made it. We would take a breather in Tennessee for a long weekend and relax. Patti had rented us a cabin on top of a mountain. It was a nice change of pace driving up a mountain rather than walking, quicker too. I was thinking maybe we should have just driven to Maine.

Patti had driven up with one of Matthew's fraternity brothers who met her at the cabin she had rented. He was going to take Matt back to Knoxville for the weekend. My son would rather go back to school than spent a nice weekend with his father and stepmother. Crap, I would have done the same thing, but I missed my beloved too much to go without seeing her a second longer. At least that's what I told her.

Matt had talked to his friend and they were still about an hour away from getting to us. Our packs were leaning against a wall and we were reclined against them and relaxing knowing our vacation had begun. The tourists stared at us like we were an attraction. "Look at the hikers Honey, see how dirty they are?"

Others looked at us like we were beggars or a nuisance that had to be walked around. Not that Matt or I cared. These well fed, well rested, clean shaved, wonderful smelling people were as equally strange to us at this point. What wasn't strange was a voice that seemed to cut through the busy visitor center, ringing in my ears, like when Quinn scratches the chalkboard in Jaws. Well, my great white shark was here, the predator that's been stalking me for weeks now, "Yo Matt, Peterman, what's going on?"

"We're heading into town, got a ride into Pigeon Forge for two days and some R&R."

"Mind if I catch a ride? Thinking of taking a day off."

"Rides not here yet, if you want to get in quicker you can try hitching."

"How you getting in?"

"Wife's picking me and Matt up and we're taking two days off to relax. She rented a small cabin, fixed budget, Matt will be sleeping in the living room on the couch, but after the trail it will seem wonderful to him." I was not going to tell him she had made arrangements in Pigeon Forge to stay in a beautiful three-bedroom cabin with a hot tub. Matt was ecstatic. The only place he could spend more time in then a shower was a hot tub, I don't know what it is with that kid and hot water.

"I don't mind waiting with you guys, it will be nice. Can't wait to meet the missus," and with that Psycho threw his backpack down with ours, laid back and lit a cigarette. He pulled his hat down over his eyes, "Wake me when our ride is here."

"If you fall asleep, when you wake up, we might be gone." Babysitting was becoming annoying.

"Peterman, you do that to me?" He seemed shocked at my comment.

"Damn right Skippy." Ignoring me, he fell asleep.

Eventually we saw Patti pull into the parking lot in her minivan. Matt started kicking Psycho to rouse him from his sleep, I would have left him there sleeping. She pulled around to where we were sitting and parked the van. She was with Matt's buddy and both their eyes grew wide seeing how ragged we looked. However, my deeply devoted wife, the light of my life, jumped out of the car and ran to hug me, but backed away when she neared me and held her nose and said, "Jesus Christ, you guys stink."

My wife had known about Psycho from my emails and letters sent home. Now she was going to meet him, and he does not make very good first impressions. In fact, he never makes a good first impression. When she pulled up and saw us standing there with what appeared to be a homeless man, she had quite the quizzical look on her face.

"Hey Hon, great to see you, I've missed you desperately. I'm looking forward to a few days with you off the trail." All I was really thinking was, it's booty time for Bob. "This is Sarge, a well-adjusted guy we met on the trail. We're going to give him a ride into town." Sarge was the most common name Matt and I would call him to his face. We weren't about to go calling him Psycho to his face.

We piled into the van, Patti and Matt's friend upfront, Matt, Psycho, and me in the back. Patti drove into town with all the windows open and the air vents blasting at full power trying her best to suppress the powerful stench. It didn't work. The two upfront could not get used to it, but it was unnoticeable to us. They gagged while their eyes watered all the way to town. We took Psycho to a cheap hotel. When we dropped him off and he asked if he could join us for dinner, Patti responded and told him, "no problem." She still did not know this was Psycho.

After dropping off Psycho we went to a beautiful cabin. As soon as we arrived my son jumped into a shower, and with the prospect of going to Knoxville for the weekend and partying with his friends looming over him, he took the shortest shower to date. My wife engaged me in a conversation about the unbelievable smell that the three of us had brought into her car. She couldn't wrap her head around it. My wife, who is a nurse, said that in her thirty years of nursing between corpses and people crapping themselves, she had never smelled such a pungent stench. Gee, it seemed normal to us.

That night we went to a restaurant that was reasonably priced, I hoped I would not have to pay for Psycho's dinner, or so I thought. When the check came Psycho thanked me for his dinner. Patti by now was aware of who he was, and was cautious about dialogue with him, but he was not so cautious, no filters for Psycho. He told her she's my ball and chain, she was my old lady, how she needs to take better care of Matt and me, and so on.

Matt left us earlier, eager for the city life again. The cabin was mine and Patti's for the night and I took full advantage of it. The night was legendary, as was I. I lit up her world. Ron Jeremy has nothing on me, well not nothing, you know what I mean. I was a love God.

The next day Patti decided to wash everything Matt and I owned, sleeping bags, tent, clothes, if it could be put in a washing machine, she did it. We went to a laundromat in Gatlinburg and banged around town for the day. Guess who called and wanted to go with us, I get tired of leading the reader on like this, because you already know. We stopped by his motel and picked him up. He was now starting to grow on me.

Gatlinburg is quite the place if you have never been there. Mullet heaven. It's like the Island of Misfit Toys from the Rudolph the Red Nosed Reindeer series. We had lunch, restocked, did the laundry, and headed back to the cabin for more booty time. Bob needed more booty time, Patti wanted to wash the backpacks, but it is not recommended to put them into washing machines. They were the only items left that still had a horrible odor attached to them. Another method that is not recommended is filling a hot tub with soap and water and putting on the jets to wash them out. I guess if you were going to do that, a rental cabin beats doing it at your home.

Being able to do her husband's laundry again really got her going. It must have given her a sense of purpose again to cook and clean for me. She came into the bedroom so I could fulfill her every sexual fantasy. It did not take long. Not because of me, mind you, but because she doesn't have many fantasies. Sexually repressed, I suppose.

We could have played lost hiker and forest ranger, me being the ranger of course. "Oh, Ranger Bob, I am ever so lost in these great big woods. Can you help me find the big white blaze? Of course I can ma'am, I happen to have a big white blaze right here." Use your imagination.

After several minutes of intense lovemaking I smelled soap. I got up and looked in the porch area and I saw what she had done to our backpacks. Soap foam was building up and starting to spill over the side of the hot tub onto the deck. I turned off the jets and pulled them out. The packs had shrunk slightly and would not go back together the way they should. Patti had removed the internal framing, which I am quite sure you are not supposed to do. This was not good, our bags were stuffed as it is, and making them smaller wasn't what one would call helpful. Over the next day I continually tried to stretch them so they would fit together once again. After a day and half of stretching I finally got them back into place.

Matt found the whole story hilarious when he was dropped off later that afternoon. He must have had a great time with his friends, he was still sweating out the booze. His morale did seem a bit uncharacteristically high, even after multiple attempts to bring him down by taunting him with the following day's mileage. I think it was down time we both needed and we each relaxed in our own way. I didn't ask about his weekend; he didn't ask about mine.

That evening, Patti, being the thoughtful, kind, considerate wife she is, announced she was surprising us both with deep tissue massages. I was excited by the idea, being naked on a table except for a towel, a gorgeous woman working my body with her tiny, but strong and soft hands, continually kneading my wanting skin. I didn't want to over think this for fear of getting an erection while this sensual massage was being done. That could be embarrassing.

The doorbell rang, my anticipation grew, my heartbeat quickened and then, what the hell was this? A German couple walked in, husband and wife, the wife

108

having more facial hair than the husband. Hansel and Gretel on steroids. Both were a good two hundred and fifty pounds. My excitement turned quickly to fear and any worry of an accidental erection was erased, and my "boy," he had issued a full retreat. No nakedness for me.

Siegfried and Roy set their massage tables up in the living room. Matt and I sat by nervously watching these two get ready. It's not an over exaggeration to say they look like caricatures. Our Amazonian Fraulein kept shooting smiles over my way, where was Psycho when I needed him? I swear she was licking her chops while awkwardly pumping lotion into her hand. "Ya, so who is first?" Matt was backing away shaking his head, but I beat him to the punch.

"Why don't we let the lad go first? He's never known a woman's tender touch."

"That's very generous of you father," he replied through clenched teeth and staring daggers into me.

"Okay zzen, hop up on zee table mein little pup." Gretel grinned and off Matt went, probably too afraid of what would happen if he said no. I waited until her husband finished setting up his table and let him have his way with me. I surprisingly felt safer in his care.

Now let me tell you about a deep tissue massage. They work you like a speed bag in a gym. There are no fingers gently toning and relaxing your muscles, no soft hands at all, but sharp elbows prodding and probing your body, looking for muscle tissue to destroy. I was grunting and groaning like a hog buried in mud, the pain was excruciating. I looked at Matt and I could swear he was asleep. Maybe he passed out. He would later tell me he wasn't asleep but rather he did black out due to the pain, literally playing possum. When Ivan was done with me I climbed off the torture rack, my legs rubber beneath me, and crawled onto the couch. I was one beat up puppy.

Before leaving Goebbels and Himmler told us not to drink alcohol or go into the hot tub for at least two hours. Thanks to them ripping our muscles apart for an hour we had an increased blood flow. They warned us if we "drank or got in ze hot tub" we would become drunk faster. Hell, I don't think Matt let them finish their statement before I heard the sound of two beers being cracked open. He handed me a beer while heading to change into his swimsuit. I had to make sure my son was safe, so I once again sacrificed and joined him in the hot tub. We wouldn't want him to drown. It just so happened we did also get drunk faster now.

Survival Note: No deep tissue massages while hiking.

We hit the trail the next day, both of us sorer then when we had come off the trail. So here was another learning experience; if you are into domination and torture combined with severe lasting pain, try one of these massages.

Patti picked up Psycho and took him back to the trail with us, it wouldn't be safe for Gatlinburg if we left him there. The three of us set off with a sigh leaving civilization behind once more. Psycho seemed to be the only one who was happy to be going back into the great green fog. Matt and I beat Psycho to the next shelter. Even by the time Matt and I got there the shelter was crowded, but it was big. This shelter was one of the Nantahala style, there was a huge overhang over the shelter with a long shelf for cooking. Matt and I threw our stuff down to claim our spots on the wooden floor.

As usual, Psycho came in and pushed my stuff aside to get the corner. I was getting used to this by now, there was no sense arguing with him, it's just wasted breath. He set up his stove on the shelf and began cooking his dinner and lit up a cigarette. The three of us were startled when we heard yelling coming from behind us, "No, no, put that out, put it out!"

We looked and coming into the shelter from the water source was a sixtyish five-foot two-inch man wearing a hiking kilt. His name was Frog Croaker. He told us he got this name from hearing what he thought was a bear nearby one night and warned everyone in the shelter that he would handle it. Upon exiting the shelter, he stepped on a frog and it croaked in more ways than one, thus another trail name is born. There was no bear.

As Psycho puffed on his cigarette again, Frog Croaker jumped up and down and started yelling at him some more. He put down his water and ran twenty-five feet down the trail, demanding Psycho put out the cigarette, as he was deathly allergic to cigarette smoke. Psycho was having none of it. It started to get ugly with some name calling and arguing, I thought I was back on the force observing a domestic dispute. Frog Croaker was yelling, "I'll die, I'm allergic to smoke, I have sensitive lungs."

Psycho wasn't exactly the diplomatic caring type. "I bet you are sensitive, you liberal shit, and I don't care how allergic you are, I didn't take a bullet in the gut in Nam to not be able to smoke in the fucking woods."

"You don't understand. You're being insensitive." That wasn't the smartest thing for Frog Croaker to say, but I managed to talk Psycho into going out of the shelter area to smoke. Frog Croaker returned with a smug smile on his face feeling triumphant.

"You believe this guy Peterman? Probably a fuckin' draft dodger and he wants me to put out my smokes. God damn fuckin' midget."

"Yes," I commented, "but you handled it like a chemically balanced adult, for the most part, and for that we are proud."

People continued to pour into the shelter as the evening progressed. Hikers were coming in and trying to squeeze into the shelter. It got so crowded that Matt and I decided to camp that night at the bottom of a small hill where there was a tenting area. Problem was there were fifteen Boy Scouts down there. After our last experience we weren't thrilled about being around Scouts again. This, however, was a much more pleasant experience than the last time. These kids were what I pictured the scouts should be. When they found out we were thru hikers they bombarded us with questions and shared their dinner with us. They were polite kids, they cleaned up after themselves, perhaps most importantly, they crashed earlier than us.

Matt and I went up to the shelter to sit around the campfire and talk with fellow hikers, we also wanted to check in on Psycho. We got to the campfire in time to see Frog Croaker sitting around laughing and storytelling. Psycho was sitting nearby scowling at him. Frog Croaker didn't seem to be having any trouble with the smoke from the fire. This did not escape Psychos notice. "Hey, er, Frog Croaker, you doing alright there? I mean that's a lot of smoke your breathin' in, it'll be a hell of a time getting you rescued out here." Frog Croaker's smile disappeared which seemed to please Pyscho.

"It's only cigarette smoke I'm allergic to. It's got chemicals in it." With that he got up and went back into the shelter to turn in.

Well, let's just say Psycho can't let sleeping Frog Croakers sleep. He tends to hold a grudge. As he lit up a cigarette, there was a bit of twinkle in his eye, and he said to me, "let's see if it does kill him." He walked to where Croaker was sleeping in the shelter and started blowing smoke in his face. Thank God there was no reaction.

Hikers midnight comes fast so it was time for me and Matt to turn in. Since Frog Croaker wasn't dead, down the hill we went.

After we packed up the next morning we checked to see if Frog Croaker was still alive, and thankfully there was still a pulse. As we were leaving a Ranger came into the camp area. He was on horseback and had a semi-automatic shotgun draped across his lap. He told us that there was a wild boar in the area that had charged some hikers yesterday and he was looking for it. Boars are a major pestilence in the southeastern United States. They range from the tips of Tennessee down to Florida and over to Texas. Throughout these mountains they can grow quite large. Farmers and landowners take precautions in these states and along the trail, there are fences with ladders and gates built in designed to keep the pigs out but make it easy for hikers to get over. We felt there was no need to see anything from the swine family, especially an enraged steroid enhanced Porky Pig.

I told the Ranger there about my encounter with the deer on the trail. He told me that it's a little-known fact, but some deer and elk are what they call opportunistic carnivores. No one will ever believe me when I say I had an encounter with a flesh-eating deer.

1,967 miles to go.

Chapter 13
The Road Kill Grill and Lounge

Matt and I had a mail drop set up at the Road Kill Grill and Lounge. It was a small restaurant and general store that doubled as a hiker hostel as well. We were out of the shelter ahead of Psycho this day and didn't tell him we were stopping there. Perhaps at last we might finally be free. You come out of the woods onto a winding country back road about a mile and a half away from the grill. Most hikers, including us, had no problem walking the distance, especially for the "trail famous cheeseburgers." That doesn't mean we weren't lazy at heart or that we didn't try to avoid walking, we did avoid walking whenever possible. We waited about thirty minutes to hitch a ride but not a single car came by. We thought if we started walking maybe we could at least hitch part of the way there. Besides, we didn't want to wait any longer for fear Psycho would catch up to us. It really didn't matter to us walking down to Road Kill Grill, we were staying the night and the Hiker's Guide said they had the best burgers around, and I'm pretty sure that there wasn't anywhere else to get a burger within twenty miles.

The Hikers Guide is an excellent companion and it gets better every year, however sometimes it's not always clear. We followed its directions to get to Road Kill Grill but when we hit a four-way intersection we erroneously thought we had to go straight across.

As we started down the road we heard a deep southern voice from a porch that was attached to a dilapidated wooden shack. I've seen refrigerator boxes used as homes in better shape. I know it seems like a stereotype, but that's how back country this place was. There were glass panes missing on the windows and there were plastic bags taped up in their place. The door was hanging on one hinge, it had never even been painted. There were rotted cars and other indiscernible machinery spread across the lawn. A typical southern mansion.

There on the deck standing on the few planks of splintered board left, stood something that shook my faith in the human race. It was a male, about thirty years old, three-hundred pounds, with a beard like the guys in ZZ Top. He was wearing a sleeveless t-shirt and overalls, the ones that have the straps that go over your shoulder, but only these were cut into shorts. Like a typical southerner, only one strap was attached over the shoulder. He had a baseball cap on backwards and a can of beer in his hand. Not that it's a bad thing, but it was not yet noon. To cap the whole thing off was the scraggliest looking bloodhound sitting next to him. This was a scene straight out of the "Hills Have Eyes."

"You boys don't want to go down there. Your kinfolk may never see you again." It smacked with that southern redneck drawl, very monotone, and scared me. It was a threat.

"Hey, uh, we're looking for the Road Kill Grill," Matt chimed in.

"Well don't look that way city boy. It ain't down that way." This is real, he turned and spit the biggest brownest phlegm ball I've seen to date. Chewing tobacco, I hoped, if not, I'd recommend he see a doctor, but we would have to save that conversation for another time.

"Which way would you suggest?" I was hoping he understood the bigger words like suggest.

"Down that a' way be healthier if ya keep your feet moving." He pointed up the other road. "Don't know why you people gotta come down here and piss in our yards. I don't come up to where y'all live and stomp through your shit, do I?"

"Hey, I didn't piss in your yard." Got to learn to think before speaking.

"Don't you get smart with me boy."

"No sir, I wouldn't dream of it, don't think there's much a chance of that happening." Again. Think.

"Yeah, and what's that suppose to mean?"

"Nothing." How do they say thanks down South? "Mucho gracias." I don't know why I said that, I think I was too far south.

We retreated down the road. Matt asked in his naive boy's voice, "Hey Dad, why do you think he didn't want us going down that road?"

Ah, the naivete of a college boy. "I can only assume, being the deep south, that there were moonshine stills, maybe a field of marijuana, inbreeding, cabbage patch kids, people screwing sheep, or vice versa, God only knows." It wasn't long before we could see Road Kill about quarter of a mile up the road, so we stepped up our pace and turned into their driveway

Survival Note: Never screw with deep wood rednecks.

"Yo, Peterman," was heard from the back of a pickup truck that had just turned in as we did. Son of a bitch. Matt and I thought we lost him and here he was arriving the same time, plus he got a ride. The gods are definitely against us. He was all smiles and laughs as he dismounted from the truck. "Hey, didn't know you guys were coming here, thought I might have lost you Peterman."

He must have a tracker in one of our bags, it's the only explanation. I must check.

116

Matt and I strolled into Road Kill Grill, paid for our evening stay, and of course to eat their world class cooking.

The store itself was a small stone building with a dining room that was straight out of the seventies. The most abundant thing in the store were cigarettes and Dolly Parton memorabilia. Dolly is the pride and joy of this part of the world. The tables were the old wood that look more like plastic and the seats were bright fire truck red. The tables needed to be scraped clean and there were flies as big as birds buzzing our ears. I'm thinking to myself, thank God I can't see the kitchen. To be honest, had this been the real world I would not have eaten here.

They didn't bother hanging their health inspection certificate in a conspicuous place, not that I wanted to see it. It didn't really matter though, for trail food this is 4.5 stars. Matt and I ordered the deluxe burger, hoping it was beef and not some roadkill animal, or worse a person that went down the wrong road. It was "PFG" anyway.

Psycho sat in the booth with us looking forlorn and hungry. "Hey Sarge, you gonna eat?" Matt asked. Matt is such a Christian, so full of compassion and love for his fellow man.

"I only got ten bucks and I want to stay here tonight so I need the money for that." Big surprise, he has no money again. He always had that sad look, like the whole world forgot about him. It was pathetic, but I'll be damned if he wasn't good at it. He had mastered making this silent downtrodden face that you know has gotten him some sympathy a time or two.

"Here's five bucks, get a burger, will you."

"I can't take money from you Peterman, that's not right."

"You're screwing with me, right? You're about fifty deep into me already, and now you develop principles and pride? Get the damn burger, it's not a loan, I'll treat you."

"You're okay, Peterman, you know that?"

Matt and I picked up our drop packages so we could restock and headed to our cabin. Psycho also had a package waiting for him there, which was a convenient cover for him stalking us. He saw a package for Frog Croaker sitting on the rack and he started taping his used cigarette butts to it. He is a sick man. One could only imagine exactly how his mind truly works.

It was here in Road Kill Grill that I met a gentleman with his wife who were picking up some odds and ends, and believe me, that's just about all there was in this store. He started up a conversation with me, "I can see your thru hiking the trail, is that right?"

"Yes sir, started in Georgia, going strong." I was hoping he was going to offer some type of trail magic.

"You should know that some of the shelters you'll be staying at have metal roofs."

"Okay, is that good or bad?" I asked.

"Point is, my wife over there and myself sheltered in one two years ago during a lightning storm. I understand they are quite safe when you're in them, but when this storm let up my wife and another stepped out to get water and a bolt of lightning hit the shelter. The two outside went flying. I ran over to her, got her heart started again, and got help from the rangers. She was in the hospital for almost a week. Lost complete hearing in one ear and she used to have beautiful long hair, now it's all curly and coarse."

"Sorry to hear that." I didn't know if he was pulling my leg or not, but her hair looked like that of Little Orphan Annie.

"Just make sure you wait awhile after a storm if you are in one of those shelters. Better safe than sorry." He was very serious throughout his tale, so I figured a word to the wise and would heed his advice.

Survival Note: Fear lightning.

Now it may be hard to believe a lot of this, but it is the truth. Road Kill had tenting pads and several cabins that had a couple of bunks in each of them. They were about eight feet by eight feet square, with stacked bunks on each side. They were smaller than an actual prison cell. Matt and I got cabin two, the "Jungle Room." I am not making this up, there was a big sign over it saying, "Jungle Room," named after Elvis and the cabin was painted like a jungle inside and out. It also doubled as the honeymoon suite. A honeymoon suite with six bunks? Being in this part of this south I assume it's possible that people did honeymoon here. Maybe the guy we crossed down the road marrying his dog?

Best of all, for once the skies parted and the sun shone upon us, Psycho was in cabin one.

Off to the back of Road Kill Grill was a river that ran past the property. There were picnic tables close to the river for hikers to use and eat at. Psycho was busy doing Psycho stuff, we sat at the picnic table with a hiker named Pat. We talked for a bit over a few beers we managed to scrounge up in the Grill.

Pat told us he was a section hiker. He explained to us that he, like many people who tackled the trail, didn't have the time to give the trail a go all at once. He would take off work a week or two at a time and pick up where he left off. We met him at Road Kill, meaning he had put several years' worth of hiking in to get to this point and he was only two-hundred-thirty something miles, so roughly two thousand to go. Pat was in his mid-thirties, so we calculated he'd be about sixty-five when he finished. That's a lofty goal.

We told him about Psycho and our time with him. Matt told him about how we ended up out here, how I was a retired cop and our trials and tribulations. Pat found our stories hilarious to this point and probably assumed we embellished a bit. He didn't know us well enough yet to realize we were only speaking the truth. Matt and I enjoyed talking with Pat, it was a welcome breath of fresh air after the past few weeks with Psycho. We had almost forgotten what normal conversation was like.

Pat had only been on the trail for a few days when we caught up to him. He told us he had been hiking with some younger kids who seemed to be about Matthew's age. The two guys who looked to me like your run of the mill hippies, were just that. They came and sat down with us and had a few beers. Matt, Pat, and I were finishing up our dinner, when one of the hippies whipped out a joint. He lit it up and started puffing away while the other hippie looked at us and asked, "Hey, do you guys mind if we smoke?"

Even if I did mind, it probably would have been smarter to ask before lighting it. I was a bit worried about Matthew being exposed to the "Devils Weed," a nubile college boy like him is easy prey to hippies and cults.

"I don't mind," Pat said, then pointed at me, "but you may want to ask him, he's a cop." This kid's eyes grew like the Grinches heart in that moment. Hippie instinct must have kicked into high gear because he flicked that joint with such accuracy and precision that I had never seen before. His joint was in the river in a second flat and was washed downstream. No cop was going bust him.

"Guys, I've been retired for a few years now, I could give two craps what you do. We are also out in the middle of the woods, what could I possibly do anyway?" Realizing now the gravity of his mistake he looked at Pat.

"Pat, not cool man, not cool," anguish was on in voice.

"Hey, I didn't flick your doobie into the river, you did that one all on your own," Pat said with a chuckle. I knew I liked this guy. He might be as sick as I was. Very cool. I must attract these people. Psycho had come over to eat with us and joined us. After an hour or so Pat leaned over to me and said, "You weren't kidding about this guy."

No, no I wasn't, I said to myself.

Matt and I got up to turn in for the night. There were six of us there at Road Kill Grill that night; two hippies, Matt and myself, and Psycho and Pat. Pat assumed he was with the hippie kids but when we got up and told us he was in cabin one, Matt and I looked at each other and then at Psycho. Psycho was in cabin one and the biggest shit eating grin spread across his face.

"Hey Pat, me too!" He got up with Pat and started to lead him back to cabin one. I swear I heard banjo music start playing at that moment. Pat looked back at us in despair as he was led into the tiny cabin with Psycho.

We found Pat sitting with Psycho the next morning eating breakfast. Pat had a bit of glazed look going on. Psycho was doing his normal thing, smoking cigarettes and drinking his black coffee. Matt couldn't help himself, I really don't know where he gets it from, "Hey love birds, how was your night together?"

Pat chuckled nervously, Psycho stood up, "It was good, wasn't it Pat? Nice and relaxing." He gave Pat a slap on the back as he walked to his cabin whistling Dixie.

"Shit man, I was only kidding, you look like you've seen things," Matt said questioningly.

"You guys really weren't kidding. He's quite the character."

The evening before we had discussed with Pat our hiking timetable for the next couple of weeks. He was more or less on the same schedule as us and asked if he could tag along. It would be nice to have someone else around, besides someone was going to have to corroborate our stories. Pat is a real person and his identity has not been changed to protect him. Even after everything we told him and he witnessed that night he still wanted to tag along.

1920 miles to go.

Chapter 14
A Trail Name is Born

Though we were now out of Great Smokey National Park it was still a pretty busy piece of the trail. The day after leaving Road Kill Grill we ended up in a shelter with twelve other people. The problem here was it only slept six. It would be a big problem on the horizon when Psycho came in. Psycho didn't carry a tent; he would want the shelter. Pat, Matt, and I were early enough to claim spots, but Psycho wasn't. The man had to stop multiple times a day for smoke breaks, he also never uses walking sticks, which as we discussed early on, makes hiking much more difficult and slower. He would usually stroll in an hour or two behind us, huffing and puffing while reaching for his cigs.

Well, as predicted, once he saw there was no room at the inn his Psycho switch kicked into overdrive. He began arguing with me, getting increasingly louder and louder. "What the hell Peterman…" followed by crazy statements about Vietnam and Iraq. I saw what he was doing, I think he forgets at times that I was a cop. De-escalating situations was my job for thirty years. Not that it mattered, this was all a show, and it was working. He was trying to scare people out of this shelter to open a spot for himself. I'll be damned if it didn't work. A young couple on the other side of the shelter packed up their bags and headed up the trail a bit to camp. Psycho turned to me all smiles as he unrolled his sleeping bag in the now vacant spot. This was Pat's first true taste of Psycho in the wild.

All he could do is stand there and shake his head in amazement.

There is a common prank on the trail among people who travel in groups or with friends, and that's to sneak weird things into people's backpacks without them noticing. Man, are people pissed when they realize they were carrying extra weight all day. Long distance hikers live and die by ounces. Before leaving Road Kill Grill, Matt had packed a Gideons Bible in the bottom of Psychos pack. When he found it later that evening he did not see the humor in it.

I think if there is one thing we should have known about him by now is his twisted mind would not be outdone. He spent the entire night reciting parables from the Bible to us at the campfire. He would say, "Hey Matt, you know the Lord says," and read some random passage whether it made sense or not. No one in the shelter was real happy having this scraggly old fart sitting at the campfire proclaiming the word of the Lord. In hindsight it was not a good idea to put a Bible in his bag, Matt should have put a rock in his bag instead.

Our new hiking order with Pat along is Matt still in front, eating spider webs, me behind him, and Pat taking up the rear. One reason Matt took the lead all the time was for some reason Mountain House meals at night and Pop Tarts in the morning gave me unbelievable gas at times. Matt chose the webs over the constant gassing. Pat fell victim to my odorous expulsions, spending some mornings for about an hour or so bitching about my condition. This went on every day till Pat had to leave the trail.

Matt would continually bust out laughing every time he heard Pat behind him exclaim, "Jesus Christ

Peterman, you really need to see a specialist about that problem. What died in your ass?"

While we were hiking and talking to Pat the next day, Matt and I were trying to come up with a trail name for him, it's funny what you can spend hours talking about on the trail, yet he is just a regular guy. He said he never got a trail name because he hadn't really done anything wrong yet, so it was hard to nail him with some humiliating trail name. A trail name that's deserved, albeit embarrassing. It was our goal. I knew he liked beer, his name was Pat, so we reversed it and named him Tap, as in a beer tap. I know, it's lame, but calling him Pat wasn't going to work. He was pleased with the new name, but inside Matt and I knew it wouldn't stick. We would come up with something.

Our next destination was Hot Springs, North Carolina. The night before we got into town we spent at a shelter with twenty-one churchgoers. The tent had to go up, there was no room in the shelter, even Psycho could not get in. In this kind of scenario Psycho opted for the solitude. Matt and I had concerns because Psycho had made it known to us in the past he did not really care for religious people. We all agreed it would be best to avoid the shelter entirely. We tented far from the shelter to prevent interaction between the looney tune known as Psycho and the God lovers. All he had was a tarp, so he would string a rope between two trees and throw his tarp over it. He said, "I've slept in the damned jungles of Vietnam, I can sleep on this bullshit dirt."

He set the tarp up by our tent, maybe he thought it would shield him from all the religion going on around him. Well, whenever we set up a tent, you know it is going to rain, and it did. Tarps don't work well in the rain. You think a dry Psycho is bad news, you should see a wet one. That "bullshit dirt" turned to "bullshit mud."

Finally, we reached Hot Springs. This was another "Trail Famous" spot along the way. The whole town at best is maybe five-hundred yards long. We stayed in a fleabag hotel because it was cheap and that's all that really mattered to us. The shower head was all crusty and rusted, with only three little streams of water coming out of it, but at this point seemed like the best shower we ever took.

Psycho got his room, thankfully a few doors down, and it became his habit to sit in the doorway of his room on a chair with the door open. I believe he did this so he could watch us when we were going somewhere. Watching us, he saw us leaving, and joined us in going out to dinner that night at a pub, the only pub on the main street. Matt picked up a new trail name, "Four Brew."

Matt and I had a pizza which both of us agreed was the best pizza ever to grace this green earth. That, or it's the first pizza we had in who knows how long. We were drinking with dinner and after four beers Matt fell asleep at the table, hence "Four Brew." When we left the restaurant all the beer we had drank was put on Taps bill, and although I gave him the money for ours, Psycho thought Tap had drank that many beers by himself, and he was now onto preaching the sins of drinking to Tap.

"Do not get drunk on wine, which leads to debauchery, instead be filled with the spirit," Psycho said, of all people, quoting the Bible. It might have been the Bible we put in his bag. He never ceases to amaze me, going all biblical on Tap.

"Sarge," Tap said flatly, "I am filled with the spirit. The type of spirit that's 80 proof."

"You're going to hell, Tap. There is no hope for a soul such as yours in this world," Psycho said laughing.

"Well goodnight guys, we're going to hit the sack. Sarge, don't stop until he accepts the Lord," I chimed in, and Matt and I made a beeline to our room while the sermon continued.

Fun Fact: The town was used as a POW camp during WW1, many of the prisoners found it so hospitable they wanted to stay.

The next morning was an unassuming one, it was a beautiful day, and all four of us were taking a "zero" day in this sleepy mountain valley town. I will admit it's a beautiful area, but there isn't much to do. Matt and I were going to check out the towns name sake, Boiling Springs, but first on the menu was breakfast.

We met Tap and Psycho again in the only diner in town. A small rustic diner, the tub of lard sitting by the grill, bacon sizzling away, home fries stacked to the side, and of course grits boiling. I ordered what I thought would be the safest breakfast to eat. Unbeknownst to us, it would be our last breakfast with Tap.

While we ate, we were watching some news channel on a television mounted in the corner above us. We didn't get to see much news, but one of the big stories was the birth of a baby panda in some unnamed zoo. Matt, feeling grouchy and tired from his four beers and lack of sleep let go a tirade about the poor harmless pandas.

"I can't believe this is even newsworthy. You know what pandas are? They are nothing but big stupid useless animals and they can't even breed by themselves, they need our help and now I'm stuck having to watch panda porn. Some creatures are not meant to live on this earth."

Tap replied, "Rough night? Come on Matt, you got to admit there pretty cute and lovable."

I immediately saw it coming, Tap should have kept on eating and kept his mouth shut, but he didn't know Matt that well. The silence was but for a moment, and then it came.

"That's you! That's your new trail name," Matt said excitedly, "you're not Tap anymore, you're Panda." And thus it was spoken, and thus it was done. This is how real trail names are born.

I repeated, "Yeah, big, dumb, stupid useless animal. That seems about right."

Meanwhile Psycho was howling with laughter, elbowing Panda in the ribs. "Boy they got you pegged. Panda it is. I think I knew a Panda once in 'Nam."

The argument by Tap/Panda to forego this trail name meant nothing to us. It stuck with him for the rest of his time on the trail and in all likelihood, his life. In fact, when I talk with him or see him, I still refer to him as Panda. His wife even calls him Panda at times. Psycho thought it was hysterical, if only he knew his "real" trail name.

The actual hot spring itself is right on the edge of town at a resort. They cleverly pump the mineral rich water into hot tubs, which are surrounded by privacy walls. They are hot. We could only stand to spend a few minutes at a time in the tub without being boiled alive. Had we stayed in we would have looked like shriveled prunes. At last I found the one place with hot water that Matt couldn't spend an hour in.

An interesting side note; the woman who set us up in the hot tubs had lived in Hot Springs her whole life, she was fifty-seven years old, and had not traveled more than twenty miles from the town. I could not imagine that. She said everything she needed was right here. It's hard to believe she and I exist in the same reality.

1,846.3 miles to go.

Chapter 15
The Town that Hung an Elephant

We had a relatively peaceful few days hiking into Erwin, Tennessee. Relative being the keyword here. Against what would seem to be the prevailing wisdom, I had eaten some really spicy food the night before we left Hot Springs. I had several tacos, this was the only time in the entirety of my life that I had Mexican food in a place where there were no Mexicans, my system was not ready for it.

I woke up to a fire burning in me that had started the night before. I certainly was not expecting the heat that was imposed on my ass the next morning during what was luckily an over the water Chapter 5. We started out of Hot Springs, but my butt cheeks started to chafe something awful. I was sore and walking bowlegged. The friction between my cheeks was so intense each step I took looked like I was sending smoke signals out of my ass. I didn't understand what was happening. I never got blisters on my feet, but I couldn't imagine blisters being worse than this pain. My pace was slow and excruciating. Panda noticed my discomfort as he hiked behind me and asked what was wrong. "Bob, why the hell are you walking like broke back mountain?"

"Tacos. The God damn tacos. I feel like I passed a ghost pepper that was lit on fire out my ass. My can is burning up, it feels like my butt cheeks have sandpaper stuck between them, and we still have eight more miles to go."

"Well, I told you not to eat spicy food before the trail. I would have thought you'd be ahead of this learning curve." Panda was obviously enjoying my discomfort, but as always, he was still breathing in my gas, only now it was heated and lethal.

"Hey, I'm not the one that gave you that trail name, Matt was. Have some sympathy for me. I ate some tacos and now damn it, I have Montezuma's revenge." A tear ran down my cheek, the cheek on my face, but if my ass could cry it would have. The closest thing to satisfaction I could get was taking a shot at him and his stupid trail name.

"Don't you hiking geniuses have any Glide?"

"And what the hell is Glide, Panda?"

"It's like a deodorant stick, but it is a thick coating type of lubricant." Panda dropped his pack and reached into one of the zippered compartments to show me. "This is Glide." He was holding up something just like he had said, a deodorant stick

"You put it on your chaffed areas and it immediately soothes and lubricates." Panda was beaming that he knew something Matt and I didn't.

"Well give it to me and let me try it," I had my hand out to Panda.

"No way. You're not rubbing my stick of Glide up and down your ass crack. It's just not right dude."

"Come on Panda, I'm in pain." And believe me, I was.

"Tell you what. I will carve a little piece off the top of this stick so you can rub it on your red swollen ass," Panda was now laughing. The things these big stupid Pandas think are funny are not funny to humans.

I took the little piece he gave me. "Have you rubbed this on your ass? I don't want it touching me if it's been in your crack. I don't see any fur stuck to it." Always time for humor.

"Funny. I used it under my arms when I chaffed there. And really? You're the one with the campfire in your pants, not me. Beggars can't be choosers, buddy boy. Use it or not."

I dropped my pack and then went a short distance into the woods, yanked down my shorts, and rubbed this substance up and down my ass, coating my cheeks and the sphincter area. This wasn't a time to be shy, I got all up in it. Within the time it took me to walk back to them, I noticed all the discomfort had gone away. This stuff was a miracle. My cheeks were slick and ready for action, some hardcore hiking action that is. I wanted to buy stock in the company, I wanted to buy the company. This stuff is a hiker's gold, believe me. You can always learn something new on the trail. I keep it at home now. When we hit a hilltop with signal, I called Patti.

Survival Note: Never eat real spicy food before hiking long distances.

"Hey sweetheart, I need you to order something for me and send it in the next drop."

"Sure, no trouble. What do you need now?"

"Well, there's this stuff called Glide. G-L-I-D-E. Order two sticks for us."

"What's it for? Never heard of it."

"It's a lubricant, and, no, not sexual. For chaffing. It's amazing. Mail one for me and one for Matt."

"What's chaffed, honey?"

"If you really want to know, my ass. So, I need two, Matt's ass is not going anywhere near my Glide stick."

"How is Matt? Do I need you to send proof of life? Haven't heard from him at all. No one has."

"His frat house has, that's for sure. Get that ASAP please. Love you, miss you. Got to go, don't want to use up the battery."

"Miss you too honey." If you ask me, she still lacked sincerity.

Continuing, now comfortably on our trek, we stayed in a shelter with three sisters, all in their seventies. They told us they would get together once every summer to hike in the mountains and had done it for the last fifty years. These old broads were hiking together before I was born. The shelter slept six, but Psycho still had the three sisters squeeze together so he could have more room. This trip is starting to get really funny. On a side note I am beating Matt in Gin Rummy to date 20,235 to 19,380.

The Golden Girls pulled out early the next morning as we were having breakfast. We had never really noticed before, but Psycho was always the last one out of camp. We never really connected the dots at the time, but due to his wound from the war he waited for others to leave before he attended to his personal matters. It was the most considerate thing he had done. Well, that was all until today. Psycho walked into the woods to do a Chapter 5.

Matt and I were eating breakfast around the campfire. The coals were still glowing from the night before, so Panda started throwing some sticks in to stoke the flames. Panda was awfully pleased with himself, "See here Four Brew," he said mocking Matt, "you're not the only one who can get a fire going."

Panda was giggling to himself, but Matt was quick to respond, "Just like a big dumb stupid panda to think he started a fire that was already lit, that's like putting lettuce on a cheeseburger and saying you cooked it."

We all laughed at that comment, even Panda, as Psycho walked out from behind the bushes. Matt and I had already gotten up and were cleaning our bowls out, Panda was still sitting and staring at his roaring accomplishment. Psycho began to throw some paper into the fire. Once again, the Gods spoke, and the winds shifted. Panda was sitting and still eating his breakfast by the fire. The smoke was now blowing directly into his stupid Panda face. Psycho was just merrily throwing this paper gingerly into Panda's fire without a care in the world. If Psycho had done this before, we had never seen it.

Matt jabbed me in the side, "Dad, is Psycho throwing what I think he's throwing into the fire, and if yes, am I correct in saying Panda is now breathing it in?"

It's like my whole life had led to this one perfect moment. I could see Matt was holding back with all his might, moments like these are rarely gifted to us. I looked over to Panda, "Hey Panda, you should get a load of what Sarge is doing right now."

Panda looked up to see Psycho tossing the paper into the fire all the while humming to himself. "Hey Sarge," Panda lectured, "you're supposed to pack your garbage out."

"I don't want to carry that, it's the paper I wiped my ass with, it's full of shit."

Panda jumped up and yelled, "Wait! What! What the fuck is wrong with you? Burning shit paper? Oh my God, I'm breathing it in! I breathed in your shit! God damn it! You're really fucked up man!" He was one pissed off Panda.

Matt and I were laughing our asses off. "Hey Panda, it's in your lungs now. How did Sarge's shit taste? Oatmeal and shit for breakfast. Hey, that could be the breakfast of champions." Tears were flowing down our eyes and we were doubled over.

"No, no," Matt said. "It could be the breakfast of pandas. And pandas probably do eat shit. And father, I do believe you are being a bit insensitive to panda culture. Who are we to judge their ways?"

"Hey Panda, Sarge's shit or my gas, which has more flavor?"

We did not let Panda live this incident down, not ever. Not to this date. We loved that moment.

The trip into Erwin was a lot of climbing, which included scuttling up and over some boulders. The weather was a total crapshoot, it would rain then stop, rain then stop. In a lot of ways that was worse than constant rain, just as soon as you thought it was over it would begin right back up, so eventually we just gave up on our rain gear.

Psycho made a detour into a town to get some cigarettes, and again, according to him they chased him out of town. This time, he says, it was because he was calling them hillbillies. Banned again. The guy is really starting to rack up the banishments. Matt and I slowly started to believe his story. He was acting moody and carrying on in a way we hadn't seen before. The whole time he is setting up at the shelter, getting water, preparing dinner, he's yelling "the trail sucks and all hillbillies blow." We were sure something happened in town, but he would not tell us what happened.

As Psycho is going off on his tirade two new hikers came up the trail into camp. One of the guys asked Matt, "Is this guy staying in the shelter tonight?" Matt just cracked a smile and nodded in the affirmative.

Unfortunately for this random hiker Psycho had heard him. "Yes, I am and it's none of your fuckin' business," he said while charging toward this now frightened man. Pointing, he said, "I'll be sleeping in that God damn corner right there." They, being normal people possessing common sense, moved on.

We are starting to smell worse, whatever effect washing our possessions had is long gone. You get used to your stink, but we noticed it more now as it got a lot hotter, and on the windless humid days you can feel yourself basting in your own juices.

The trail doesn't go through Erwin, Tennessee like it cuts through Hot Springs. You must either walk or set up a ride. The town is not a short walk from the trail but it's a popular destination for hikers and there are several people in town who will come and pick you up. We didn't go directly into town since Erwin itself is off a highway that runs north to the Tri-cities area, so there was an Econ-Lodge beside the road that we walked to. The hotel had a pool which pleased Matt to no end.

I actually got to shower first as I think Matt bathed in the pool. Panda was sticking with us, but once again we lost Psycho. The three of us chowed down on pizza and beer while lying in our air-conditioned hotel rooms. We were starting to like Panda, he's like us, he likes to drink and act stupid. Life can be good at times.

As I said we were on the outskirts of Erwin and called a shuttle service in the Hikers Guide, Ms. Janet. Ms. Janet was yet another instance of something or someone being "Trail Famous." If you were a thru hiker you knew Ms. Janet, she gave rides and ran a hiker hostel. She pulled up to the motel and the three of us made our way over to her. I opened the van doors and heard, "Yo Peterman."

Psycho was in the van. The son of a bitch was grinning ear to ear, "Thought you lost me, eh?" I kept our plans for the future vague, but it didn't matter, Psycho was hiking on anyway. We spent our day just banging around town and were picked up by one of Matt's frat brothers for dinner, a guy they called "Tree." I guess you can get a dumb nickname without hiking the trail. He was six foot four, so I guess in frat house logic that makes you a tree.

Now as we get into Erwin itself, I must address this chapter's title. Erwin is the town that hung an elephant. I must first tell you the story of the elephant so you can understand Erwin. When I first heard the story of the hanging elephant in the Thru Hikers Guide, I had to look it up before we got there. I give credit to Blue Ridge County Publication for much of the information that I found, which I assume is true. In fact, Erwin should have been named Ervin, after the person who donated the land for the town, but a misspelling by the post office changed that.

The story goes that Sparks World Famous Shows was a circus, albeit a small one, and was unable to compete with Robinson's Four Ring Circus or Barnum and Bailey. The owner of Sparks, Charlie Spark's, would try to get people to attend by hosting a parade in town prior to the circus performance. There were animals and employees, some of them freaks, some not so much, and they would march down the main street in town to the excitement of the crowd.

On his posters, Sparks billed Mary the elephant as the largest living land animal on earth. Bigger than Jumbo from Barnum and Bailey by two inches, she was also dangerous, having killed a man before. All hype for his circus show

On September 11th, 1916, as the story goes, a man named Red Eldridge was hired by Sparks as a handler for Mary. Then, by most witness accounts, on September 12th, 1916, Mary killed Eldridge in Kingsport Tennessee. There are several versions as to how it happened, much of it being lost to history. All versions of the story include Red poking Mary with a pointed spear/stick which back then was an important handlers' tool. The assorted renderings of what occurred go on to say she wrapped her trunk around Eldridge, threw him to the ground or into the side of a soda stand, and then stomped on his head, crushing it. Another version by some was that she sank her tusks through him, or yet another, landed a fatal blow to his head with her trunk. Whatever was the truth, Eldridge was in fact killed by Mary. She became known in the town and press as "Murderous Mary."

It was decided by the local population she had to be destroyed. Public uproar was huge. The biggest gun in town did not work, five shots did not faze her, there needed to be another way, electrocution was out, there was not enough power on the local grid.

On a side note though, in 1903 an elephant was electrocuted at Coney Island in New York, for killing a handler. Mary was not to be the first murderous elephant to be put to death by humans. Dismemberment by chaining her to two opposing trains was discussed, as well as crushing her between two trains was considered. The final recourse, and the easiest, was to hang her from a derrick crane used for lifting trains onto the tracks. The hanging was free to the public at the railroad yard in Erwin.

Which brings us to September 13th, 1916, at the Clinchfield Trainyard. Mary was to be put to death. The crowd was said to be about twenty-five hundred, an incredible crowd for rural Tennessee in those days. The hanging itself was a circus event. They wrapped the first chain around her neck and hoisted her up, the chain snapped causing her to fall to the ground. The chain was far too small and thin. Her hip was broken by the impact. A heavier, thicker chain was used, and up she went again. She was left hanging for an hour, kicking, until dead. She was buried in the train yard in an unmarked grave, and the town of Erwin wants to forget this event.

Most the townspeople do not like talking about something that was sort of embarrassing and happened over eighty years ago, so of course the young boy could not let it go. Everywhere we went and everyone we met in town he had to start asking questions about the hanging elephant. We heard that at one time there was a bar in town called the "Hanging Elephant." I would have loved getting that t-shirt as a souvenir. Most people would just not talk about the elephant and would just call us "damn Yankees."

1,842.2 miles to go.

Chapter 16
Slack Packing

After walking around town all day and filling up on some nasty fast food we walked to Ms. Janet's house. She was going to give us a ride back to our motel. Ms. Janet was a lady after our own hearts, she was very friendly with a touch of sarcasm. We told her how we were headed back out in the morning and would need a ride to the trailhead. That's when she introduced us to the concept of "slack packing." She astutely pointed out that there are only a few places along the trail where this is possible.

Slack packing, Ms. Janet explained, was when a person would stay in a town or hostel and would be dropped off at a trailhead and picked up at another point further up the trail the same day, thereby allowing them to leave behind the bulk of their gear and carry only that day's provisions. Matt obviously thought this was a great idea. We could eat in town every night and sleep in an actual bed.

"Hey Panda, what do you think, you're the one out here on vacation?" Matt asked.

Panda answered as only a panda can, "Well, it's okay with me. I'll never pass up a chance to shit over water."

The next morning Ms. Janet brought us some day packs which were nothing more than a regular backpack that you would see any kid wearing to school. The beauty there being you needed to carry your water, some snacks, and lunch. Everything else we could leave behind. The three of us decided that we would only take one bag and share the load, each one would wear it for a few hours.

"You know Dad, I think Panda should have to carry the bag longer. He is the closest thing out here to a pack animal." That didn't fly with our panda pack mule.

We hopped out of the van and Matt took the first shift with the day pack. At this point Matt and I had been walking almost daily with anywhere from thirty to forty pounds on our backs. We had been doing this for weeks. It's hard to describe the feeling of hiking unencumbered for the first time. It's almost like when you see those videos of astronauts walking on the moon, each step feels like a little hop. We were hopping down the trail. The other noticeable advantage was speed. We were covering ground quickly without our packs.

This slack packing was a great concept. I could do this every day. In fact, at one point, I had heard rumors of a guy that was doing just that. I never met the guy, but I heard there was a retired couple and that his wife had an RV and was his "support team," so to speak. She would pick him up each day, when roads allowed, or every couple of days when she could. He never really had to carry full weight. I could have done that if my wife were not such a dedicated nurse refusing to give up her work for me.

Ms. Janet picked us up at the designated roadside. The three of us had to wait around a while, we had made real good time, and we were usually chipper after a day of easy hiking. We went back to our hotel and checked-out, we would spend the next few days slacking from Ms. Janet's hostel. Her hostel was basically her house with a couple of rooms with bunks for the hikers that stayed there, it was still better than most the places we slept.

We continued slacking the next day, as we were still within Ms. Janet's driving radius. It was another lighter than air day for us. Matt would lose his Four Brew moniker that day seeing as he unwittingly stepped on a box turtle. I must admit a box turtle is the last thing you would be looking out for on a mountain top at five thousand feet. At last, he became "Turtle Stomper."

Now fortunately, or unfortunately, depending on your outlook of the world, that name didn't last long. When you spend a lot of time outdoors you can begin to sense changes in the weather and know the rain is coming. We could smell it. It was a strange atmospheric scent that would get stronger before the flood. Because of this we picked up the pace hoping to make it to our pick-up spot before it began.

Matt was leading the way and moving quickly on some flat ground. There was a log down over the trail which Matt stepped on to get over, which is by no means unusual, however this log was home to a resting hornet's nest. I think you know where this is going. Needless to say, Matt took a few stings to his leg earning him the newest nickname, "Bee Sting." I admit it's not the most creative thing I've come up with, but who cares?

We were not far from pick up, maybe half a mile, which was good because Bee Sting's leg was starting to swell up something fierce. Hiking will give you good calves, but they shouldn't look like cantaloupes. We managed to get to our pickup spot, a small church right off the trail. As we got there the skies opened up and it started to pour.

We could tell Matt was in some pain, but he was toughing it out. Panda and I still hurled insults his way but we were much nicer than usual, besides we needed something to do while waiting for Ms. Janet. We waited and waited, for over an hour and she didn't show up. Two other hikers had shown up coming down the trail to the church and were dripping wet. They were also waiting on a ride to pick them up. Ms. Janet still had not come in when their ride appeared. It was a smaller car, belonging to their friend, so there was no chance of us catching a ride with them, but there was room for at least one.

With my paternal instincts being as high as they were, I approached one of the guys, "Hey man, can you take my son into town with you? His leg is swollen, he is in quite a bit of pain."

"Nope, can't do."

At this point I was still being polite. "You've got room for one more, come on, don't be a dick." I couldn't believe they wouldn't take him into town. "I'm not asking you to take all of us, it's a little hard for him to walk."

"I told you no." He repeated. This is not the type of thing that is typical on the trail.

"Fine. It would be a real shame if you were to pull out of here and get t-boned in that little shit car of yours by a gasoline tanker truck and become pinned down as you watched the gasoline from the tanker start spilling around your now crushed car. You cry and beg for help as I walk past and all you're going to hear is "nope, can't do it," as I drop a lit cigarette on the ground. That or I could just kick your ass now."

He had pissed me off at that point. Well, they didn't take Matt into town, there was no crash, I did not kick his ass, but they did look sufficiently terrified, so at least we got something out of it.

We waited for the rain to subside before deciding to start walking to town. None of us were particularly thrilled about it, but we couldn't wait all day. We hadn't made it far when we saw Ms. Janet's rival shuttle service show up. He was gracious enough to give a ride but would only do so if he could drop us a few blocks from her home, Erwin turf wars being what they are. Turned out Ms. Janet's van had broken down, it's a good thing we didn't wait.

We slack packed the next day as well and everything went off without a hitch. Ms. Janet dropped us off and as we were getting out of the car her dog jumped out with us. "Don't worry about him, he'll follow you guys. He'll disappear and pop back up, but he'll be there at the finish line." Sure enough throughout the course of the day this little dog would vanish into the woods and appear an hour later three miles down the trail. Then again, I'm sure he could track our stink for miles. She was there at the end as well as her dog.

There were three other hikers that were bunking down at Ms. Janet's that night. Two guys and one woman. They sat outside with us for a while and it became clear real fast that these three people sucked. It seemed they had no humor or joy in them at all. Every attempt at pleasant conversation was shut down by their trivial bullshit.

They told us their names, but we didn't remember them or care. Instead we, once again, we ascribed our own names to them. One guy was simply "Nerd," because he was a nerd. The other guy had abnormally large canine teeth, hence the name "Snaggletooth," unlike Nerd, Snaggletooth was a dick. Last, but not least was the girl, we called her "Bitch," I don't think much of an explanation is needed.

The night before we left Erwin, to continue our odyssey, Ms. Janet questioned me as to what I thought about as I hiked the trail. I told her that since Matt and Panda were hiking with me, and on occasion, Psycho, we mostly chatted on and off about different things, most not making any sense whatsoever. I did tell her that going uphill, I sometimes would sing 100 Bottles of Beer in my head, trying to finish just as I got to the top. I also explained to her that I had been playing an Xbox game

144

prior to my going on the trail. It was a volleyball game in which you had your choice of several luscious female players. As you progress through the game you could buy the girls skimpier outfits. There was a rumor going around that if you finished the game in a certain time frame, I think it was a half hour, the girls would appear completely naked.

I finished that game four or five times in the time frame stated, but the girls never got naked. I found out later on it was an April Fool's joke, damn kids and their Internet. I told Ms. Janet that since the girls never got naked, I would play the volleyball game in my head and the girls would undress as they played. I know, I am a sick bastard, but it passed the time. I only did this on steep uphill climbs when I needed a distraction from my misery.

I didn't know what to make of the look she was giving me. She gave a hearty laugh, "Christ Bob. I ask every guy I meet that question. Thousands of people have come and gone from my shuttle, and that is the most bat shit crazy thing I've ever heard. Probably the most honest too. You would have to be some kind of asshole to make that up." Little did she know.

The next morning Ms. Janet dropped the three of us off at the trail. When I strapped on my pack, Ms. Janet leaned out the driver's side window and yelled back to me, "Hey Bob, start getting the girls undressed, it's a long way up hill." Off she went.

Matt looked puzzled. "Dad, what did she mean by get the girls undressed?"

"Long story son, it involves nudity. These are your formative years, I wouldn't want to warp your fragile little mind."

"Well I want to know then," Panda chimed in.

"For a species that has trouble breeding without help, I think it's better you don't know either." I wasn't going to try to explain the whole Xbox thing. They would think I was stupid.

I should say however I did accomplish one big thing on my list while in town. I finally got some earplugs to drown out Matt's snoring.

1,827.1 miles to go.

Chapter 17
Wet Coeds

Of course it rained all day again. We read in the guide that water sources might be dry in some spots depending on rainfall, so you plan accordingly. No such problem to date, I've never seen so much rain. The first shelter we came to we stayed at.

I didn't pay too much attention to shelter registers, but each shelter has a notebook or some such implement for hikers to write in. This serves a multitude of purposes. If you get lost the authorities can locate the last shelter you were at, and it gives them a starting point to look for your dead rotting corpse scattered among the bear shit. It would help my wife collect on my life insurance that much quicker.

Some hikers draw pictures, same picture register after register, some leave messages for hikers behind them, others write praises to God, poems, it goes on and on. We would sign in just in case we got lost, besides it gave the lad something to do while I set up camp for us. Matt loved to read the stupid sayings aloud to me while I cooked our dinners.

"Hey, Dad, you got to hear this last one."

"Go ahead Matt, it can't be any worse than most the other shelters writings."

"Oh, it is. It was written yesterday and says, "I pulled in late tonight and I am very tired. I had to hike fast because there are three very, very, bad men following me. They want to hurt me. They are Peterman, Panda, and Silvertoes. They are extremely dangerous, run if you see them." It was signed Huff and Puff."

I started to laugh. "Well did he at least spell all the big words correctly?" Panda was chuckling in between his bites of bamboo. Literacy was severely needed in these registers. It was hard to believe the majority of hikers are college kids and most cannot spell or use proper grammar.

Two hikers pulled into the shelter and started unpacking. One went to sign in the register and told his buddy about Psycho's entry. "Wow, wonder if that's real?"

"There's some real nuts out here, that's for sure," the other said.

"I agree with you guys," a knowing smile on my face, "we have met some real psychos on the trail."

We had some small talk and they introduced themselves by their trail names and asked what our names were.

"I'm Peterman." I responded.

"They, er, well, they call me Panda." His head was hung low and it was almost a whisper, he was ashamed of his name and the way it was earned. This made Matt that much prouder of having bestowed it up on him.

"I'm Silvertoes." This was Matt's most commonly used trail name at this point, due to his blisters and constant use of duct tape on them.

"Shit, is this entry true? What did you guys do to him? Why would he write this?"

Matt spoke up, "Well I guess that depends on your definition of what true is. We are very bad men, but he's more likely to hurt himself then we are."

"Hey, he's unbalanced. A wacko. You need to meet him." I answered. To my amazement, they started packing up their stuff and said they were going to the next shelter.

Matt couldn't let it go and yelled after them as they left, "We can find you there too."

"Hey Matt, wouldn't it be funny if Psycho is in the next shelter. They would have been better off here."

Matt decided the entry in the register cast us in a bad light, no shit, so he added an entry that went, "Peterman, Panda, and Silvertoes are trying to find the writer of that entry because at night he stole all of our food and shit in the campfire. If you see him, stay clear of him, he is probably some deranged psycho from an asylum."

Panda asked, "How many times you guys going to mention the shitting in the fire?"

"Forever," Matt and I answered him in unison.

In a shocking turn of events we were stuck in the rain again. We had plans to continue hiking further, but Matt and I were, in every way, defeated by the rain that day. We sloshed into a shelter very early in the afternoon and were soaking wet and freezing. The idea of going any further was ejected from our minds the second we stepped under the shelters canopy and didn't feel buckets of rain pouring on our heads. Unfortunately, this had a sadder consequence, we had to release Panda into the wild.

Panda was scheduled to be picked up the next day at a highway intersection the trail crossed past the next shelter. He had to continue on in order to maintain his schedule and make his flight home. He hung with us for another hour hoping the rain would let up and we would go with him, but it never did. We took advantage of our last minutes together, not reminiscing about the good times, like friend's would, and doing what we do best, cracking jokes at Panda's expense.

I started, "Well Panda, we hate to see you go but you've run out of bamboo and will simply starve if you stay any longer."

"Yeah, that and you should really see a doctor, I'm pretty sure you've developed shit-lung disease by now, it's a very serious medical condition," Matt added.

"Well guys, I'd love to stay but I've got a special lady friend waiting at home."

"A SLiF, you didn't tell us you had a SLif," which is what we still call her to this day.

"I look forward to your email and updates fellas, who knows, maybe I'll be back." And like that he disappeared, a Panda in the mist. Matt and I would be back at each other's throats again.

We spent the afternoon deep inside our sleeping bags trying to dry off and stay warm. We were the kind of wet and cold that you can feel in your bones and with nothing resembling a hot shower for miles around, hiding in our bags was the best we could muster. We had hung our wet clothes up inside the shelter in an attempt to let them dry out. We read our books, wrote in our journals, and continued our running game of Rummy, which I was still winning. Regrettably for Panda leaving, his timing was as bad as his face is dumb.

Later in the afternoon, what I can only describe as three gorgeous well-endowed coeds, came dripping wet into the shelter. Well, I could describe them better but for the sake of keeping peace with my wife, we'll leave it at that.

"Hey, you guys don't mind if we stay here with you tonight, right? We really don't want to go any further in this weather," the tallest coed said, she being the tallest because her well-toned legs went on forever.

"Of course not, the more the merrier," I answered as I rolled Matt's tongue back into his mouth.

"Do you mind if we change really quick, it's wet out there, and our clothes are soaked," one girl asked. I've seen so many movies that start this way. Matt was already up moving some of our clothes over before she even finished asking. You can imagine the thoughts that raced through my mind. Did they need help changing? Wet t-shirts can be a real bitch taking off. And exactly what did they mean? How much clothing was coming off? Are they doing it right here?

While we were talking to them one at a time turned her back to us as if it was nothing, stripped off her t-shirt and sports bra, and put on a nice tight dry shirt. These are the moments on the trail that make it worthwhile. I had to wipe the drool from the corner of Matt's mouth. The boy really needs to get laid. This was another of those, "I love the trail moments." We entertained the girls the rest of the night with our stories of the trail and our many days with Psycho.

Survival Note: Coeds in wet t-shirts can boost your spirit.

Sleep was good that night and there were dreams aplenty. Normally I toss and turn but that night I slept peacefully. In the morning it was still pouring rain and it was time for a Chapter 5. There was no privy at this shelter, so I had to cop a squat in the pouring rain, I chose Position 3. Normally it's best to shit in the morning before you are completely gross and sweaty again, but in this weather it didn't matter. Nice way to start a hike, but cleanup was easy.

I came back to Matt chatting up these young ladies, he does make me proud sometimes. "So how far are you hiking today? We might end up at the same shelter again," he asked, hoping to get another night with them.

"Actually, we are getting picked up today at a logging road about five miles in," one girl replied. You could see the disappointment written all over the young neophyte. I could hardly blame him, they were much better to look at than I was and all the women you see thru hiking at this point are just as furry as the men.

We set out, following the three girls and admiring the view. We heard later on that three Playboy girls were section hiking the trail, Matt and I not knowing if these girls were the three. I think so, in my mind anyway. I like to think we hiked with Playboy Bunnies.

Next was Roan High Knob shelter, which is the highest shelter on the trail, over six thousand feet. The guidebook says it's the year-round coldest shelter on the trail. When the girls got off, as they said they would, Matt had a little less pep in his step, I think he was beginning to miss the real world. He forgot what women looked like. To make matters worse it's a pretty rough climb up and it was pouring again. This was about as bad as I've seen it on the trail when it comes to water rushing down the path. We were up to our ankles in water, climbing even higher into the storm.

The shelter at Roan High Knob was a rustic cabin that at one time had served as the Fire Wardens quarters. It had a loft up top and was quite spacious. The temperature continued to drop with what seemed like each passing moment. We set up our sleeping bags on the bottom floor and went through our normal routine. Then without a moment's notice all hell broke loose.

A storm blasted through the cabin, not the weather, but rather a dozen or so kids between ages nine and eleven. To top it off there were only two counselors with them. Kids being kids of course, they were filthy, disgusting, and smelly, but luckily, they all wanted to sleep upstairs. Matt and I would have the whole bottom floor to ourselves.

Matt read the journal in the shelter. "Hey Dad, an entry from the Panda."

"What's your favorite big dumb animal have to say?"

"Says, Silvertoes and Peterman, good hiking with you. Keep me updated. Gonna try to come back, signed your furry friend Panda."

"It would be cool if he came back. Gotta let him know about the coeds. If he was there we probably would have had panda schmool all over the shelter."

Matt was lying on his back reading and the kids were being rowdy above him. It felt like each time one of those slimy little bastards moved debris would fall from between the boards and all over us. After an hour of this Matt sat up, his eyes had the look of a man who has had enough. He stood up mumbling to himself, "The hell with this," and started digging through his pack. I was curious enough to ask, "You're not planning on burning this place down?"

"That's not a bad idea, but no I've had enough of this crap, it's not going to stop all night. I'm putting up our tent."

I couldn't argue. It would be better than having dirt rain down on us all night. We've had enough rain that day. These little bastards would not go to sleep. The earplugs were not helping either. Finally, I'd had enough and talked to the counselor. "Excuse me ma'am," she couldn't have been more than twenty-two and did not wear a tight t-shirt, "as the delightful as these little buggers are, we'd like to get some sleep, otherwise my son over there, well he's good at getting wet wood to burn." I don't know why I said it, but it did the trick.

The next morning, we awoke to proof that this was the coldest shelter on the trail. There was snow on the ground. I hate it when the guidebook is right. This was the second time we encountered snow and the last. The snow disappeared very quickly as we descended the mountain.

1,808.3 miles to go.

Chapter 18
Freak Patrol

O ur next stop was Over Mountain Shelter. If you ask Matt, he'll tell you this was one of his favorite places we stayed. It's stopped raining so our moods were gradually lifting. It was our first few days without Panda or Psycho around, but it was not yet quiet. We had overheard the counselors talking before leaving the previous shelter that they were meeting the second half of their group at Over Mountain, who were hiking the opposite direction. Christ almighty.

The shelter itself is a big red barn and was used in a movie, "Winter People," a thriller type movie. Our evening was setting up more like a horror flick. It was by far the largest shelter we had encountered to date, easily capable of sleeping several dozen people. We already knew it was going to come to that. There is a lower level as well as an upper level, then to the side overlooking the valley below is an eight-foot raised platform underneath the barn's overhanging loft. It's really is a beautiful place.

We set up our tent on the riser off the side of the barn by the campfire pit. As expected, the eleven people from the previous shelter appeared, with a group they knew coming from the opposite direction with eleven more kids. Twenty plus germ producing kids in all. Might as well kill me now.

The old barn easily slept that amount of kids, and they all piled into the barn yelling and screaming, running around, most of them climbing into the loft over the deck we were tenting on. The thing that pissed me off was the four counselors pitched their tents down the trail away from the barn, and after dinner the kids were left unsupervised at the barn with us, the thru hikers.

I noticed a familiar scent wafting in the air that was caught from time to time on the evening breeze. The odors were emanating from the direction of the counselor's tents.

"Eww, I think I smell a skunk," one of the kids cried out. It was no skunk, rather sweet Panama Red. There was no mistaking that, years on the force you learned that odor well. Matt just chuckled and pretended not to be envious. I'd have been stoned too if I had to spend a week hiking with these kids.

Matt picked up yet another trail name at this shelter. The kids wanted a campfire and were not allowed to have one because the counselors were not supervising them. Matt, always the hero, took over, and after sending the kids out to scavenge firewood, and several tries with what was mostly wet wood, he got a huge blaze going. He failed to tell them it was because of the fire sticks I bought him, which were essentially napalm.

He sat at the fire with the kids, basking in his newfound popularity. I heard one kid say to Matt, "you are a fire starter." Matt liked the name and chose to be called Firestarter. After all the names he had we agreed to go along with it for now, you never know.

The closer we got towards dinner the more the shelter began to fill up. This is a popular hiking spot with heavy access. Some weekend warriors came and set up on the other riser, the kids were all set up in the loft.

I'm just setting the scene here for the upcoming altercation. Just a little before dinner, into the shelter wandered the "Bitch," "Snaggletooth," and the "Nerd." We had started calling them the "Freak Patrol," perhaps it was a bit mean, but Bitch was a Bitch and the others suffered for it. While we hiked, we spoke of how they could be an action comic. The Freak Patrol versus the Toxic Avenger, that would be quite the movie. Just one of the more stupid things you discuss while hiking.

They were not at all pleased to see us. Bitch almost got renamed "Sourpuss" for her reaction at seeing Matt and I standing there. They came out onto the deck, as they understandably did not want to be in the barn with all those kids. Bitch came storming over to Matt demanding he take down the tent so she could have some more room, mind you she had plenty, she just wanted more. "You guys need to take your tent down now," she barked in Matt's face.

I give my son some credit, he has a pretty even temperament, most of the time. He doesn't anger easily, however once he does he can go a bit nuts. His hospital bills prove that. I hope he at least won some of those fights that required a trip to the ER. As you can imagine I was a bit concerned when he looked her dead in the eyes and calmly said, "No."

Bitch turned bright red and began to rant at him, "You're being inconsiderate and rude having that tent up. We'd have a lot more room if you took that down."

"Sorry. We were here first and you still have plenty of room, put up your own tent if you'd like, there's a reason I put ours up," Matt replied to her. He wasn't getting mad, he was enjoying himself making her miserable.

Our tent was right up against the edge of the deck on my side. Yes, the tent did use more room than our sleeping bags would have, but there was plenty of room in the other places for the Bitch to set up. Had we truly been taking up all the room we would have moved outside to make room for any other hikers. Our tent had a zipper flap on each side of the tent, so each person could enter or exit the tent without disturbing the other. The Bitch put her sleeping bag right up against Matt's side of the tent, where the space between them would have been, instead she left a huge space on her other side. This was purely for spite. Matt, if he needed to get out during the night, would have to step on her sleeping bag, or her, to get past. This created a problem.

"You know you're blocking my side of the tent if I have to get out," you didn't hear him say it, but you could sense he wanted to end the sentence with "Bitch."

"Too bad. Take the tent down." She was curt, lying on her back with her arms crossed, atop her bag.

"Not happening lady. I get up sometimes at night, you know small bladder syndrome and all."

"Tough. Piss yourself."

I was really starting to enjoy this.

"I'll tell you what, if I do have to go I am going to unzip this flap and pee on your sleeping bag."

"Hey Matt, give her the Bambi speech." I just wanted to hear it again.

The conversation ended there. Matt got up and walked across her sleeping bag, I thought she would take the cue and move, but no such luck, she was standing her ground. I just hoped that Matt didn't need to get up during the night. It could make for a very interesting night.

It started approaching hiker's midnight, so we got into our tent on the platform. Since Firestarter retreated to the tent there was no one left to tend the fire, which sent a multitude of kids up into the loft.

They were loud but I had earplugs, it didn't much matter to me. I could feel Matt was moving around, I looked over to see him smiling ear to ear. He was chuckling and pointing up. I looked up and could see the clouds of dust pouring down from above us, and to make it better, covering the three stooges next to us. He motioned for me to take out my earplugs. I did.

"Stop moving around up there, dirt is falling on us," we heard the Bitch yelling for the next thirty minutes. Every time a kid moved, she yelled for them to quit messing around. Kids being the gross little things they are were giggling above us.

"Hey lady," Matt cooed, "hence the reason for the tent. Sweet dreams."

The Freak Patrol was up before at six the next morning, banging around and making as much noise as possible to wake us and the kids. I think they wanted to get as far from us as they could.

1,801 miles to go.

Chapter 19
Noises in the Night

Continuing north takes you over Little Bald and Big Bald in the Roan Highlands. A bald is an enigma, it is a mountain and it should be covered with trees but instead there are grassy meadows. No one truly knows why.

This part of the hike goes straight through cow pastures with these long-horned steers that stood as tall as we did. It was intimidating at first, rodeos and bullfights flashed through my mind with the cowboys and Matadors being flipped up into the air by these horned monsters, but they completely ignored us.

The twelve-inch wide dirt trail cut through these meadows that were full of grass about knee high. Every once in a while you would be walking down the trail to find a six-foot bull with horns that stretched five feet across standing smack dab in the middle of the path. You had no choice but to go around him, and as you did so you soon learned what cow patties were. They looked like Road Kill Grill's burgers which made me wonder. You couldn't always see them due to the height of the grass, so I liken it to trying to walk through a minefield. When you stepped on a fresh one, boy, did you know it.

It was also at the end of this meadow that we found a sick fawn curled up in the grass. We heard from a group of kids moving south that they had seen it the night before and how cute it was. The counselor's either didn't know or were smart enough not to tell the kids the truth. It was abandoned by its mother. It was clear it had been there more than a day. Now this should prove that regardless of what you have read here, I am not in fact a heartless bastard. I got some cell service on a nearby hilltop, but due to spotty reception, and this being the days before internet everywhere, we couldn't get through to anyone. I resorted to calling my daughter Kathy and had her find the number of a local Ranger station near where we were. After several calls I finally got in touch with the Ranger. Their response simply was, "nothing we can do, haven't you ever heard about the circle of life?" Were these assholes quoting The Lion King to me? Walt Disney is rolling in his grave. As sad as it was, there was nothing else for us to do, we moved on.

A day or two later we were quickly approaching the Virginia State line. We had a particularly long day and evening was approaching quickly. We were still about a mile or more from the next shelter, and so we decided to camp that night by the Elk River.

You come out of the woods into an open field for about one hundred yards or so next to the river. Mind you we had gone shelter to shelter since our first night on the trail, but this was much better maintained site, so we went for it. We were only about six feet from the river, which was flowing fast. After dinner we hung our bags in a tree near the water and called it an early night. We would need an early start to make up for the lost mile that day. I put in my earplugs, as was now my habit, and closed my eyes the second dusk set up on us. Matt said the sound of the river would lull him to sleep, however he would have no such luck as usual. My eyes weren't closed for long before Matt woke me up.

"Dad wake up. Dad, did you hear that? Dad? "Matt was vigorously elbowing me in the side.

"Hear what? I have my earplugs in."

"There's something out there. It sounds like it's snorting."

"We're by the trail, could have been a horse and rider going by. Maybe your own snoring woke you up. Get some sleep."

Twenty minutes later he's shaking me awake again. "Dammit, I'm telling you there's something outside our tent!"

"Well go out and take a look."

"There is no God damn way I'm going out there, it's dark and I don't particularly feel like being mauled to death."

"Then unzip your flap and take a look out with your flashlight."

"No way. Something will drag me out of the tent into the night and you will just go back to sleep."

"That's a very likely possibility, in fact that is what I'm going to do now." As I was putting my earplugs back in, I heard this loud snort. It couldn't have been more than ten feet from the tent. "Shit, that's a bear, or best scenario, it's a boar."

"Yeah no shit," Matt said. "What are we going to do?"

"I'm thinking with your blisters I could outrun you. That's Plan B. Let's try Plan A first and do what they say, let's make a lot of noise and hope whatever is out there doesn't shred our tent or us apart."

"Great plan, sounds real reassuring. Especially with whatever it is making noise is on my side of the tent."

"That's why I took the riverside. All I have to worry about is your man-eating beavers."

Now if you were standing nearby, it had to look and sound ridiculous, flashlights waving around inside the tent, two guys yelling, "get out of here," banging whatever we could find to make noise, till Matt found his whistle and deafened me. We sat in silence for the next half hour, just listening, finally feeling safe enough to sleep.

I worried the next morning our bear bags may be missing or dragged off somewhere. They were supposed to be "bear proof," but I've seen what bears can do. Luckily due to my expert abilities, our bags were safely hanging from the tree. As we hiked out, we saw bear scat on the trail, maybe fifty feet from our tent. We hoped that we scared the shit out of that bear, but we were also glad pieces of us weren't in it.

Survival Note: If something outside your tent is making noise and you are afraid to look, then don't.

Virginia was getting nearer, and we were anxious to get there, it's a huge milestone.

One shelter we were staying at along the way was full of holy rollers. I swear we must be filled with the Holy Spirit because we attract these people. It seems a lot of religious people are out here on the trail. I guess God must be a hiker. We met two of his spiritual beings about two miles from the next shelter. They were at a stream getting water. The book had this listed as a water source, but we were still a good clip from the shelter. They told us the water supply at the shelter was dry, nothing but a faint trickle and impossible to fill up a bottle from. These two had carried down a bunch of water jugs and we're filling them up for the group they were with.

Finally, a stroke of luck, something went right for us. These righteous men had saved us an additional four miles round trip for our water supply.

Matt and I filled our jugs, plus we each had a two-gallon collapsible water bag, so we filled those as well. Normally we would just fill those and use that to fill our bottles. We didn't need that much water, but being equally righteous men, we thought of the group at the shelter, over twenty of them in total, and how they might need some extra water. This also meant we had an extra eighteen to twenty pounds to carry for the next two miles. Of course, this being the Appalachian Trail, it was all uphill, a gentle uphill, but still uphill, so it was a bitch of a walk with the extra tonnage.

We got to the shelter thinking we would be hailed as heroes for bringing life giving water, but God never misses an opportunity to play a joke on Bobby Boy. Or maybe he's after Matt, that's probably it.

The water source was not dry, it was cool, clear, and not more than fifteen feet away. For my son you would have thought this was the end of the world. He was not happy, saying something along the line of "what kind of God would do this to me?" I now knew God was after him and not me. It worked out in the end anyway, as our faithful friends had made too much dinner and they shared it with us. We never turn down a free meal, besides it was "PFG."

Since we were tenting, we decided to get up at four in the morning, it was a full moon, and almost like daylight. We talked about hiking by moonlight and figured this was the time to do it. It was amazing, the landscape takes on an eerie, almost spooky feeling, but at the same time seems soft and iridescent, as if you were in a light fog. Conversely, we tried hiking part of one night with no moon whatsoever. Pitch black. We hiked with just our head lamps. Now that is just nuts, you are constantly watching for blazes, looking down at the trail, back up for a blaze, and every time you hear a noise you swing around to see what it might be, only to hear a noise in another direction so you swing over in that direction. You constantly think something is behind you. The worst is when you hear a noise and you look in that direction and see two red dots looking back at you. No idea whatsoever what it could be, and you really don't want to know. Add to that the thousands of spider eyes glowing as your headlamp hits them, and it was game over. First spot we hit after an hour of night hiking we pitched our tents and crawled into our safe little cocoons

We hit a small campground a few days before reaching Watauga. They had cheap tenting sites, something like three bucks a night. However, a private single room cabin was ten bucks a night. We also never pass up a mattress. I know it sounds repetitive, but Matt jumped into the shower, only this time I didn't have to worry about the hot water. This place had community bathrooms and community showers. He could sleep in there for all I cared.

I walked over and did the laundry and decided on pizza for dinner. Mainly because I didn't have a choice. There was nothing around this area and pizza delivery was the only food we could get, other than if we opted for our trail dinners. Never pass up the chance to order pizza I always say. I had Matt call in the order, an extra cheese, meatball, and onion pizza. As Matt was finishing the order I had a crazy thought, "Hey Matt, ask them if they'll bring us some beer. A twelve pack of Corona, I'll make it worth it."

Matt just smirked and shrugged. "Excuse me sir, my dad wants to know if you'll deliver some beer with our pizza? A twelve pack of Corona?" I couldn't hear the other side of the conversation, but I imagine it went something like this;

"I'm not sure we can do that. There's got to be some laws against that."

"Sir, I totally understand, but this is America dammit, land of the free."

"Well since you put it that way, how could I possibly mount an argument?"

To my astonishment, the pizza girl showed up with a double cheese meatball and onion pizza and the twelve pack of Corona. She looked at me and asked to see my ID, my jaw about hit the ground. She laughed and handed me the beer, "I'm pretty sure you're old enough." Not all heroes wear capes and as promised she was rewarded. I thanked her. She told me that the owner mentioned my request and that she too was a hiker, and enjoyed beer after a weekend hike, so she fulfilled our request. Besides, let's not kid ourselves, she wanted the tip.

We ate our dinner in the little gathering room they had. There were a few board games and a small TV/VCR combo on the counter. The only VHS tape that would work was an old Tom Berenger movie, "Last of the Dog Men." There were worse ways to spend an evening on the trail.

We left there to hike over Watauga Dam, an earthen dam. I must admit it is a cool thing but there is not a chance in hell I'd live anywhere near this thing. I'm sure the people who built it knew exactly what they were doing, but it's essentially a well-groomed dirt mound that is holding back an entire lake. However, that didn't prevent us from stopping for a photo op.

Fun Fact: Watauga Dam, is the second largest earth dam in the United States at 318 feet.

Down the trail we hit some fifty-foot waterfalls and took a nice swim. Some of the waterfalls on the trail are breathtaking. I prefer waterfalls and rapids to the scenic overlooks. Something about them that seems calming and soothing to me.

1,743.0 miles to go.

Chapter 20
Carry Me Back to Old Virginny

It's always hard waking up on a thin blow-up mattress and throwing yourself back into the woods. You never quite get used to that. Matt always took it hard too, he was pretty moody these days. We continued on step after step. We stopped for a snack by the side of a country highway, it was late afternoon and we still had a few miles to go. Two other hikers popped out of the woods behind us and I struck up a conversation with them. We gave them the rundown of our story and they said they were thru hikers as well. What was odd about that statement was they didn't have packs on, not like ours anyway. They were slacking. It turns out that had we turned left the night before, instead of right, we would have come upon a rather popular hikers' hostel. Sure enough, I consulted the book and it was right.

A couple of minutes later a car pulled over with a young lady behind the wheel to pick up the two hikers, so I asked her, "Got room for two more?"

"Sure," she said.

I've rarely seen my son happier, he even grabbed my bag and put it in the trunk of her car for me. We all got to talking on the drive back about our experiences to this point. Her name was Bear Claw and she had also been a thru hiker. She was temporarily running the hostel while its owner was away. She shuttled the four of us back to the hostel, which was a nice cabin in the woods. There were several other people staying there, some passing through, some working for stay, and some out hiking the trail.

We had put up all our belongings and Matt was tending to his feet. The blisters never seemed to let up for him no matter what he did. There was always a general consensus that his shoes fit yet he was always blistered. Matt sat outside at a picnic table on the porch and pulled his boots off. One of the other hikers was watching as Matt grimaced pulling off all the duct tape from around his toes, hence the Silvertoes moniker.

"Holy crap!" one of the hikers shouted. "I've never seen so many blisters, it's like your blisters have blisters. How are you even walking right now?"

"Gingerly," was Matt's response. "You may want to look away 'cause I'm getting ready to drain these things."

That did not deter his new friend. "This might sound a bit weird, but do you mind if I watch?"

"If that's what gets you off pal, knock yourself out."

Matt was practically a surgeon by this time when it came to draining blisters. He would pull out his sewing kit, the irony being he still doesn't know how to sew and would heat the tip of the needle. Once he found the tip to be sufficiently sterile, he would insert it into the bubble of flesh protruding from his skin. This other hiker was watching very intently even leaning in closer to Matts disgusting feet. Just our luck to run into "Son of Psycho," another complete nut job. After draining them Matt would let his feet air out for the night.

We still had to eat our rations but that didn't matter much, this was an unexpected boon for us. We had discussed slacking for the next two days with Bear Claw, and of course, for a small donation she was happy to do it. We slept that night in bunks upstairs in a communal area. They had several books lying around, a sort of leave-a-book take-a-book situation, Matt and I each took one for when we continued north. It was common to find books in shelters, why carry the weight once you were done? Somebody else always takes it eventually. Then there were people like Psycho, when he read a book, he would rip out each page as he read it, throwing it into the fire, thereby reducing his weight as he goes. As least that's how he put it. When Matt asked Psycho why he did that as opposed to just leaving it behind for someone else, he replied, "Fuck 'em, that's why." Christ was I starting to miss Psycho?

We did a short hike the next day only doing about ten miles. It only took us a little over four hours to complete this section and Bear Claw was there to pick us up. We got back to the hostel and cleaned up, and when we came out Bear Claw was out there with another girl taping a pattern to the hood of her car. It took a minute or so to figure out what they were doing, but slowly it started to take shape. They were going to paint a bear claw onto the hood of Bear Claw's car. Some serious hippie shit right there.

Matt and I were just idling about watching when Bear Claw spoke up, "You guys gonna stand there and watch or earn your keep?" And with that I think Matt fell in love, though it seems he falls in love with any girl that doesn't smell like a hiker. She handed Matt and me some brushes and put us to work.

We painted her car for the rest of the afternoon and then lounged around reading and catching up on our journals that evening. We "zeroed" the next day as well and as far things went it was rather uneventful those next few days.

We were still a few days off from Virginia, but we were in a good place after the last few days. The area is rich in waterfalls and some of them are right along the trail. It's a popular tourist area so we stopped to get our feet wet. Matt and I had a bit of a funny encounter here as we were hiking out of the park. We ran into a family of four with two young kids headed down to the waterfalls, all of them in denim shorts and flip flops. They stopped us and asked how far it was to the waterfalls. Matt and I mostly judge distances these days based on time. After thinking about it for a few seconds Matt answered them, "I don't know Dad, probably about a mile, right?"

"Yeah, sounds about right," I answered him, "not that far down the trail, maybe twenty minutes."

Well, to see their faces when we told them that, it's what we must have looked like on day two. It's like we told them the President had been shot. This was another "I love the trail moment." We rolled our eyes and chuckled as we walked past them. Amateurs. "It's not that far, it's worth it." I may have had a bit of an air of superiority. It was only a mile after all.

We saw the Mount Rogers National Park sign, so we are now in Virginia. Hallelujah. We are headed to Damascus for a couple of "zero" days. It was only a few miles into Damascus where we had planned downtime anyway. On our way into town we walked through a small field with some tall grass on each side. Matt was leading the way and as usual not really paying attention to anything but the next few steps in front of him. Had he glanced to the side he would have seen the massive black snake coiled up about two feet to his right. It was a six-footer, maybe bigger. I shouted to Matt to stop for a second since he was about ten yards ahead. I was able to tell its size because I did the one thing you should never do. Here is what I learned, but never seemed to follow, never poke a snake with your hiking pole.

It is quite remarkable how a thing with no legs can move so fast. The serpent launched at my pole giving me a series of mini strokes. I threw the pole down and backed up as this slithering serpent headed straight at Matt. Even though I was still in an adrenaline-fueled panic, I was still able to see the humor in my son throwing down his poles and sprinting up the trail. The backpack doesn't allow for an actual burst of speed, so it was more like a waddling jog. The snake gave chase for only a few seconds before heading into the grass.

"Don't fucking poke shit with your pole!" he screamed at me. He was a bit flustered in that moment, "that thing looked like an Anaconda. I've had too many animals tried to kill me, and we've only just reached Virginia for Christ sake."

"Hey, it came at me first you know."

"You're the nitwit that poked the damn thing in the first place. It should have come after you."

Survival Note: Let resting/sleeping animals alone.

Damascus is both the most proverbial and literal gateway to Virginia, the most well-known town on the trail, and maybe the most hiker friendly. Damascus hosts the trail festival known as "Trail Days," which is usually in May. Hundreds of hikers swarm into Damascus, whether active hikers, past hikers meeting old friends, or people who are thinking about hiking, the town and the area in and around it are packed with these people. So much so that people camp everywhere, along the sides of the road, people's yards, the town parks, everywhere. You just have to be careful of the police. There are lectures, music, food, and equipment vendors, just to name some of the activities. If you can make it to trail days in Damascus it also means you are on a good pace to hit Katahdin before it closes. We did not make it in time for the party.

Before I get into the town of Damascus itself, I want to address a few of the equipment changes we made there. There were some pricey expenses, but I suppose we'll chalk it up to the learning process. First was the stove, our MSR with fuel canisters had to weigh over two pounds. The nozzle needed to be constantly cleaned, it had to be pumped, and the fuel was in steel canisters. A lot of weight and a lot of space in our bags that could be put to better use. I got a little titanium stove about the size of a soda can top, maybe a half inch thick. It had legs and a potholder. It could fit in my shirt pocket when folded up and had essentially no weight to it at all. It burned denatured alcohol and would boil two cups of water in three minutes. It was amazing, and the fuel could be carried in a plastic soda bottle. This is what Panda had used and it was pretty much a no brainer. We were boiling water out here, not making three course meals. Once I became aware that this was an option, I don't know why a person would spend money on anything else.

The next item to go was the two-man tent. Out went the days of sleeping side by side in a tiny stale nylon fart chamber. We, and by we, I mean me of course, bought two Big Agnes one-man tents. The two tents weighed less than a two-man tent, and we each had our own, no more crowding into a tent together. We called them our little "green coffins." They were shaped a little like the old western style coffins and the inside was not much bigger than one. Nothing would fit in there except you and your sleeping gear.

The next big change was food. Pretty much the only dinners we had for the rest of the trail were all Mountain House meals. All our mail drops would now contain these wonderful, nourishing, and most of all easy to cook and clean up meals. Since Matt was keeping the trail named Firestarter, I bought him some fire-starting sticks, he really didn't need them, but it irked him in just the right way to make the money worth it. It's the little things in life that bring joy to a father. Those were our major purchases. Our packs were continually getting lighter and smaller, and we were getting stronger.

Matt and I stayed in a beautiful B&B on the main drag of Damascus. It was run by a friendly woman who laid down the house rules when we walked in. We finished all our chores and our routine maintenance and sat on the porch with our Coronas watching all the different people and hikers going by. We were taking two "zero" days in Damascus, they were going to have some type of firework display the next day so we figured why not, besides we weren't out here just to walk, it was an opportunity to "see America," or some crap like that.

It was the first day there while we were sitting on the porch playing Gin Rummy, now 42,367 two 42,003, the kid is getting better, we saw Psycho go strolling by. Like a lot of predators his vision is based on movement, neither Matt nor I moved a muscle.

"Hey Dad, is that who I think it is?" Matt whispered to me.

"Shit, he's caught us again," I said with a chuckle. Things always get interesting when he's around.

"Where do you think he will stay? Any chance he can afford it here?"

"There are lots of places around town, he'll find the cheapest." We thought he was ahead of us, but he must have been a day behind us instead.

Matt and I met an English woman who was also staying in the B&B with us. She said she was a journalist from across the pond in England. She was doing the Transcontinental Trail by bike and writing a story about it for her publication. And I thought what we were doing was stupid. I always wondered if we were mentioned in her story since she spent a couple of hours interviewing us.

I loved talking with her, her British accent, and she used terms like, "I'm quite the bird, dog's bollocks, full of beans," and my favorites were, "blow me" and "knock up," the first meaning surprising or something to that effect, the other means waking up. She said to us, "knock me up in the morning and I'll have breakfast with you." Well blow me, who knew?

Anyway, the town is truly hiker friendly to everyone except Psycho, I guess. He spotted us by accident the next day, he was walking through town with his pack on. He stopped and started bitching to us that he was thrown out of the hostel, which was part of a church, for smoking. He said he was smoking his cigarette outside minding his own business and someone told him he could not smoke there.

"Peterman, I'm telling you man, I said okay, and I finished my smoke. This guy gets all pissy 'cause I'm not putting it out that second. That asshole must not have any idea what a pack of these cost. I told him to blow it out his ass."

He was ranting that there are no true Christians anymore. We don't even ask him why anymore, but he always has an excuse, never his fault, he's just misunderstood. I mean a church asked him to leave. He decided he would sit the day on the porch with Matt and I deciding what to do, that was until the owner of the B&B, that sweet old woman, told him to leave, he was bad for business. We found out later he ended up stealth camping the next two days by the Laurel River on the outskirts of town. Probably waiting to see when we were leaving.

That afternoon Matt and I had lunch at a burrito shop that was about a block and a half from the B&B. We ordered our lunch and a couple of Coronas. We hadn't had burritos in a while, it was good we were staying in a house with an actual toilet, but more importantly free TP. We ordered a second round of beers and the girl gave them to us and eyed Matthew suspiciously. She nodded at me and said, "I know you're over twenty-one, how about him?"

Just my luck, Matt would be the first hiker arrested for underage drinking in a burrito shop. Matt chuckled nervously while eye-balling the door, as if he was going to make a run for it in his Crocs.

"He's twenty-one, I'm his father. You'll have to forgive us we're not used to carrying our ID's on us, they're always in our bags. It's a hard habit to break."

The waitress just smiled and nodded, giving us our Coronas. Matt let out a long sigh of relief. He wouldn't have to become a fugitive from the law just yet. We finished up and headed home for an afternoon of some R&R.

At the fireworks display that night, the Fire Department had it set up too close to the crowd, dangerously close if you ask me. The fireworks were going off too early and exploding directly over the crowd. Everyone looking up were getting cinders in their eyes. Not very well thought out by the local Fire Department. While we were watching the display of sparks and explosions in the sky above us, Matt yelled and grabbed his lip. I looked at it, and man, it was swollen instantly. It looked like his tooth might have gone through his lip. A beautiful blonde woman was standing next to him and she was looking at him with a face of disdain.

"Jesus Christ Matt, what did you do?"

"Nothing, look at my lip."

"Did you grab her ass and she hit you? I saw the way she looked at you."

"Maybe it's because my lip looks like a golf ball and it's bleeding."

"What happened to you then?"

"I don't know. I was watching the fireworks and something hit me in the face."

"And it wasn't her fist? Is Psycho around?"

"It's not so funny. Why does this stuff keep happening to me?"

When the fireworks ended, we found decent size pieces of what appeared to be wax chunks around the area on the ground amid the remains of the fireworks. Probably, when one of the rockets exploded which used the wax as a sealant it hit Matt in the lip. What are the odds? Although I did not let him know I was a bit concerned, I had never seen a lip swell up that big, and believe me I split a lot of lips in my time, and not all of them my own.

The next day the swelling had gone down considerably, and I decided to go to the local Fire Department to let them know of their blunder. The Fire Department was closed, no one was inside, all the doors were locked. Well, off to the Police Department so it doesn't happen again. Closed. A note was on the door that no one was on duty inside, but if someone is in need of help or a police officer, there was a phone number for one of the cops at home I guess.

That night we had dinner at a small restaurant on the edge of town. It had a continual contest running, whomever ate the most of whatever was on the menu got to name it. Hanging on the wall were pictures of hikers that had come through and built these massive sandwiches and named them for themselves. That is until the next person comes along and beats it. By the time we got there the BLT now had over a pound of bacon on it. I told Matt go for it, but warned we were pulling out of town the next morning. Whatever havoc that sandwich would do to his stomach, he'd have to face it outside and away from the comfort of the B&B. He ultimately relented to his own wisdom and refused to do it. Now that I think about it, I should never have talked him out of it, then again, I wouldn't want to walk behind him after a meal like that.

Well rested and with great trepidation and remorse, Matt and I again packed our bags and strapped them on to begin the heartbreaking walk out of town. These small towns continue to amaze me.

1717.3 miles to go.

Chapter 21
Horses Have Feelings Too

It's a long hike through Virginia, you are constantly looking at the maps and the trail guide, hoping the state will eventually end. It does by far have the most trail miles of any state. It's like you are never going to get out of it, yet you persevere, always saying to yourself, "am I there yet?" because at the end of Virginia is West Virginia and Harpers Ferry. Party time.

The first night out of Damascus was again all uphill, Matt and I were in a shelter by ourselves, and then in came Psycho. We thought he had left a day earlier because we had not seen him in town the previous day. Psycho told us he saw us leaving town so thought he would join us.

"Hey Sarge, where were you? We didn't see you in town after Aunt Bee threw you off her porch."

"Yeah, thanks guys. Friends would have left with me." Psycho seemed disappointed we did not give up our soft beds, showers, and other amenities for him. "That town sucks anyway, they don't know how to treat hikers."

"You mean they don't know how to treat you. It's listed as the friendliest town on the whole trail for hikers, you just have a way of pissing people off."

"So what, hillbillies, all of them. I slept by the river where you're not allowed. I showed them. I came in and out of town without being noticed, 'Nam style. Jungle."

"Where you could watch the trail?" I asked.

"Damn right. I didn't want you boys worrying about me, so I waited for you."

Since we were the only three there, Matt and I set our coffins up in the shelter against Psychos grumblings.

Hey, we gave him the corner. Anyway, we wanted to try our new tents out, and believe me, they were small and cramped. We also realized we were stuck with him again for some time. Good thing I hit an ATM.

The next day as we were hiking we found the trail to be quite crowded, there were a lot of day hikers, section hikers, two and three-day hikers, and bicyclists in this section, probably because of the Virginia Creeper Trail, as it was known in this area.

On the summit of White Top Mountain, we met twenty college girls who were taking a break, so we joined them. I'm starting to like college girls myself, and Matt was thoroughly enjoying himself. The female species seemed to intrigue him somewhat. God bless his tiny virgin soul. Several of the girls were talking about the movie "Grease," and for the next half hour they spent their time teaching me the dance "Hand Jive." I still know it to this day, not that it comes in handy for anything. You do that on a dance floor, and everyone looks at you like you're an idiot. It's hard to slow dance to anyway. For those who remember American Bandstand, I give it a seven, hard to dance to but a nice beat. It's sort of like being able to do the whole "Thriller" dance, why would you want to.

The shelter we hit that night was over Mount Rogers, Virginia's highest peak. They don't take you over the peak at 5,729 feet, they only take you to 5,500 feet, but the good news is they have a side trail that will take you to the summit. Yeah, like that was going to happen.

Thomas Nob Shelter is a rather large shelter, I guess because of the amount of hiker traffic in this area. It was two stories tall, with a sleeping area upstairs. It could hold sixteen, unless Psycho came in, then it would have to hold seventeen, and he came in, but by the grace of God, the shelter was not crowded.

179

It was in an area with wild ponies, which again made this area very popular for overnighters. These ponies were feral of course but had no fear of humans. They were not the skittish little horses the dumb wanna be cowboys had on the trail. These would come right up to the shelter looking for food. Never feed the wildlife was the rule, but you always had those assholes that don't listen.

We don't know if it's a legend or not but we heard that in one of the National Parks some parents had put honey on their child's hand to get a cute picture of a bear licking it off, just to have the whole thing go horribly wrong and the bear maul the child's hand. You always heard stories like that along the trail.

At this shelter, I had phone reception and thought it would be nice to say hello to the wife and rub it in her face that I was still out here. I sat on top of the picnic table in front of the shelter and dialed her up.

"Hey Hon, its me, the Daniel Boone of Calabash."

"So how are things going?"

"Pretty cool. I'm at a shelter in Virginia with wild horses, and one is standing right in front of me, maybe two feet away. It's making me a little nervous though. It's just staring at me."

"Make sure you take pictures."

Matt was standing in the shelter looking at me and said in a soft voice, "Hey Dad."

"Matt, I'm on the phone with Patti. Can't you set up your own stuff?"

"Hey Dad." Again, a little louder.

"Hold on Patti, let me see what Matt needs, I might need to tie his shoelaces or something."

Patti's response, "Glad to see you two are getting along so well, it's like the very first day you left. The bonding working out well I assume?"

"The kids helpless without me."

"He's the seed of your loins dear."

"Don't remind me. What is it now Matt? Zipper stuck? Don't know what Mountain House you want for dinner?"

"That horse you think is so cute standing in front of you, look underneath him."

I glanced underneath the horse now that my attention was off Patti, and this beast standing in front of me had, for lack of a term that would fit better, a full hard on. A massive erection. Maximus Cockus in Greek circles. Now I was really nervous. The horse was actually licking his lips. Is that normal for a horse? I slowly slid across the table and jumped into the shelter, Matt laughing the whole time. There was a rail a few feet in front of this shelter, so as this horse approached he could not come right up to the shelter and have his way with me.

"What's with that horse?"

"I think he likes you Dad. Maybe he thinks you're the horse whisperer."

"Funny. You think it's a homo horse?" I was never politically correct.

"Maybe he wanted to hump your legs like dogs do."

"Oh great, a one-ton horse straddling my leg soaking me with horse jizz."

"Better than being attacked by him, like the deer, boar and snake."

I made a lot of noise and motions, the horse took his sweet time, but eventually left the shelter area. In this particular shelter, the water source was a spring in a big field about three hundred yards behind the shelter. It was in a large fenced in area with a gate so the horses could not get in and ruin the water source. I needed to get water, so I started across the field, only to look to the left and see that damn horse standing on a hilltop looking at me. The stupid horse started a bit down the hill, so I broke into a fast stride, ran to the fenced in area, then did a dive over the fence and tucked into a somersault on the other side. I stood up and looked and I swear that stupid horny horse was laughing at me. I took my time filling the water bag, waiting for my equine lover to drift away. I hurried back up the hill to the shelter.

Survival Note: All feral horses should be geldings.

The next day, with some more trepidation, mainly because I didn't know where Flicka was, we left the shelter hiking through a few miles of open fields with stallions roaming about. Some were even the little Shetland type ponies.

We met a young girl on the trail who was hiking with her dog. I don't know why people do that to their pets, but what I do know, she was probably the hairiest girl Matt and I had seen to date. I know the books say for girls to go natural on the trail, but it was something we were not used too. Armpits could be braided, legs that look like a chia pet, facial hair like my grandmother's. The horse looked better groomed.

She told us that at the shelter she was at the night before a group of five male hikers in their fifties came in, ate, then hunkered down for the night, only one of them did not wake up in the morning. Apparently, he died peacefully in his sleep. Rangers came in on ATV's and then called in a helicopter to take the body out. One of the other hikers, for some unknown reason, covered him with his sleeping bag, only to realize he had let the chopper take off with the sleeping bag, and now was without a bag. Not real bright.

Interesting fact I just learned from this young hirsute, there are approximately one-hundred-sixty-five thousand white blazes on the trail. I should have had Matt count them to keep him busy. Speaking of numbers, Rummy is now 67,462 to 67,395. I'm leading but it's tightening up.

1682.4 miles to go.

Chapter 22
Only You Can Prevent a Forest Fire

There was high bear activity in the area of the next shelter. This was evident due to all the bear scat we saw along the trail. To make things worse the next shelter was heavily wooded right up to the front of the shelter. The beasts could sneak in close without you seeing them. It had a fireplace built into it and as is with all shelters the front was open. It looked as if it was a cabin and they had taken the front wall down. Matt loved it, Firestarter was in his glory with a fireplace he didn't have to take ten extra steps to get to.

Fun Fact/Survival Note: An interesting fact I was told by a trail runner, bears smell like wet dogs. I don't know if that's true, but I was mindful to keep alert of that particular pungency.

One of the other chores assigned to Matt now was hanging the food bags. We discussed this a bit earlier. It's not that difficult for a normal person, but my son is special, so very special. At some shelters, especially in areas with heavy bear traffic, there are specially designed places to hang your food bag with a systems of pullies, that are proven, mostly, to work. Others had bear boxes that locked. Since bears do not have an opposing thumb, they simply cannot open them. The dumb creatures would try but fail. That would have been a problem for Panda.

In the shelters without a food bag system, which is by far a vast majority, you would need to throw a line over a tree branch, at least five feet from the trunk, and about twelve feet off the ground, so you could hoist your food bag up and out of reach of the bears...simple. Right? Not so for Matt.

First, it would take inordinate amount of time for him to find a branch. We're in a forest for God's sake. Then he would take one of our carabiners, tie it to a line, and try to throw it over the tree branch. These carabiners have no weight to them whatsoever, they are aluminum, so it would continually full short, or worse it would get caught in the smaller brush and branches around the tree. The one or two times he got it up to the branch, it never had enough weight to come down the other side so it would get caught in the tree. I would then have to cut the line, we lost the carabiner, and I would have to do it myself. I think he did it on purpose to piss me off, but it always amused me to watch him for that half hour or so trying to succeed. We only ever got one carabiner back from a Good Samaritan.

It was at this shelter we had another Psycho encounter/near death experience. I am telling you I do not make this stuff up. He came in after Matt and I had set up for dinner. He still had an MSR stove with the fuel canister and pump. He said he had no money to update his stove. I was not loaning him any. He set it up on the picnic table and pumped up his canister, this is a normal thing most hikers do on the tables outside of the shelters. In fact, a lot of the tables you see have burn rings on them from the stoves that get a bit too hot. He turned it on, lit the burner, and started the stove. Psycho is not the most graceful cook you'll ever see, but he put a pot of water on the burner and turned to get his food ready as the water began to boil.

Well, much like some rockets the rubber seal on his fuel canister had gone bad and fuel was leaking out. The fuel canister was seeping fuel onto the table and pooling

185

over by the lit portion of the stove. Psycho spotted the fuel flow any yelled to Matt and me, "If the flame hits that fuel tank, that tank will blow!"

Well Psycho, the ever-heroic Marine, threw his body between the bomb and us. He was full of finesse and singular focus. It was no different than jumping on a grenade. He deftly smacked the boiling pot of water off the stove, removing a potential missile from hitting us. He then slid around the side of the table grabbing the bottom of the fuel tank and tossing it tomahawk style into the woods just before it would explode.

That's how he would tell the story and does to this day. That's not what happened. So, we will pick up from the last truthful event. Rewind.

"If the flame hits that fuel tank, the tank will blow!" Psycho was in a panic

"No, it won't. Just drag it out of the way and clean up the spill," Matt replied.

"Matt is right, the tank would need to sit in the fire for quite a bit to explode." I started to walk over to his stove.

What does this Einstein actually do? He did jump up and smack the pot of boiling water, which he incidentally sent flying right at me, while in the process spilling the water on his hands and shirt. He did grab the fuel canister, but he didn't throw it like a hero. He barely tossed it ten feet away. He didn't even manage to get it behind a tree to protect us from the blast. Now if you never heard one of those MSR stoves while it was running, they sound like a small jet engine. This can be a bit alarming if we weren't so accustomed to the sound at this point.

Matt and I are standing there, dumbfounded by what we just saw, speechless, and all we could hear was the whooshing of the stove coming from what was barely a stride into the woods. Psycho is standing there like he just saved the world. Smirking.

"Hey, shit head, just what the fuck are you thinking? You just threw a lit stove into the woods. One that's leaking for that matter."

"It might have blown, and then we would be dead, so the way I see it you should be thanking me."

"You are certifiably insane, you know that? The stove would not have blown, you ass. But now we are faced with a potential forest fire."

"You don't know Peterman. I've been around explosives. Besides it might burn out."

"Being exploded in Vietnam does not count as an expertise in demo," Matt interjected.

"How the hell did you survive this long without some type of help? You do need to be in the woods, I now see why you are out here, you can't survive in society. The only problem is you're not good for nature either. I get why you had your own padded room."

"Relax Peterman, we're safe and besides forest fires are a cleansing part of nature."

"It's also real rich that the guy who just threw his burning stove in the woods is telling me to relax."

Matt, thankfully had hurried into the woods and recovered the stove, still lit, and shut it off. We went over and doused the area with water to make sure we did not burn to death during the night in a Psycho fueled forest fire. I still had my repair kit from our stove, I gave it to him so he could fix his stove. I should add that to his ledger, he's costing me more than Matthew.

Survival Note: Never, ever, throw a lit stove into the woods.

Much to Psychos chagrin we survived that night.

1,664 miles to go.

Chapter 23
Blisters

We continued our monotonous hiking and we arrived at Partnership Shelter after another day of ups and downs. It's located right next to the Mt. Rogers National Park Headquarters, so this should be the flagship of shelters. It was clean, slept sixteen with room to spare, had a flush toilet, and a hot shower attached. It also had a pay phone and you could use and have pizza delivered. It's not hard to figure out by now where Matt headed to. I went over to the Park's Headquarters and got an ice-cold soda. Now I usually don't drink soda, but on the trail, it was a luxury. I sat and talked with the two female Rangers that staffed the building and asked about the trail ahead. That being done, questions answered, I walked back over to the shelter. More hikers had come in and Matt was still in the shower. The other hikers had taken numbers to see who was next, just like it was in an old-time deli-counter. Since I had ordered Matt out, they let me go in next. Three minutes, like an egg, and I was done, I think my wife would agree with that.

We hadn't planned on meeting Patti here, but Ol' Sivertoes struck again. Matt's feet, as much as they look like Hobbit feet, do not share the same endurance. He was suffering from another severe bout of blisters. I really don't know how he does it, it's like he hadn't been walking for the past twenty years. I know we've joked about blisters having blisters, but he really did, the poor bastard. When you get blisters like that, they take on other worldly properties. The balls of his feet were one gigantic blister, and they were a translucent reddish color. The rest of their physical properties resembled that of a waterbed, you could poke them and just watch the fluid beneath rippling about. He would drain them; you could see the beginnings of a new blister forming underneath. They then would harden up and become callouses, but somehow those callouses would rub off and the whole process would start over again.

As enjoyable as it is to pick on the lad, he was in a lot of pain, and that's not fun for anyone. Toward the end of the day he would be moving so slowly I was able to drop my stuff off at camp and go back and carry his backpack the rest of the way. I know it was heroic of me, but I was only thinking of my son. I never had much trouble with blisters, it was hard to empathize, but his feet looked gross enough to know he needed to stay off them for a while. I called nurse Patti.

Even though she wasn't technically supposed to be "retired," she was, so it was easy for her to drive over to us at the drop of a hat. We called her from the shelter and told her to meet us in the town of Marion the next day. It was the nearest town to where we were. One of the female Rangers was kind enough to drive us into town as her shift ended. We wouldn't get to order pizza to the shelter, but that was fine as we now had access to all the food Marion had to offer.

We settled on a greasy spoon diner close to the motel we found a room at. It's funny to think about distances when you are used to walking all day. The diner was close but still at least half a mile away. Most people, in most situations, would drive that distance. Even with the blisters that was a laughable distance for us, we may have moved slow, but it was easy.

True to its look, our meal was greasy, and once again luck was on our side. We ate our fill as we always do when we hit towns. Marion, however, is a bit further off the trail. They see their share of hikers coming into town, but the trail doesn't pass through it. We were obviously hikers and the waitress struck up a conversation, so as we always do, we shared parts of our story. An older couple at the table next to us heard us talking and commented about how lovely it was for father and son to do this, blah blah blah. That conversation came back around to Matt's feet, and Matt played up the helpless cripple that can barely walk part very well, putting on quite the display making his way to the restroom. He limped on both legs, let his knees buckle a few times, and held onto the backs of chairs for support wincing in pain. It was a breath-taking performance piece, it was so good I felt the need for a cigarette afterwards, and I don't smoke. It worked, the older couple insisted on driving us back to our motel. And the Oscar goes to....

Thank Christ we got a ride home because that food does not sit well in a hiker's digestive track. You become accustomed to the routine food and greasy meals like this lube up the innards. I was thankful for the ride and I was thankful for, as Panda says, "getting to sit over water." I never take flushing for granted anymore.

Patti pulled into town in the early afternoon the next day. It's funny, as far as we've walked and for as long as we've been out in the woods, we were still only six hours from home. That's kind of depressing to think about. It really makes you think about how long it took to get anywhere before cars.

She brought us our next mail drop, we still took advantage of having a car around and did some shopping. After spending the kind of time we had out on the trail, walking into a grocery store can be sensory overload. It's important to be disciplined, so I went straight for the

Corona and some limes. We got a few luxury items that we don't normally get, like food that expires.

We decided Matt would rest for a few days and I would slack for a while since Patti was around with the car. You might think it nice to rest for a few days, but Marion isn't exactly a tourist destination. There was little for Matt and Patti to do all day aside from drop me off and pick me up. The only thing worse than hiking all day is being stuck in a hotel room all day. This hotel did not have a pool, much to Matt's dismay.

"Slacking" alone was a wonderful experience for me, hell, hiking alone was a new experience for me. It's easy to cover a lot of ground alone without a pack, but you also must keep in mind that there won't be a ride for you at the end if you move too fast. I had stopped to rest at a shelter about a mile or so from the road Patti would be picking me up at. Knowing I still had about two hours to kill before she picked me up, I rested. I leisurely perused the log searching for signs of those we had met along the way, namely Psycho. I had not run into him while slacking which meant he had already passed us, or he hadn't made it this far yet. There was no sign of him in the logs, I don't know if what I felt in that moment was relief or disappointment.

I continued in my solitude, one man surrounded by nature, a pillar of sanity alone with his thoughts. In those hours alone I became a master of my domain, a bastion of serenity and calm. I was, in those moments, Planet Bob, a world unto himself.

My tranquility, however, was shattered upon entering a clearing in the woods. I came out to the road where Matthew and Patti were waiting diligently for their redeemer. Now that I was there, their day could finally begin. I walked up to the minivan and slid open the passenger door.

"Hey Peterman! What's going on?" Psycho was sitting in the other seat in all his glory.

Matt was smiling wryly, clearly seeing the shock on my face. "Yeah, we got here early thinking you'd make up some time being alone and guess who popped out of the woods about ten minutes after we arrived? Well you really don't have to guess, do you?"

"Yeah Peterman, Patti said I could have dinner with you guys tonight. She's a nice gal Peterman, a real keeper. Matt told me about his feet and you slacking for a few days, so I think I'll join you. We don't need you losing your marbles out here all alone."

And just like that Planet Bob was smashed by a Psycho asteroid. It was a planet killer, an extinction level event, no serenity survived. Again, I don't know if I was feeling relief or disappointment.

"Where are you staying? You got money for a room?" I was still imploding.

"Yeah, monthly VA checks plus your loans. I haven't forgotten I owe you a few bucks Peterman." That shit eating smile again.

Since I was slacking Matt had plenty of spare time during the day, he asked around town to see if there was anything to do. Given our remote location we didn't hold out too much hope. It was quite serendipitous for us that Marion was stuck in the sixties. They still had a drive-in movie theater. The movies wouldn't start until sundown which in these summer nights gave us plenty of time to eat dinner and make it to the show.

Dinner was nothing remarkable and we were all pumped for the movies. It would be a welcome break from our routine, which even when staying in towns like this meant going to bed when the sun went down. However, there was one routine I was not about to break. On the way to the theater I had Patti stop at the grocery store, I bought a Styrofoam cooler, a ten-pound bag of ice, and a twelve pack of Corona. By the way, I am not now, and have never been an employee of Corona. I figured this would be the best way to enjoy the movie and with Matt the apple didn't far for from tree. Psycho, of course, disapproved, but who cares? Damn AA people.

"You know Patti, I've been watching these two on the trail. They drink a lot." His voice was that of a person who seemed concerned.

"You're right Roger." That's his real first name. "I've preached to him, but does he listen?"

"AA would be good for both of them."

Screw you Pyscho, I thought. "Hey, hold up Hon," I yelled to Patti as I put the beer on ice in the rear of the car. "Be right back."

Into the store I went and came out with another twelve pack of Corona. "That should do it, now we have enough. I tend to drink more when Psycho acts holier than thou."

We pulled up to the Park Place theater and paid our admission. The place looked as rundown as they come, like it hadn't been painted since the day it was built. The grounds were tiered so each car can see over the one in front of and below it. It was a good system. Patti backed into a spot in the middle of the second tier. Her minivan had rear facing seats and speakers in the back. It was perfect for us but that meant Psycho and Matt were out of luck. Patti being the angel she is had brought collapsible chairs for them to sit in. They had to share a portable radio to get sound, as the audio was broadcast through an FM frequency.

We were really there to see the second show, it was a Terminator movie and the kind of thing Matt and I like to watch. This being a family establishment it showed a kid's movie first as part of the double feature. It was some stupid Eddie Murphy movie. It wasn't any good and this was evident because when I looked over toward the end of the movie, Psycho had the radio all to himself and Matt was sound asleep with several empty Corona bottles at his feet.

Psycho and I slacked another day before Matt was finally ready to strap on the boots again. We ate one last dinner together and turned in early knowing we had to plunge back into the abyss the next day.

1,653.3 miles to go.

Chapter 24
Still Virginia

Patti dropped the three of us off where Psycho and I had left off. We offered to go back and redo the parts of the trail that Matt missed, but he was being gracious enough to allow us to continue on where we left off. We were scheduled to meet Patti in a couple of weeks anyway so there were no prolonged goodbyes. She spun the car wheels and left us in a cloud of dust, left hand extended out the driver's window waving goodbye.

We hiked on for the next few days with nothing much to report. We spent our time with nonsensical conversation, heavy breathing, swatting at bugs, and sweating grotesquely. God damn mountains. All day, every day. Then something interesting happened.

As I've stated before I'm not particularly religious but there are some things I can't explain. This was the first of my run-ins with the supernatural. Matt and I were hiking, and I was leading the way, both metaphorically and literally. Now if it were just me, I wouldn't mention it and just assume that I'm crazy, but Matt was there, and he saw it too. We came into a pine barren toward the top of a mountain and there in the center of the trail was this white orb floating above the trail. This stopped me dead in my tracks since it was only about thirty feet away.

I turned to look at my son who just shrugged with indifference while witnessing this phenomenon. I decided to approach hoping maybe I'd be raptured away from this God forsaken mountain range. Maybe it was aliens, I would have gone for a probing or at least tossed them the boy for their experiments. It hung in the air and moved away as I approached gliding gently between the trees but

196

never hitting them. Then it just disappeared. To this day I have no idea what it was. My heathen son argues it was a cluster of gnats or something with sunlight reflecting off them, which I grant is a perfectly plausible scenario. However, I like to think I know the difference and besides it looked too intact to be a reflective swarm of bugs. We made the mistake of asking Psycho what he thought it could be when he showed up at the shelter later.

"Peterman, man, I'm telling you, I see those things all the time. You're a marked man, Peterman. They're probably watching you now too." So now I've got that going for me. Maybe I should add aliens to my list of things after me.

We continue to meet eclectic groups of misfits all along the trail. There were a different set of players along this section. There was "Smelly Socks," it's easy to guess why this person was trail named this. There was "Nine Fingers," his pinky missing from birth. "Snake Bait," bit twice by snakes, luckily for him they were non-venomous. One I loved was "Look at Me," a cross eyed hiker, funny to look at and to talk to. "Tourettes," he was always cursing about everything, he and Psycho were interesting to listen to. "Headlights," her nipples were always hard, she was another personal favorite of mine, and last but not least "Ariel," from The Little Mermaid. She thought she was trail named this because of her long flowing red hair. Nope, she smelled like a fish. As I said earlier, take a trail name with you because people on the trail loved to label other people, or maybe it was just us, either way it was your name.

We hit another fleabag motel the next day, it was owned by a husband and wife, both Pakistanis. Their cleaning staff consisted of two redneck women, tipping the scales at three to four hundred pounds each, with very few teeth. I charmed them while I sent Matt for some beer next door. They did all our laundry for us, sleeping bags and all, and I slipped them a six pack. They loved it. Then Psycho rolled in and changed the whole mood of the place as only he can. They placed him in a room at the very far end of the hotel. He sat in his doorway, facing our room, his usual position, waiting to see what we were doing. He also managed to piss off my two new friends because he kept complaining about his room, the pillows, his sheets, anything and everything. As always, he followed us to dinner, it was like having a faithful dog by this time.

Off we go again. Patti is meeting us in four days, so we need to get to the pickup point in time. We're saying nothing to Psycho about the pickup. As the days ticked by it began to grow noticeably warmer and by warmer, I mean it was fucking hot. Then there were the bugs, the damn bugs. They were coming out in force and boy do they love the smell of shitty sweat drenched humans. As annoying as the bugs were Matt took the brunt of it. It must have been his undefiled sweet virginal blood. Hey, it's fine with me if he has to be the virgin sacrifice to keep the insects clear of me.

Maybe flies live longer in the wild and are able to grow larger because these sons of bitches were huge. These things looked like they were at least a half-pound a piece and could have made a filling meal. They would continually divebomb our ears, sounding like a chain saw when they buzzed by. I don't know what the obsession with ears are, but I seriously thought of wearing my earplugs, the constant droning reminded me of my wife, but like I said Matt had it worse.

The gnats and no-see-ums were driving Matt to the very brink of insanity, in fact that's partly how Firestarter really came about, he started campfires because the smoke would drive away the gnats, but nothing was worse than the black fly and horsefly. This combo was my son's undoing. I got a front row seat on several occasions to my son's freak-outs. If a fly started buzzing me, I would hurry up to get closer to Matthew hoping to pass the bug into his orbit, so to speak, and it would work more often than not. Adversely when I saw him being strafed, I would linger back just enough to go unmolested. These suckers were so big they would occasionally get tangled in his hair during their kamikaze runs. He would lose his shit. He'd start swatting at it with his arms flailing all over the place, but his walking sticks were strapped to his wrists, so they too are flying at his head. It really made for quite the hilarious scene.

Another time, and this is true, a horse fly followed Matt buzzing his head for over a mile. One take away from this experience was that it was clear we were in much better shape physically, because in his fit of fly induced insanity, he took off at a full sprint with all forty pounds on his back to escape his winged demon. The leviathan was not dissuaded by his encumbered burst of speed and continued its pursuit. The last straw came when the fly swooped straight into Matthews ear. It went ever so slightly into his ear canal buzzing the whole time. Even thinking about it now gives me the shivers. That was the point where Matt decided it would be a battle to the death.

Matt threw his walking sticks down and ripped his backpack off letting it fall to the ground. He untied the knot on his bandana, its primary function is to collect sweat, and spun it up like one would do with a towel in a locker room to whip someone in the butt. I'm standing there, countless miles into the Appalachian Trail wilderness, watching my man-child son fight a horse fly.

The interesting part of the whole thing was that it seemed like the fly knew exactly what he was doing. Matthew was bobbing and weaving attempting to pop this fly with his do-rag, as if it were a whip and knock it out of the sky. He would miss and the fly would counter, buzzing in at his face and ears. Matt would strike, the fly again would parry and counter. Incredible. Finally, and with great dramatics Matt backhanded the fly as it swooped in on him sending it tumbling to the ground. You would have thought he had just won the Super Bowl. He was screaming and beating his chest. It made me sad to know that in that instant I was witnessing my son's finest moment, which was him defeating a horse fly in single combat. As this poor dazed insect looked up at him the last thing it saw was the treads on his hiking boot. Stomp. Dead.

Every once in a blue moon Psycho would leave the shelter before we did in the mornings. We would eventually overtake him at some point in the day due to his numerous cigarette breaks, but on this day, we found him sitting in a field eating his lunch. This was not the type of field Matthew and I would have stopped in, anything where the grass is above ankle height is just inviting trouble. Naturally trouble is what Psycho found. When he showed up at the shelter he was covered in ticks. "Hey yo, Peterman, Matt, someone come help me get these little fuckers off me."

As you can imagine Matt and I wanted nothing to do with it. "There is not a chance in this world I'm coming near you or those ticks. You shouldn't have been lying in the weeds," Matt told him.

"Ah, come on, I'd do it for you."

Psycho began picking them off one by one and dropping them onto the shelter floor. It would have been nice if he had crushed them after he dropped them, but nope, not Psycho. He would just pluck them off and send them on their way. This nut job was really hard to read sometimes. It's like he doesn't think about his actions whatsoever, or the consequences for that matter. Matt and I decided to sleep in our tents that night. I already have two bloodsucking leeches I call my children, I didn't need any more attached to me.

The next day it was the "Summer Solstice" which is naked hikers' day. We were not getting naked, not with all the damn biting insects, hell, we weren't getting naked anyway, bonding between father and son only goes so far. We were hoping for the best, naked girls. That did not happen, but we did past two middle aged women day hiking, wearing only bandanas covering their breasts and groin area. They were hiking the opposite direction of us, so as they passed, we turned around to look and saw two bare asses. That was the full extent of naked hikers' day.

The most interesting thing to happen in that stretch of days was meeting another father and son duo out on the trail. They were simply Frank and John, it was their first day out and they had not picked up trail names yet. The thing that set them apart was John had cancer and it was his dream to hike the AT. His father Frank was able to take him out for a short section hike. John was also about college age, so I likened him to my son. Not because of the cancer, but because he, much like Matt, probably did not belong out in the wilderness. I give Frank all the credit in the world for doing what he was doing for his son.

John wanted to get a better view of the world around us and took a blue blazed trail. He thought it was a shortcut to a scenic view. Well, not so much. Frank did not go with him, because like me he had to care for his child by setting up camp for the two of them. Frank finished setting up and came over to Matt and I were. I asked him, "Where is John?"

"Oh, he took that blue blazed trail, it's a shortcut to a side trail with great views."

"Uh, oh," Matt muttered.

"Yeah, Frank, that's not a shortcut, it's a loop trail that goes back to where you guys came onto the trail," I told him.

I pulled out my maps and showed him exactly where we were and the trail that John had gone on and the one he mistook for it. Clearly, John was not a strong hiker due to the cancer and Frank looked distraught, as you can imagine any father would. It was still early enough in the afternoon to keep him from panicking, we still had a few hours of sunlight left. Matt and I agreed to help go look for him, each of us taking a different trail, the AT, the loop trail, and the scenic trail. We planned to meet back at the shelter after two hours if we hadn't found him. Luckily John was found by his father shortly before sundown. He realized after about a mile that he must have taken the wrong trail and began to make his way back. They made it back to camp before we did having come back up the AT.

Matthew and I arrived back at camp a short time later, it was that magic hour just as the light was beginning to fade. We walked the last few hundred yards together hoping Frank had better luck than we did. Instead of being greeted by Frank and John we were greeted by Psycho sitting on the picnic table smoking a cigarette, "Hey, where you assholes been?"

Frank and John came walking over and Matthew and I were both relieved to see them.

"Well, besides being a hiking God, I have been part of a search team," I told Psycho.

"Oh yeah? Well what did you find?"

"I found your God damn running tab that you owe me, that's what I found."

"Easy Peterman, easy. Just having some fun with you, these guys explained the whole thing. I saw your stuff here and asked if they'd seen you guys. You boys are a class act."

I couldn't argue this point. The rest of the night was wonderful, Firestarter built us one of his famous fires and we laughed and joked with Frank and John until it was time to turn in. Frank and John hiked out the next day. We wished them well before they left and made sure they were on the right trail home.

1,626.3 miles to go.

Chapter 25
And Still in Virginia

Along certain stretches of the trail horses and hikers share the path. It was at this particular junction in Virginia where we came across an abundance of them. Some of the riders we came across were out for the day and some out for a weekend ride. Some of them were nice people and others were complete assholes. Honestly, I think it would be a blast to take a horse out into the mountains for a few days and ride some back-country trails. Most of these people however thought they were Roy Rogers or Wyatt Earp, maybe even a few Buffalo Bills, but they looked more like Deputy Dog. Some of these idiots were wearing the ten-gallon hats and dusters, boots with spurs, and other ridiculous accessories, and this being June.

We learned very quickly that horses are skittish around backpackers, the backpacks make us look larger and different from the normal people they are accustomed to seeing every day. When a group of riders are coming down the trail, they are supposed to stop their horses and let the hikers move past quickly to keep the horses calm. It's a nice sentiment but when you have a one-ton animal on a two-foot-wide trail it gets complicated. Especially when there are steep banks on both sides of the trail.

We had that problem once, high up on a mountain, and the horses were having none of it. I guess they didn't care for our looks and smells. The lead horsemen stopped his group to let us pass but his horse had other ideas, as Matthew attempted to pass the horse started to stomp at the ground and Matt would not get any closer to her. I can't say I blame him. We ended up having to climb down the mountainside about fifteen feet or more so the horses could pass without incident, or injury to us.

We came to learn that these were mostly guided tours, which explained a lot. They didn't have the etiquette you would expect from an experienced back country rider. They had no regard for where their steeds were pissing and shitting. That's a problem for the water sources at the shelters. The shelter we stopped at had a group of riders and the whole place smelled of horse shit, and we had just gotten used to smelling like shit ourselves, and we didn't need to add this to the mix. There were signs posted everywhere about keeping horses clear of the water sources and so what do we run into? If you guessed a horseback rider with his horse peeing in the stream where we were getting water, then you were right. I asked this faux cowboy if he could read English. We seemed to clash immediately, was it me? I asked if he was literate, which I hoped he was, getting no response I then explained it like I would to a child.

"You see the signs here that say N-0 H-0-R-S-E-S. That means horses are not allowed. If you can read, then why is your horse peeing in my water source?"

His clever response was, "Oh yeah, what are you gonna do about it?"

"Well, it would appear that there is not much I can do about it, aside from pointing out your reading deficiencies. If you wouldn't mind though, it would be great if you could give me your home address so I can defecate in your water supply." Where was Psycho when you needed him, he would just blow smoke in this guy's face till he left.

Survival Note: Get your water upstream from trails allowing horses.

The next water supply was a mile and half away, this made our decision simple. We would hike to the water source and camp there for the night and leave these John Wayne pretenders behind us. Even Matt was on board with the extra distance. Sure enough, it began to rain, but at least Mother Nature had the graciousness to allow us to get camp set up. Not enough graciousness, mind you, to permit us our dinner. With nowhere to light a stove we were relegated to cold cereal with powdered milk. It was essentially the same as going to bed hungry. Matt and I each climbed into our respective coffins and chatted back and forth a bit before calling it a night.

After a few more days of rain and shine and up and down and over and around we were ready to meet Patti again. We had a normal day's hike ahead of us, twelve miles to the dirt road we agreed to meet at. Well, good God in heaven above, if that's where she is, we were ecstatic. There was an extra pep in our step knowing that there would be a hot meal, hot shower, and a soft bed waiting at the end of our day. Bobby Boy would also get some much-needed booty once again.

Our plan was to meet at one PM, or so we thought, but that would be too easy. We were in the dog days of summer on a Sunday in July, and man it was hot. Unbearably hot. We waited on the side of the dirt road for a while but there was no shade around without going back into the woods. We were dying. Literally dying. We had to cover ourselves in our green trash bags due to the voracious bugs and their relentless assault on our flesh. For two hours we sat by the side of the road waiting for salvation, only to be forsaken.

"This is bullshit, I can't handle this anymore, we have to move," Matt broke the silence. He was right.

"Okay, well the main road isn't too far, we can start heading that way and Patti should be coming from that direction anyway, so it's better than just sitting here and roasting."

We gathered our things and headed down the road. The worse part of being out in Bumfuck, Virginia is no cell reception. No matter which way I walked there was no signal on my phone. Matt wasn't having any luck either, we were both in a black hole of cell phone coverage. We wouldn't normally expect to have coverage out here, but we were pissed off, hotter than hell and hoping for some luck.

We got to the intersection where the guidebook said there was a store. Well the book wasn't wrong, the store was there, however the book did not mention hours of operation and it was closed. Not just closed, but out of business. Of course, the hiking gods never miss a chance to kick a man when he's down, there was no pay phone. To my eternal dismay even the soda machine out front was empty. It's amazing how a small thing can make your day better, a cold soda in those moments would have done wonders for our morale.

I spotted two farmers, if that's what they were, in a yard a short distance from us, and walked over to them while Matt laid under the shade of the closed stores awning. I greeted them and told them of our plight and, naturally, my concern for my wife. I asked them where I might find a phone I could use to check in on her. Now mind you, though I was on the other side of their fence, we were only about ten yards from the house, which one would safely assume has to have a phone. Not to mention one of these two hayseeds had a satellite looking phone hanging from his hip. These two numbskulls had a ten-minute discussion as to where the closest pay phone might be. As I listened to their conversation, I was forced to assume that combined IQ was somewhere in the forty range. Impressive. Now I see why the south lost the war.

The conclusion from this great meeting of minds was that the nearest phone was, not counting the one in their house or on hayseed number one's hip, at another store about five miles or so down the road. As I said before, we walked down from the mountains and we were now in Virginia farmland. It was July and it was steaming. However bad you imagine hiking all day in the mountains to be, hiking across hot black asphalt is worse, especially during the hottest part of the day. To make matters worse there was no shade anywhere, only misery. Patti, I swore, would pay for this. I walked back over to Matt and broke the news to him, "Son, we aren't quite done hiking just yet. Five miles to the next phone."

As you can imagine, his reaction was less than favorable. I swear it was so hot the souls of our shoes were starting to melt, and our hiking sticks were poking holes into the road. Hitching was out of the question, there was no traffic coming or going from where we were. With heavy hearts we carried on to what we could only hope was a store with a phone.

It's hard to tell exactly how far we had made it up the road when we were coming up on a double wide trailer jacked up on cinder blocks. Sitting outside was another of the deep south's prominent citizens and his dingy mutts by his side. He watched as Matt and I made our way up the road at all turtle's pace. As we approached the front of his palatial estate, we heard him say to his mutts, "go get em' boys," and motioned and the dogs toward us. Well, those mutts took off from the makeshift porch and raced across the yard toward us.

Matt and I had become pretty proficient with our folding knives but this is not how we saw ourselves using them. I flicked mine open. I took a step forward to shield my son from the brunt of the attack, because let's face it, that's just the type of guy I am. At the last second this redneck jackass whistled for his dogs and called them back laughing hysterically the whole time. What in the actual fuckedy-fuck is wrong with these people? If someone in New York had done that I would have shot them, and here's this asswipe in stitches laughing. It was not that funny. This is why horror movies take place in the south, it's people like this guy. Given our surroundings this wasn't the time or place to pick a fight, we just kept on our way an I made a mental note to one day return and burn his piece of shit trailer to the ground.

The day was getting longer, longer than it was supposed to be and we were running short on water. We passed another house, one that wasn't supported by cinder blocks, with a young teen outside washing his Jeep. We were melting at this point, my son was a walking puddle and I wasn't far behind. If my calculations were anywhere near correct, we still had roughly two miles to go and that's banking on the two hayseeds actually being right about where the store was. We stopped for a moment and motioned for the kid to hose us down. I half expected him to refuse, considering the other run-ins we had with the locals here. He obliged us, and man let me tell you, it was nice. He let us cool off for a minute under the cool shower of water and we shot the shit for a while. I told him about his neighbor down the road and he found it hilarious. What's that old Foxworthy joke, "you might be a redneck if...?"

To the young man's credit, he did give us some ice-cold water and told us to hang out while he finished

209

washing his Jeep and he would air dry it by driving us to the phone. Again, we were ten feet from his house, but no mention of a house phone. Do these people still use smoke signals, I just don't get it. He did deliver on his promise though and took us the rest of the way. Matthew thanked him profusely as though he just volunteered his kidney or something.

We've finally got to the pay phone and I called Patti, it went straight to voicemail. It was now past five o'clock and our patience was completely shot. I left her a message as to where we were with a tone that suggested she should hurry. I'd be remiss in my husbandly duties if I didn't mention I was a bit worried for her safety, but only a bit. Matt and I sat under what shade we could find drinking a beer and waiting, hoping she got my message. We sat there discussing scenarios that could have taken place:

1. She's crashed.
2. She's dead.
3. She left me for someone else and this was payback.

We decided that option three was probably the most likely. Patti did finally show up and our day had been much longer than anticipated. She began to explain why she was late, but I told her it was best she not speak with me at the moment. The fuse was short, and it was lit. I grabbed a twelve pack from the store and Patti began spraying down our backpacks with Febreze, she had wised up after previous encounters. She started toward me with her perfumed spray, but I guess the look in my eyes suggested it would be best not to. She jumped behind the wheel as I cracked open a beer for the drive to the motel.

Matt had his own room this time, so his shower time was none of my concern. I went into my shower straight away to wash away the ridiculousness of the day. It's incredible what a hot shower does to one's mood. It calmed me down immediately. Now that I was once again serene in both body and mind, I asked Patti what had happened. She went on to explain that she had gotten a flat tire and the only place to get it fixed on a Sunday in the deep south was at Walmart, while the nearest Walmart wasn't exactly near. Compounding the matter was the fact that there was no cell phone reception anywhere. Murphy's law, if something can go wrong it will. I hate that guy Murphy.

We would be slacking for the next three days while Patti was around to drop us off and pick us up. We went from north to south and were able to cover some big miles in this section having twenty plus mile days. I also gently reminded Patti not to wash our backpack's in the tub while we were gone. It just wasn't worth readjusting everything, our packs were familiar at this point and you don't want to jeopardize that.

1,534.8 miles to go.

Chapter 26
We Get Boared

Matt and I had another delightful run in with the wildlife on this section of trail. We were minding our own business, zoned out as usual, when Matt stopped dead in his tracks. I almost ran into the back of him. Above us, on the uphill trail ahead of him, maybe ten yards or so were two small piglets. Matt started to make a joke, "So this is where baby back ribs come from. I've never seen bacon in its natural habitat."

It would have been funny if we knew momma pig wasn't around, but they are never far from their babies. So while Matt was mapping out the cuts of meat on these piglets, the brush started rattling and out popped this ugly, angry, behemoth. This sow was huge, at least three hundred pounds and four feet long. She was pissed that we were in the area of her children.

Fun Fact: Feral hogs are a big problem in the South, and they have been known to be aggressive. Wild boars can eviscerate a man and have been known to kill hunting dogs, and even the occasional hunter.

"So, what do we do?" Matt asked. Just as he asked this ill-timed question, the little piglets started toward us and momma bolted pass them gunning straight for us.

"Oh shit, get behind a tree quick!" Was all I could squeak out. I guess momma hog didn't like Matt's jokes about eating her young. As soon as she was just about on top of us she split off at the last second and led her piglets into the woods. Matt and I quickly moved past where they ran into the brush, hoping to put as much distance between the happy family and ourselves.

When we were a few yards pass where they had entered the brush, momma poked her head through the thickets, snorting at us and thrashing about shaking the bushes it was semi concealed in. I also checked off another box on my list of wildlife that has tried to kill me since this undertaking. Hogs, snakes, horses, and deer, oh my!

We continued slack packing south, maybe it's your psyche, who knows, but it did seem easier, like Carl said, downhill. It could also be argued that we weren't lugging thirty-five pounds on our backs. One thing we didn't consider was who we might run into heading south.

A few miles further up, I was leading, and stopped to point out to Matt some turkey chicks about twenty yards up the trail. Cute little buggers. We watched for a few minutes when out onto the trail came the hen, at least I think it was. We started toward them figuring they would waddle into the woods. Life is just not that easy. This overstuffed Thanksgiving dinner decided we must represent danger to the chicks and started running down the trail right at us. People say wild turkeys can't fly, that's bullshit. This thing launched itself at us, wings flapping, about four feet off the ground, with a look of death in its eyes and a screech that would make your balls shrink. I jumped to the side and thought for sure it would impale itself in Matt's chest, but he too jumped to the side and avoided certain injury or death. Go back two paragraphs and add wild turkeys to my list.

Another attack loomed ahead. We could hear it's huffing and puffing a mile away. It was no surprise to see Psycho come around the bend in all his scrawny glory with his old metal frame backpack that was too old twenty years ago, and boy was he happy to see us.

"Yo, Peterman, Matt, you guys are going the wrong way, you two idiots get turned around or something?"

"Something like that," I replied.

"Oh man, you got no packs. You didn't tell me you were slacking Peterman. Where you guys staying anyway? Is Patti around again? I think she really likes me you know, knowing I'm out here watching your backs."

"Yeah, well, where were you about fifteen miles ago when a boar tried to put its tusks through our backs?" asked Matt.

"Well you guys slip past me every now and then, I'm not as spry as I once was." He was lighting up another cigarette.

"We'd love to stay and chat but we're getting picked up and heading back into town." I said this with a bit of superior tone.

We finished our day and loaded up into Patti's van, but not before changing our clothes, taking a Febreze bath, and stuffing everything we had in two fifty-gallon garbage bags. We were all smiles heading into town without any hiccups this time. Patti told us she thought she screwed up again and was waiting at the wrong place because she had seen a pickup truck heading into town with some hikers that had hitched a ride. She thought it was Matthew and I and we were pissed from having to wait again.

We cleaned up at the motel and got ready for dinner. There was a unique classy restaurant in town called "The Bank" which is, as the name implies, inside an old bank. How's that for an innovative name? Matt and I were dressed in a set of clean clothes Patti had brought with her, freshly showered, and feeling good that summer evening. We were leaving to go to dinner, when, lo and behold, Psycho is sitting in the doorway of a room at the end of the walkway, smoking. Turns out the hitch hikers

Patti saw was just one hiker and that was Psycho. What are the odds of that?

"Yo, boys, is it dinnertime already? Give me a minute to grab my stuff and we'll go."

He invited himself to dinner. It's not surprising really, but he didn't quite look or smell as fresh as we did. Patti didn't want to go to "The Bank" because of his offensive odor. After driving around for a while and not agreeing on another venue, or finding anything decent that was open, we landed at "The Bank" anyway. We asked, as we had become accustomed to, to be seated away from other patrons in an attempt not to mitigate Psychos stench upon other diners. This staff accommodated us by seating us in a private room, upstairs for hikers, which was probably just a large closet they put a table in.

It was a decent enough dinner, but we broke some news to Psycho. We would be jumping off the trail for the next few days to go to my daughter Kathy's wedding. I could swear I saw a tear roll down his eye.

We dropped Psycho off the next morning at the trailhead and it was like the final scene in "Harry and the Henderson's." I stood there as Psycho lingered, and like in the movie I said, "Go on, get out of here, can't you see we don't want you anymore."

"I can't go with you?"

"No, it's just family." I was being curt and to the point.

"I'm not family yet?"

"No, not yet. We need more time, you understand. Matt bringing home another man would cause problems." I was hoping humor would work on him.

"Oh, I see. Okay. Yo, Peterman, Firestarter, see you down the trail." Psycho made a whimpering noise and faded into the dense greenery around us.

1,519.5 miles to go.

Chapter 27
The Trail Gets Lonely

Kathy's wedding went off without a hitch. It was held at a lovely B& B in the Virginian countryside and was a very small event with only the immediate family attending. While we were off the trail, Matt learned of a friend's passing and we decided that he should jump off the trail and pay his respects. We would make arrangements for him to rejoin me in a couple of weeks when it made sense. Gin Rummy was 73,974 to 73,623, the boy is still coming after me.

After two days I was back in action, sans Matt. Patti was sticking with me for a few days since we were close to civilization. I naturally took advantage of this situation and "slacked" for those days. Patti decided she wanted to test her mettle a bit and do some brief hiking. The opportunity arose when I came to a place known as Dragons Tooth, which was a jagged point of rock outcrop along the trail. It's a well-known landmark for hikers and it was close enough to the road for day hikers to come and visit. This was a perfect opportunity for Patti.

The plan was for Patti to meet me at the top, since she was coming from the parking lot on the opposite side. It was a short two mile walk for her to meet me and then we could hike back together as a happy joyous couple. Well, we've established already not much ever goes according to plan.

I will relay her account as it was related to me. Patti pulled into the parking lot at Dragon's Tooth trailhead, it was a landmark after all, so it was easy for her to find. The lot was mostly empty except for another car or two. She pulled into a spot right by the trailhead where there was tall grass leading into the woods. Now the way she tells it as soon as she stepped out of the car a four-foot Rattlesnake slithered quickly pass by her within striking distance. Did I mention Patti has, let's call it, an aversion to snakes, especially poisonous ones? I thought for a brief moment I heard the scream from where I was miles away.

I truly don't understand women, I likely never will, despite the fact I am in touch with my feminine side. Even though she had watched the snake go into the grass, she jumped back into the car and the waterworks began. Patti sat there crying until she heard, what I can only assume, was my reassuring voice in the back of her head. "Don't be a wimp. Man up. It's more afraid of you than you are of it."

Well in her mind that wasn't true, she was definitely more afraid of it. To her credit, she did, after taking a moment to gather herself, climb back out of the car. She made noises as though it were a bear stalking her, constantly looked over her shoulder as if this snake was in the mob and it put a hit out on her.

She grabbed her little backpack and gave a wide berth to the grassy area she saw the snake dart into. She was still under the assumption that this was an ambush. She did a little run for the first few yards down the path until whatever logic in her head told her she was safe. She made her way down, or rather up, the trail toward Dragon's Tooth. She said the only thing running through her mind was lions, tigers, and snakes, so she began to sing it out loud to scare away any other snakes potentially lying in wait. I just let her have that delusion.

From the parking lot Dragon's Tooth is a seven hundred fifty-foot climb in just over two miles. If anything, the adrenaline from her scare helped her out with her hike, her heart was beating out of her chest, and here I was thinking she didn't have one. Patti reached the bottom of Dragons Tooth but couldn't figure out where to go from there. It was essentially a vertical rock wall. Then she saw the iron rungs sticking out of the rock wall and the famous white blaze is pointing up.

Snakes are not the only thing Patti is afraid of, she doesn't much care for heights either. She took a minute to sweep the area for snakes and North Koreans or whatever else might be waiting to attack her, then took a seat on some rocks. She decided she'd wait for me there at the bottom. She sat and drank her water, ate her fruit, and remained ever vigilant. After a while she heard the clicking of hiking sticks above her.

"Honey is that you?"

"I don't know if I'm your honey, who are you?" the voice replied.

"All right jackass, I know it's you, come down here."

"Why don't you come up here with me, the views are lovely." I knew at this point there was no way she was climbing up here, but I still have to have my fun when I can.

"Look over the edge and you'll see why. It's a straight climb up!" She was practically yelling at me now.

"Come on up. You'll love it." I was trying my best to reassure her, but it wasn't working.

"Okay, listen, I was almost killed by a rattlesnake on the way here, and if you think for one second I'm going to get myself killed climbing up there you are nuts. I hate heights and I'm beginning to hate mountains. I think you should just get down here."

"Almost killed by a rattler? Huh, this ought to be good." I climbed down into my wife's waiting arms.

Instead of kisses I was confronted by her, "I will not meet you again on this stupid trail by myself. What if you found my body in the parking lot?"

"Well Hon, as tragic as that would be, I do have a pretty nice insurance policy on you. Your memory would live on from the edge of my infinity pool in Cabo." Besides my tending to exaggerate, she was still emotional, I think all women are. Miraculously we managed to make our way back to the parking lot without me having to take a bullet for her.

The next day when she dropped me off for some "slacking" she accompanied me a dozen yards or so into the woods. She refused to lose sight of the parking lot or where she parked the car. She had to pee, and it wasn't going to wait until she was back in town. Still, she would not let the car out of her site as though she would be sucked into the trail if she couldn't see it. There were no privies out here, she was committed to peeing in the bushes. This wasn't sitting well with her.

"There's a house over there, they might see me."

"No honey, they can't see you, we can barely see that house from here, what makes you think they want to see you anyway? Just go."

Since we were still within sight of the road the next statement was obvious, but I was hoping she wouldn't ask. "Please stop any traffic that tries to pass, they might drive by and see me."

"And how in the hell am I supposed to do that? Jump in front of a moving vehicle, lay in the road. If you would lose site of the car you could go further into the woods, otherwise just go. No one here knows you and you'll never see any of them again. Now for god's sake just pee so I can be on my way."

"What about poison ivy or snakes?"

"No poison ivy there, don't sit in the bushes anyway, just squat by them."

I went over and checked for snakes, bobcats, and mountain lions. "All clear, I think it's safe. Let's go, I'm losing daylight."

"Okay, you don't look either."

Great. It never gets easier. I missed Matt. It's like I would want to watch her pee. She finally finished her business. Leaving, I had to cross a small wooden bridge over a creek to continue down the trail. Here Patti thought it would be cute to take a picture of me as I crossed the bridge.

"Give me your phone so I can take some pictures of you crossing the bridge." Keep them happy, that's my philosophy. I handed her my phone and began to pose for a picture. Instead of hearing the normal clicking sound of a photo being snapped I heard a splash followed by an "oops."

"Oops," I repeated. I may have come off as a bit sarcastic in this instance. "Oops" is never a good thing to hear anywhere. Never

"It fell, I'm sorry."

"No, it's only my lifeline to the outside world. Nice going. I'm sure it's ruined."

"I'll get it, don't worry."

"Need swimmies? It's close to two feet deep. Hate to have another "oops."

Patti pulled off her shoes and socks and into the creek she went, somehow my phone was still powered on, so she took it with her to dry it out.

"Make sure you pick me up at the right time in the right place, I have no way of contacting you now." I wasn't really upset; my fuse had burned out long ago.

"Sure honey, don't worry." She had that Joker smile going on her face again. She told me later she had spent close to an hour drying my phone with her hair dryer. I'm surprised she didn't melt it.

Survival Note: Don't let anyone handle your phone near water.

After Patti picked me up, shockingly on time, we headed back to our hotel and I showered and cleaned up. Heading out to dinner, along the side of the road I saw a hiker trying to hitch into town. It was Shadow. Shadow was someone who Matt and I had hiked with several times over the past few weeks. He was called Shadow because he was always there. We swore he was using shortcuts none of us knew about. Shadow had given me the best advice I had gotten from anyone on the trail, that being, "what's your rush young man, you have your whole life." I just love the psychological shit.

I told Patti to pull over and pick him up. It was courtesy after all, you know, karma and whatnot. I knew Shadow was heading into town to the bus depot to meet his girlfriend in New York. We dropped him off at the bus depot and he thanked us profusely. After he was no longer in earshot I turned to Patti, "My God, is that what we smell like?"

"That's exactly what you smell like."

Now all the Febreze made sense. The smell was unbelievable. It was nauseating. I know you get used to it on yourself, but this was some next level shit. Now I know.

1,481.5 miles to go.

Chapter 28
Ghosts, Crap, and Stupid Questions

Matt wasn't gone very long but it seemed like I fit a whole bunch of crazy crap into a small amount of time. Some of it funny and embarrassing, some of it bordering on unbelievable and strange. Maybe the things that happened weren't so extraordinary and being alone amplified my awareness. Who knows?

Since Matt has taken a bit of a sabbatical Patti was sticking with me for another couple of days so I could "slack" some more and although she'll never admit it, she missed the man that is Bob.

Patti was taking me to a trailhead, and we had decided to stop for breakfast on the way. As usual for rural Appalachia there wasn't anywhere around to eat except for what we call a greasy spoon of a diner. I didn't mind much; coffee and a greasy breakfast usually gets the plumbing going. Today, however, my body would betray me.

My drop off point was deep in the woods off a logging road, which to clarify is a never maintained dirt path of a road. There is only enough room for one car so if someone was coming the other way one of them would be screwed. The trail crossed this road about five miles into the woods. You may not think that's very far but given the condition of the road described above, it can take twenty to thirty minutes to get to where you're going.

The plan was for me to just grab my slack pack, jump out, and get going. Well, about halfway up the mountain that plan took a turn for the worse. I had to

Chapter 5. Badly. Very badly. I've always marveled at how quickly the brain can get a signal to your asshole. I clenched up as tight as I possibly could, gripping the dashboard for support.

"Hon, find a place to pull over, now."

"Why? What's going on?"

"Coffee and greasy bacon is what's going on. If you don't find a spot quick you'll be airing out this car for a month.

"Okay, let me find a spot, there doesn't appear to be much around," her voice was too calm, I was in distress.

The sides of the road had deep gullies and there were old mobile homes on both sides of the road. I wasn't about to go knocking on Confederate Carl's front door asking to shit, nor was I dumb enough to do it in his front yard. I've learned my lesson, when it looks like a scene from Deliverance it is a scene from Deliverance. Patti was afraid to pull over anyway, she was afraid of interacting with the locals. There were herds of cows, they were just meandering all over the road, not moving till you bump them. I was sweating bullets now, clenching my asshole like it's never been clenched in all my years on this earth. My stomach was gurgling without mercy. This went on for another ten minutes as she looked for a pull off. I could taste shit in my mouth.

"Stop the fucking car!" I screamed. She slammed the brakes and I threw the door open. It was too late for Peterman. I got two steps outside the car when my sphincter muscle gave out. I was instantly flooded, both literally and figuratively. I was overcome with relief and at the same time overcome with terror at the thought of what just happened. I shit myself. Let that sink in for a minute. I am a grown man over fifty years of age and I shit my britches. I couldn't even get my shorts down. Thank God Matt wasn't here to see this.

This was not good. A warm sensation started flowing down my legs, making its way toward my boots. This was probably the first time in my life I thanked God it was a liquid shit. All I could hear was laughter roaring from the van. Patti was howling with delight with something I presume she thought she could dangle over my head for the rest of my natural life. I wasn't quite yet to the point of finding this little mishap funny in any way, shape, or form.

Patti luckily had brought supplies with her and I had all my hiking gear in the van. She was used to us showing up filthy, so she had provisions in the back of the van. I didn't wait to get back there, I stripped where I was, in the middle of the road, a few steps from the car door. Again, thank God Matt wasn't here. I took a roll of paper towels and grabbed the some wipes and began to clean myself off. I won't go into vivid details, but I even had to change my socks. Everything went straight into a garbage bag; it was a good thing I had a change of clothes in the car or this situation would have been much worse. Imagine sitting naked in the parking lot of the motel while waiting for a towel or shorts.

I cleaned myself up nicely with the paper towels, as well as you can anyway, but there was still the smell to deal with. I grabbed what I thought were baby wipes and started wiping down my ass. Turns out they were not baby wipes at all, they were Clorox bleach wipes. Clorox wipes will burn the ever-living shit out of your asshole, and that is not the way I wanted the shit out of my ass. I was screaming so loud I think I started a stampede.

"What did you do?" Patti asked, laughing so hard now there were tears rolling down her cheeks.

"Fucking wipes, these are Clorox wipes, not baby wipes! The hair on my ass is burnt off!"

"Only you would use Clorox wipes on your ass. Why would I have baby wipes in my car?" She asked.

"I don't know, they looked like baby wipes, you have everything else in the damn car, oh shit, this burns."

I just wanted to fucking die. I stank of shit and now it felt like someone shoved a lit road flare up my ass. Lovely imagery, I know. You cannot believe the pain I was in. I took some paper towels, completely covered them in Glide, God bless Glide, and shoved it in my ass crack to ease the pain and make the hike somewhat manageable.

"That's the funniest thing I've ever seen," said Patti, still wiping the tears away. "Don't worry, I won't tell anyone."

"Yeah it's hilarious," I replied sealing up the garbage bag and tossing it into the back of the van, "but you know what's even funnier? You get to take this to a laundromat and wash it while I'm gone."

She later related that the laundromat had a whole new smell to it when she left.

This is an event I'm not particularly proud of, and I blame her to this date.

Survival Note: When you feel the need to shit, do it! Don't wait!

Patti pulled out of town the next day and I continued my journey north. Let me tell you, the days definitely seem a little longer when you are by yourself. I found myself that evening being alone for the first time in a shelter. The good news is there were no mice or snakes, the bad news was there were water rats. These rats were easily sixteen inches long and they didn't just scurry across the floor like their smaller cousins, they stomped. It didn't take much to convince me to set up my tent that night.

The thought of waking up with a rat staring at me was too much. I set my tent up that night in the shelter, hoping they would not chew through it or drag it away.

The section of trail I was coming into was a very pleasant one. The trail ran essentially parallel to the Blue Ridge Mountain Parkway. It was a nice section of rolling hills and relatively easy hiking. I would pass through the scenic overlooks and picnic areas every now and again. A positive at this time of year was they were always packed with tourists. These mobile couch potatoes would be in their cars and RV's pulling over to see something scenic while I was going about it an entirely different fashion.

Naturally these mouth breathers would be curious, bombarding me with a bevy of questions:

"Are you hiking?"

"No, I'm scuba diving."

"Is your backpack heavy?"

"No, 75 pounds is never heavy."

"Do you sleep outdoors?"

"No, there is a Ramada Inn every twelve miles. For a small fee we can stay in as many as we want."

Even better than those were the questions, "Do you eat food? Do you climb mountains?" That one really gets my blood flowing as I'm sure by now you know my feelings on mountains, and lastly, "Is there some sort of trail you follow?"

I'm a patient person, but some people really test that. I did snap at one person when I was in a particular mood, he asked, "What do you do when it rains?"

"I get wet jackass, what do you think?" He just made a face and moved on. Instead of stupid questions I wish these people would just feed me or give me a beer.

Whenever wandering into these rest areas, scenic overlooks, campgrounds, or any other place containing tourists, you will see them with their picnics and barbecues, their cold beer and soda, and all the things you can't carry with you. You miss it. You miss the sweetness of a soda or the crisp freshness of an ice-cold beer. So, you beg, sort of. I prefer to think of myself more as a traveling bard, regaling people with my tales and entertaining them in exchange for food and drink.

On the trail however, it is known as "Yogi-ing." Anyone who has watched a Yogi the Bear cartoon understands. Sometimes you could really score, getting a full dinner, sometimes it came down to grabbing a handful of chips and trying your luck somewhere else. You became desensitized to asking people for food, you would see Joe blue-collar working the grill with his stupid kids running around and screaming and strike up a conversation, telling him how you are hiking the AT and make him envious it's not him, and then say, "Boy those burgers sure smell good, we don't get the chance to eat a lot of meat out here, you sure are lucky," or something to that effect. Most of the time they are swapping places with you in their minds and leaving behind their snot-nosed screaming kids, which inevitably leads to a free meal for Bobby Boy. Occasionally someone would turn you away and that was usually because there wasn't enough to go around rather than out of malice. All of this is not to be confused with Trail Angels, Angels offer, there is no begging involved.

One day along that stretch of trail it rained. I know that must seem shocking by now. I was about a mile from the shelter when the rain let up and the sun began to poke through the clouds. I came into a small pine barren and as I got nearer to the shelter, I was shocked to see a woman standing a dozen or so yards in front of me. She was pointing into the woods, it was in the general direction of the shelter, but that's not what caught me off guard. It was her clothing. She was dressed in an old blue vintage dress, like real old-fashioned vintage. Little House on the Prairie vintage. I knew there were Mennonites that frequented the area, so it was possible they were out camping for the evening. I didn't think much of it really, it just meant I'd have some company tonight. Maybe "Yogi-ing" time.

I looked up again to the spot she was standing at, but she was gone. There was a sign at the exact point she had been, pointing to the shelter a tenth of a mile or so down a side trail. I figured she was just pointing the way to camp in case I missed the sign. I got to the shelter to find it empty. I still didn't really think much of it, maybe she had to shit?

I started to hang up my wet clothes to let them dry while contemplating staying that night. A young man came into camp, ex-military, he told me he had just got out of the service from overseas, he was going to hike the AT and cross it off his bucket list. We were shooting the shit for about ten minutes or so and he asked me, "Where is your wife? I haven't seen her since we've been talking."

"Well, my wife is home in Calabash, or at least that's where she told me she'd be. Why do you ask, have you been seeing her?" It went over his head.

"Oh, well is anyone else here? I saw a woman in a blue dress pointing toward the shelter." He preceded to describe the same woman in blue standing in the same spot I had seen her. We surveyed the area and there was no other camping gear around. We were a good couple of miles from the road, and like I said it's possible there were Mennonites, they are common to this area, but a woman in that garb alone this far into the woods? That's just creepy.

We discussed what it could have been. A ghost? Apparition? Succubus? A succubus didn't sound so bad to me. We made a pact that we would each stay there that night if the other did, and thankfully the rest of the night was without incident.

Now I've seen some pretty terrible things in my time, I've been in some very scary places, but I never believed in ghosts or the supernatural. I've strongly reconsidered that position nowadays. If the last part about the woman in blue wasn't convincing a few short days later I experienced another unexplained event.

As I was coming down the switchbacks into Punch Bowl Shelter I saw a young kid, again in a blue outfit, the three-piece type they wore in the 1800's, playing by the shelter. Once again, I didn't think anything of it other than I would have company for the night. It took me another couple of minutes to finally get to the shelter, and lo and behold it was empty. There was an access road only about a half mile away, I figured a family probably hiked into see the shelter and then left. Other hikers trickled in and I didn't mention it to anyone, like I said, I didn't think anything of it.

I called Matt later that evening, so we could plan where and when he would rejoin me. I told him about the lady in blue, which he agreed it was probably a Mennonite, however unlikely that might be. I also told him about the kid I saw playing by the shelter, I don't know why I brought it up, but I did.

Matt asked, "What shelter are you at?" I told him I was at Punch Bowl and he started laughing.

"Very funny, I'm not falling for that one," Matt chuckled at me.

"Not falling for what?" I asked him.

"Try reading your precious Hikers Guide every now and then. The shelter is supposedly haunted if you believe in that kind of bull." We talked for a little bit longer and then ended our conversation.

When I got off the phone, I naturally pulled out my Hikers Guide. Turns out the little shit wasn't lying. The Hikers Guide had a little tidbit in there about this haunting which prompted me to do a bit more research.

It turns out that apparently in the late 1890's there was a schoolhouse near the bottom of Bluff Mountain. One dreary November day the teacher was running out of kindling for their heater, so, as was custom for the time, the teacher called a recess and sent out the students to collect wood to keep them all warm. When recess ended all the children returned to the schoolhouse except for one, four-year-old Ottie Cline Powell. Nobody is exactly sure what happened, but most people agree that he got lost heading back to the schoolhouse, and being as young as he was, he probably thought he would be able to see the school from the mountain top, not understanding it was several miles away. A search was mounted for young Ottie but he was never found.

It is theorized that an exhausted Ottie made it to the top of Bluff Mountain just as some freezing rain made its way over the mountains. He likely sat down to rest, fell asleep, and never woke up. Some months later he was found by a group of hunters whose dog ran up the path toward where young Ottie rested. It's rumored that some hikers have experienced a young boy at the top of the mountain say, "Hi I'm Ottie. Do you know how I can get home?" Coincidence, I think not.

Talking with a Ranger about that incident he related to me that when people go missing in the woods if they are usually twelve years or younger the majority of the search is uphill, as this is where the young tend to go. If they are sixteen or older the majority of searches look downhill. He stated that the problem is when they are between those ages that you just don't really know where to look for them. Older people tend to head downhill toward rivers and streams and follow them, younger kids think they can spot something from the top of a hill or mountain.

On another side note, I accomplished another trail milestone on this stretch through the Blue Ridge, one that Matt is pissed off he missed. I jumped off the James River footbridge into, of course, the James River. It's apparently something the local high school or college kids do for fun. Naturally after I had jumped someone told me that a kid had died doing it a few years ago after landing on a log floating just below the surface of the water. I don't know if it's true, but it put a damper on things.

1,404.9 miles to go.

Chapter 29
Buns of Steel or Cold Water Causes Shrinkage

There was one other small incident, and I do mean small, if you wish to call it that, which occurred before Matt rejoined me at Waynesboro. It wasn't a big deal, literally. I promise the puns will make sense.

Though I've been a bit of an Eeyore with a little dark rain cloud following me around since Matt left, I found there are still times when I love hiking the trail. Even though we've met a lot of nut-jobs since we've started, I've enjoyed meeting most those nut-jobs, they make the trail fun. You get to connect for a small time with all kinds of people, from all different parts of the country. Some pass you by never to be seen again, some you catch up to and others catch up to you, and in the cases of Panda and Psycho, some hike at the same pace as you do. Psycho, of course, being a special case since I'm sure he wasn't hiking at the same pace as us, but rather stalking us like prey.

Since Matt had left I had been doing an on and off pace with a young college girl. I never did learn her real name, to be honest I'm not sure I asked her trail name either. She was "Buns of Steel" in my mind and my journal. Let me tell you, she earned that nickname, and it was well deserved. Her derriere being, still to this day, one of the most spectacular behinds I have ever seen. I walked behind it for hours on the trail. It literally got me up and over mountains.

I consider myself a connoisseur, if you will, when it comes to the female butt, and hers was poster perfect. Her shorts molded to her ass, the cheeks were firm and hard, and as she walked muscles rippled through her gluteus maximus and upper legs. Even now I cannot remember her face, only those spectacular buttocks. I didn't miss Matt these days, Matt who?

As I walked behind her I often wondered how her butt got to be so perfect. Was she a softball player in college? That could explain a nice tight bottom. Was she a gymnast? No, she was too tall for that. Maybe she ran track? A tennis player? Maybe she lived on the tenth floor of a high rise with a broken elevator? I never actually had the nerve to ask, imagine how that conversation would play out.

"Oh hey, I couldn't help but notice your perfectly sculptured ass, which would make the statue of Venus blush. I've been staring out at it for the better part of the past week and for the life of me I just can't figure out how it got to be so nice. Pray tell, how did you do it?"

"Oh my God, get away from me you perverted monster."

That's pretty much how I saw it playing out. Then it came to me. She's tall, athletic, perfect bottom, she was a volleyball player! A volleyball player that would be drafted onto Bob's team in the uphill volleyball matches. In my game she was in front of me always ready to spike the ball. You had a lot of time to fantasize on the trail, there was a lot of uphill on the trail, and therefore she played a lot of ball. Again, the imagination is amazing.

I had not seen her in two days after being with her for quite a stretch. My wife couldn't believe how far ahead of schedule I was, I was never ahead of schedule, and if I was, I took an extra "zero" day to make up for it. I couldn't exactly tell her why.

"Oh, hey Honey, yeah, I'm ahead of schedule. Why? Oh, well I've been trying to keep up with this college

234

girl with an amazing tush." How do you think that would go over? She'd think me a pervert, well, just more of a pervert.

Since I hadn't seen her for two days I figured she was well ahead of me at this point. She was a stronger hiker than I was. I had struggled to keep up with her, it was worth it, but a struggle nonetheless. She started well after Matt and I did, caught up to us, and now passed us, which was a shame for lonesome Bob.

This hiking day was hot and sunny, the tree cover was less dense than normal allowing sparse beams of light to breakthrough and hit me as I walked down the path. I would have killed for a breeze, but instead settled for ninety-five degrees and one-hundred percent humidity. My clothes clinging to me as if I wore them in the shower. I was completely drained and battered from the day. It was my fifth straight day of hiking and I would not hit a town to "zero" for at least another two days. A "zero" day would have at least allowed me to shower and wash my two pairs of clothes. I was on my second pair already and they were soaked with sweat. Changing back into already dirty clothes offers no real reprieve either, they are usually damp and smell even worse from being in your bag.

On the way into the shelter there was a small flowing stream that you walked along. Eventually you reached a small wooden bridge that traversed the creek and led to the shelter. I crossed the bridge up to the generic wooden shelter I've become so accustomed to. I put my things up and did my normal chores, while still dripping wet from the heat. I decided I would go for a dip.

It was later in the afternoon, I wasn't too worried about someone showing up, I didn't think anyone was behind me, I had been doing a pretty decent pace. I walked back to the bridge where the stream widened a bit creating a small pool between the rocks. I wasn't too concerned about drying off since I was alone, I could just air out. I peeled off my clothes, dipped them several times in the river, picturing all the aquatic life downstream dying, and wrung them out. It wasn't much, but every little bit helps I suppose. It was better than smelling like a yak's balls in the summer. It was all for naught anyway, I knew as soon as I started the next day my clothes would be soaked and smelling again.

I slowly slid into the cold, refreshing, life giving water of the stream, "nekkid," as the locals might say. I laid my clothes over some rocks to dry out in the sun, planted my hands behind my head, leaned back, and let the cold water pour over me with the sun shining on my face. In this moment I was in heaven. This is how the trail was meant to be.

I felt amazing. I closed my eyes and immediately all my senses were heightened. I could feel myself connecting with nature. There was the sound of flowing water breaking on the rocks, the pine fragrance of the trees from the surrounding woods, and the pure freshness of the air. I sat basking in the sunlight feeling the contrasting warm air on my face and the cold water swirling around me. The leaves were rustling ever so slightly in grand chorus with the birds and insects singing and chirping. It was Nirvana. But then, as is Bob's life, the orchestra was suddenly silenced by the clomp, clomp, clomp of hiking boots on the wooden footbridge a mere foot above me.

Holy crap! I'm naked! My eyes shot open as the serenity and peacefulness of the moment was shattered. Time and space stopped. The universe ground to a halt. I was staring up into the sun above the bridge but staring down at me was "Buns of Steel." The universe quickly began moving again with the roar of her laughter as she realized she caught me unaware. This was not how it happened in my fantasies. That moment is still burned in my memory. I didn't want this to be real. I think this was most men's nightmare. She was pointing and laughing and the only thing that came out of my mouth was "shrinkage! The water is cold!"

Still laughing uncontrollably, she turned and walked toward the shelter and managed to choke out, "Get dressed will you, then come back to the shelter."

I watched that ass walk away like I had done so many times before, admittedly it's a tough habit to break, besides it's not like I could be any more embarrassed than I was now.

I dressed quickly, keeping my back to her the entire time, at least my butt was bigger than what she had previously been laughing at. I walked back to the shelter and before I could say a word she chimed in, "Trail names, I have a few of those for you right now."

I responded, "When it thaws out it looks bigger."

"I guess I'll never know, will I? Now about those new trail names, let's see, how about Tom Thumb? Eunuch? No, that won't do."

"You do know this isn't much fun for me." Instead I wanted to say I have a few nicknames for you but thought wiser of it.

"Oh, I know, Shrinky Dink?" She was on a roll now laughing hysterically to herself. I hate a bright sarcastic woman, especially one with a great ass. No one should have that much going for them. "Peter Peckerless, Moby Dickless, Inchworm? Oh yeah, I like that one, you'll be Inch Worm from now on."

"You have a mean streak, you know that?"

Survival Note: Never bathe naked in a cold stream if you wish to keep your dignity.

Both luckily and unfortunately that was the last night I would see "Buns of Steel." At least I left her with a story. To see her again would mean humiliation and the spread of a less than flattering trail name. I left early the next morning fully prepared to hike in overdrive just to stay ahead of her. We never did cross paths again, nor did I ever bathe in the nude along the trail again.

1,327.9 miles to go.

Chapter 30
Miss Daisy Driving Us

We had decided that Waynesboro would be the best spot for Matt to rejoin me. It was the closest town to the trail that was easily accessible, besides I'm sure Matt was anxious to get back out here. That was a subtle stab at humor if you couldn't tell. I got into town the day before Matt arrived taking a "zero" while waiting for him to show up later that evening. There wasn't much happening in town, so I tried to set up a ride for us back to the trail for the following day. It was usually pretty easy to hitch into town but finding a shuttle back isn't always easy.

It' didn't occur to me at the time, but we were looking to get back on the trail on a Sunday. Sunday is the Lord's day in this part of the country. This was the Bible Belt after all. Everyone was at church or some type of luncheon or picnic afterwards. Fried chicken, slaw, biscuits, all the "fixins." I did, however, get lucky on my eighth call, or so I thought.

The eighth number I called was answered by an elderly lady. I inquired about a ride to the trail and she didn't seem to know what the hell I was talking about. This should have been the first red flag. After a couple of minutes refreshing her memory the light bulb went off.

"Ohhh, you boys are hikers. I thought you said bikers and I was wondering why bikers needed a ride anywhere. My husband is the one who shuttled you boys to and from that path, unfortunately he passed away recently, but if you can wait until Church gets out I think it would be nice to give one last ride in his memory."

"That would be great," I replied. "We can certainly wait until Church gets out and we greatly appreciate the ride." With that we arranged to meet at eleven the next morning.

Matt showed up that evening and was a bit hard to read. I think he tasted freedom and wanted more, yet somehow he still longed for the trail and its simplicity. I also think the weight loss had become quite noticeable in both of us and I think that served as motivation for someone going back to a town full of college girls in September.

Matt and I were sitting out in front of our motel room waiting for our ride when red flag number two popped up. In pulled a 69 Oldsmobile, I think it was a Delta 88, a real sweetheart of a car in its day. This was not its day. Now when I say the car pulled in, in reality it was more like it idled in, rolling forward an inch at a time. We could barely see this woman behind the wheel because she could barely see over it.

I'm guessing her depth perception isn't what it used to be, which should have been red flag number three. When she finally saw us, she stopped the car dead, a solid fifty feet from where we were, in an otherwise empty parking lot. It became clear that she was waiting on us, so Matt and I grabbed all forty pounds of our gear and carried it to where she parked. I introduced myself and Matt to make sure this was our ride.

"Well hello boys, my name is Daisy, people call me Miss Daisy." I shit you not, that was her name and Miss Daisy was driving us.

Matt threw our stuff in the trunk and jumped in the back seat. Looking back on it now I should have done the same. Hindsight and all that.

Miss Daisy was probably about four-foot-ten and shrinking by the minute in front of us. The reason I bring this up is because the front seat of the Oldsmobile was a bench seat and she had it set to where Shaq could ride comfortably. She was on her tippy toes barely reaching the gas pedal with her arms fully extended to grip the wheel. She was practically standing up.

As she pulled out of the parking lot, I said to her, "You know Miss Daisy, you can pull the seat forward, I have plenty of room, I could be wearing stilts and still have plenty room".

"Oh, it's no bother dear, this is the way I normally drive." She was looking me dead in the eyes while talking to me. She should have had her eyes on the road instead. Red flag number four. I pulled my seat belt a bit tighter, thank God they became mandatory the year before this car was built. I turned to look at Matt and he just gave me a bit of a knowing look and pulled his belt tighter as well.

"Oh okay, well are you sure you can see over the steering wheel and dashboard?"

As soon as we were out of the parking lot and into traffic, we instantly got the blare of a car horn. Miss Daisy pulled out right in front of another car. We heard their tires screech as they swerved around us shouting the entire time. Daisy asked, "What was that noise?"

Matt was locked between fear and laughter, like those people you see in the movies who know death is inescapable and get hysterical. "Daisy, don't worry about it, I'm sure those tires screeching as their car swerved around us were more for sound effect than anything else," he said trying to be kind.

"Someone went around us? Huh, I didn't see anyone pass us?"

241

All I could think of was that scene in My Cousin Vinny when Joe Pesci was questioning the old black lady about her vision in the courtroom and she says, "I'm thinking about getting thicker glasses."

As we continued through town Daisy had me white with fear. I kept reaching for the "oh shit" handle that some cars have above the passenger side window, but this car didn't have one, that or some other poor soul ripped it off already in a fear induced panic. I had one hand firmly planted against the dashboard bracing myself for the eventual impact. Matt had seemed to accept his fate and found the whole thing quite humorous, maybe he couldn't see exactly how close Daisy was coming to killing us.

Daisy approached a changing traffic light and it played out like every action movie you've ever seen, only we weren't in a car chase or out running an explosion. We just wanted to make it back to the trail in one piece. We blew through the intersection a good five seconds after the light had changed red to a cacophony of blaring horns, screeching tires, and slammed brakes.

"Oh dear, was that light red?" Miss Daisy asked sheepishly.

Jesus, where are the cops when you needed them? "It happens to the best of us, that was a quick light anyway," I said to her.

"Well I suppose it depends on what you mean by red," Matt said while I glared him down. "I wouldn't be going towards any lights if I were you Daisy," Matt added. She didn't get his meaning.

As we tooled around town heading up toward the mountains, cars were passing us by every time they got a chance. I'm pretty sure one woman gave us the sign of the cross as she zipped past. Maybe people around town knew Daisy and her car. She was doing twenty in a forty-five mile an hour speed zone. Again, she looked me dead in the eyes, instead of watching the road and she continued her game of twenty questions. "Are you married?"

"I am Daisy, and I'd give anything to be with her this very minute." That was no lie.

"Oh, that's very nice dear."

Again, I don't think she got my meaning. "I hope to see her again in three short weeks."

"Alive, that is," Matt piped in, thinking at this point he wouldn't mind seeing her either.

"What's that dear, I don't hear so well," Daisy asked.

"Nothing," I told her, "ignore him."

I don't think she was hitting on me, but I would have lied to her if I weren't married just to be safe. Trail Angel my ass, this was a trail devil intent on killing us.

"This is my husband's car. Did I tell you that?" Daisy asked.

"What's your husband's name?" I inquired.

"Waldo."

Now I had known her husband had passed away from our previous phone call, but I never told Matt. It didn't seem pertinent at the time, I should have known better. What did my bright college educated son say next? It's not hard to guess.

"Hey Daisy, where's Waldo?" Thankfully the humor was lost on her once more, I doubted she knew of the "Where's Waldo" books. I did manage to get a small chuckle out of it.

"Oh well, thank you for asking dear. He passed away recently, he was ninety-six years old. I miss him dearly."

I think Matt would have felt bad for making a poorly timed joke but since Daisy didn't get it, he didn't feel bad. I gave him another glare anyway. I said the obvious thing at this point, "We are sorry for your loss, he must have been a great man to reel in a lady like yourself. So that makes you ninety-four then? I'm sure you've seen a lot in your day.

"Ninety-five," she replied. "I just had a birthday."

Good God. She was ninety-five and still driving. Red flag six. "Well happy belated birthday and may God bless you, and us," I hoped out loud. It was barely audible to Daisy, but Matt heard it and gave me a nod.

Then came the waterworks. She began crying, "I miss him so much!"

Tears are flowing down her face and she's trying to wipe them off on her shoulder, never taking her hands off the steering wheel. Every time she tried to wipe a tear the car swerved three to four feet each way, and to our right is a ravine that drops down fifty feet or more.

Matt's face was plastered to the window like one of those "baby on board signs." He was just waiting for us to roll down into the embankment.

"Matt, you starting to get the feeling we may end up a fireball and at the bottom of the gorge?"

"Dad, I love you."

Apparently, he was having the same thoughts I was. He was saying his goodbyes. I had to do something to keep this geriatric corpse from taking us down with her.

"So, Daisy, see any good movies lately?" I asked with a nervous chuckle.

Daisy began to laugh and the crying subsided, a good thing to, as we were much closer to the ravine than I cared to be. She was mostly back in our lane, I guess the bright yellow double lines are easier to see without the tears.

"Last movie I saw was Casablanca. That was back a way. You know, you boys are nice. Are you religious?"

"I've been praying this whole time," Matt chortled.

"Not until recently," I also replied, "how much further to the trail?"

"How nice that you pray. I don't know how much further. It seems like a long ride."

I don't think long is the word for it. On three separate occasions during this ride I saw my life flash in front of my eyes. Maybe if we went faster than twenty-five miles an hour we would be there, then on the other hand, if she were going any faster, we might be in a ditch somewhere.

"Look Daisy, there's the visitors center, that's where we need to be dropped off." Praise Jesus, I guess praying does work. He was on my side for once.

"You know boys, I could drive you a little way up the parkway if you'd like," Daisy offered.

"No!" we both shouted in unison.

"I mean, gosh Daisy, that's awful nice of you to offer," Matt cheesed it up. "That would be cheating to us, we have to walk every mile of the trail."

Daisy pulled her car into the visitor's lot and mounted the curb with one front wheel as she parked.

"It's been a pleasure boys."

We stood there collectively thinking that this tiny timid woman scared the living bejesus out of both of us. I thought I was going to shit myself again, and I think I would have been justified this time. To hell with flesh eating deer or bears or any of the other things trying to kill me, Miss Daisy was by far the most terrifying. We could barely stand after that ride. As it turns out fear is an option, and it was real.

"Daisy, can I give you a few bucks for gas?"

"No. I enjoyed giving you a ride, my Waldo would be proud."

She left us wondering, how did Waldo die? Had a heart attack in the passenger seat perhaps? I now welcome the trail and anything it's can throw at me. I've never seen Matt hustle into the woods with such passion and zeal. Waynesboro is no safe haven with this woman behind the wheel.

"Have a safe drive home," I said waving goodbye. As if that was possible. She caused me more fright in one car ride then all five seasons of the Twilight Zone. Maybe this was my Twilight Zone and I survived it. Screw you Rod Sterling.

This was a true accounting of driving with Miss Daisy.

Survival Note: On all rides never accept it if they are over eighty.

1,327.9 miles to go.

Chapter 31
The Shenandoahs

We hit another milestone, the Shenandoah Mountains. The fame and beauty of the Shenandoah's is renowned worldwide, but one thing we learned is that it's quite hard to appreciate all that beauty when you can't see it. As usual we were stuck in the green tunnel. We would get some opportunities to take in the sights every now and then, but the scenic highway probably gave a better view.

Once again, we encountered warning signs as we entered the Shenandoah's, "High bear activity due to dry weather. Can be very aggressive. Take precautions." It was a curious thing, Matt and I always wondered what more precautions could we possibly take. Could we sleep in concrete bunkers? Carry bigger knives? Not carry food with us? Sing Dolly Parton songs? My singing would scare anything. All you can really do is follow your normal routine and be sure to make noise when you go around bends in the trail so you don't catch any bears off guard.

We talked a lot about shelters, but one thing we haven't really gone into is their proximity to the trail itself. Most shelters are not right on the trail, but down a side trail a bit. It was pure torture at the end of the day when the shelter was more than two-tenths of a mile off the trail. You knew you were there, but you were still not finished hiking.

This particular side trail was half a mile to the shelter. You would have thought it was a death sentence when Matt read the sign. He still gets a bit grumpy at the end of a day's hike.

"This is bullshit," he said loudly, expressing his discontentment. "There is nothing between here and the shelter for half a mile so why in the hell can't they build a shelter here. Don't these idiots already know I'm out here hiking all day as it is? They put the shelter half a mile from the trail intentionally to screw with me, didn't they? Well it won't happen, I won't do it, I'll sleep right here just to prove a God damn point." He concluded his little tirade and sat on a nearby log.

"Well son, have you considered that there is no water here and that they built the shelter next to a water source?" I hated it as much as he did, but I wasn't about to tell him that. There are moments that make me seem wise and fatherly, I build credibility in these moments, even if I did just pull it out my butt.

"How far to the next shelter? Let's just go there," Matt said.

"Too far," I told him. I didn't really know, but we had to rip that last half mile off like a band aid and just get it over with, besides once Firestarter got his fire going, he would calm down.

Well I should've listened to the boy. We hiked into the shelter much to Matthews dismay. We thought we'd be alone since we hadn't seen anyone else out on the trail during the day. It turns out we weren't alone, and I thought I was seeing ghosts again.

There was a humanoid that came in and was walking around by the shelter. I did several double takes, making sure I was seeing an actual person this time and I glanced over at Matt, who was also staring at the non-apparition. I had good reason to suspect he was ethereal; he was the whitest man I'd ever seen. I suspect that he was albino, almost translucent, that's how white he was. He reminded me of the character in the movie "Powder." I couldn't get a good look at his hair as it was stuck under a wide brimmed straw hat. Which brings us to the second reason he could have been from the spirit world. I had already seen a ghostly lady in Mennonite garb, so this was par for the course, he was dressed as a farmer. I did take some comfort in knowing that Matt was seeing this too.

Aside from his wide brim straw hat, he had on a long-sleeved flannel shirt, blue jeans, and had a camera around his neck. It was over ninety degrees out and no sane hiker would be wearing this type of outfit this far into the woods. We put our gear up but always kept our eyes on him as he walked around the campsite.

This was the kind of situation where I kick into cop mode. Things didn't add up, even Matt could tell something was off. I glanced around the camp under the guise of looking for a place to crap. Maybe he had set up a tent somewhere, but I couldn't see anything. The shelter wasn't that big. From what I could see there was no backpack, no water, no food, and throw in the way he was dressed and the fact that we were more than five miles from the nearest road on each side, nothing but red flags. It's made the hair stand up on the back of my neck. That's never a good thing.

Matt and I both had our knives on us, but they weren't worth much. I was going to confront the guy and feel him out a bit. I turned on my phone to make sure we had a signal in the event we needed to call in air support. I turned to Matt and told him my plan. "I'm going to talk to this guy, something about him seems a bit off."

"Yeah, I was getting that vibe too. I'll wait here in case he stabs you, so I have a big enough lead to run away."

"Good to know you've got my back."

I walked up to the phantom, "Excuse me, hey, how are you doing today? You look a bit lost, are you okay? Can we help you in any way?" The questions seemed harmless enough.

"Nyet," he replied in a bizarre Russian accent. This seemed like an odd place to scout for a Russian invasion, Red Dawn all over again. "Just looking around, da, just looking." He was completely monotone, no inflection in his voice, no emotion showing on his face. He wasn't even looking at me. It would be just our luck to run into an albino Russian KGB serial killer.

There were no other trails around, just the one that led in from the AT, and the water was close by, it didn't seem this guy came in from any other direction. Here I was thinking Miss Daisy scared the shit out of me, this guy though was on a whole different level, he was every bit as alarming, even more so. I was honestly and truly worried. We kept our eyes on him and then after about fifteen minutes he turned to us, nodded, and walked up toward the mountain peak. There was no trail there, it just seemed like an arbitrary spot in the woods and he walked off into it.

"That guy was a bit freaky, huh dad?"

"Yeah, he was. Do we have a signal here on the phone?"

"Looks like it, why?"

"I'm gonna give Patti a call. I miss her."

"Yeah right, that's believable."

"Well what do you want me to say? Yeah, I'm calling her to give a description of the man who is probably going to slaughter us in our sleep. I'd like to make it as easy as possible for the Virginia State Police to find our mutilated corpses or what's left of them."

"You know dad, you sure can paint a picture with your words."

Patti had recently sent me a paperback book, "Broken Prey," which was about a serial killer in the woods who would murder men and women then hang them from trees like a gutted deer. That's not how I was going out of this world, I'm going out more like Nelson Rockefeller.

I called Patti, which was another mistake on my part. She was freaking out and wanting to call the cops. I had to explain to her that my would-be murderer was probably nothing but it's better to be safe about it. Now she wanted an update every hour as to whether this guy came back or not. I wasn't about to do that, so I just told her the reception was bad and I'd call her if we were alive in the morning.

Matt and I set up our green coffins, still under the glamour that they added an extra layer of safety. Coffin may have been a fitting term considering the day's events. Matt and I called it quits at about nine, we were still the only ones at the shelter, and it was getting dark. I didn't put in my earplugs, I wanted to be able to hear anyone coming. I wasn't trying to stay awake all night, I just wanted to hear death approaching rather than wake up to a knife plunging into my heart.

I awoke to Matt unzipping my tent. He startled the shit out of me and was lucky I didn't stab him right there.

"Dad, I hear someone walking behind the shelter."

Unlike the last time I wasn't about to ignore him and just go back to sleep. I sat up and we both listened intently. It was hard to make out over the normal sounds of the forest, but someone was definitely shuffling around behind the shelter. We both had our knives out and moved toward the end of the raised shelter floor. The shuffling was moving around the side of the shelter toward where Matt and I were crouched and waiting. No commie serial killer was going to sneak up on us. All of a sudden from the other side of the shelter a red light washed over us and we heard a soft voice, "Oh, hey guys, sorry if we woke you."

Well before that sentence was finished Matt was screaming bloody murder and clutching my shirt. Another red light came from around the same side of the shelter and there were now two of them in front of us.

It turns out it was a brother and sister out hiking together. Matt leaned back clutching his heart as if it was about to explode out of his chest. He let out a long string of expletives that no child should utter in front of their parents and laid back with a sigh of relief. He began chuckling, they clearly got the better of him. The brother and sister explained they took a wrong turn earlier which set them back a few hours and were just now getting in for the night. We spent the better part of that next hour just bullshitting with them. We got some good laughs out of what happened, especially at Matt's expense, but truth be told we were happy to have some others there with us. We explained what happened at the shelter earlier. They were staying no matter what. We had safety in numbers, or so we thought.

Matt got to give out his second trail name that night. The only food the sister had brought with her for that weekend hike were saltines, which is a great way to die on the trail. Matt dubbed her "Crackers" which she seemed to embrace readily enough.

I called Patti the next morning, although I called an hour later than I said I would. I figured I would let her worry a bit, strengthen our bond, love is like that. In reality all I did was dash her dreams of an insurance payout; love is like that too. She told me she had the Waynesboro

Police Department's phone number taped next to the phone in case I did not call. She bitched at me that I scared her and she did not sleep because of it, even though I was the one who would be getting murdered while she was in our king sized bed made of feathers basking under the A/C. I often wonder if she is as much of a bullshit artist as I am.

We continued our way through the Shenandoah's. As far as the hiking was concerned these are golden days. The trail itself was relatively easy, relative being the keyword of course. There were lots of up's and downs, but there are always lots of ups and downs, nothing but ups and downs, but these were hills and not mountains, so we considered this to be reprieve.

1,322 miles to go.

Chapter 32
Rude People, Not Us, Never

We got off at one point to retrieve a food drop. Our package had been sent to a motel about three miles off the trail. We had planned on stopping there for the night and a six-mile round trip is an extreme side trip for us. We hoped, as we always do, that some kind stranger would see us hitching and take pity on some rag-tag hikers, no such luck on that day.

It always amused me every time something like that happened, because even though I was annoyed by it, you would think it was the absolutely worse thing to ever happen to Matt. I fully expected him to just lay down in the street and die. We would find that hitching would become harder to do the further north you got. We picked up our food drop at the motel and the owner was kind enough to give us a ride back, a gesture that was most appreciated by both Matt and me.

We were coming upon a stretch of trail that had two luxurious lodges right on the trail. Both very well-known tourist stops. There are very few places along the trail where this occurs, and it is glorious when it happens. You hear so much about us being off the trail that it may not be understood just how much we are hiking and the distances between these places, you can go a hundred miles or more before coming across some place that is not a cheap motel. These two lodges were a good day's hike apart.

On our way to the first lodge we were walking into an incredible fog. It was unbelievable, we could not see ten feet in front of us, and when that happens the trail becomes difficult to follow. Imagine trying to follow white blazes in a thick fog when you can't even see the trees they're painted on. We developed a system so we would not get off the trail. One of us would stay at the last blaze we saw while the other would go ahead looking for the next blaze. When he found it, he would call back and the other would follow up. It was slow, but we didn't want to drift off the trail, not in this fog. To find your way back would be difficult, to say the least.

There was also the creepiness factor. When the fog is thick the forest is unbelievably quiet, and that can be unnerving. Shapes in the distance resembled anything you imagined them to be, such as all types of creatures and other unrecognizable things until you are right on top of them. We need to stop watching science fiction horror movies.

"Matt, you take the lead now. I've been doing most of the looking for blazes," I was having trouble with the fog.

"Oh, sure, you want me to be the bait?" We had been talking about movie creatures, and now he was whining again. He was right though; he was better bait than me.

"You ever see the movie "The Crawling Eye?" It's an old one," I asked him as I scanned the woods.

"No, was it in color? Or did you confuse black and white TV for fog?" The kid could be a real smart ass at times.

"Funny guy. It's about a fog that kept rolling onto a mountain top where a group of people were stranded in a lodge. Then these huge crawling eyes with tentacles would come out of the fog and start taking them and killing them. Since you never saw it you don't have to worry about it."

"Crawling eyes? That's what you're worried about? How about missing the blazes on the trees and getting lost?"

"Crawling eyes are more terrifying. Childhood movies can stick with you, ya know? That's why we only let you watch Sesame Street, and even that scared you, you were frightened by Big Bird."

"Is that supposed to be a joke? It's a seven-foot talking bird with a weird voice, of course I was scared. The Native people called them "Terror Birds." Look it up." He was right on that on, great comeback on his part.

Matt and I caught lunch in a shelter we were passing by. Matt was back to reading the registers again and this one seemed to have a bunch of odd sayings written in it, each hiker trying to outdo the previous. Stuff like, "I like my women like a summer's meadow, hot and steamy." As Matt and I continued up the trail we came up with sayings of our own. I liked, "You can't shape death while you're still alive," it made no sense whatsoever. Another I came up with has an R rating, "I liked my women like golf, one hole at a time." Again, being repetitive, you have a lot of time to kill on the trail and the conversations don't always make sense.

We finally strolled into Big Meadow, one of the two lodges along the trail in the Shenandoah's. It is a beautiful place. The lodge itself has a very rustic look, a mix of stone and timber. The inside had a large dining hall that continued to exemplify the rustic cabin look. It was all gorgeous wood from ceiling to floor, well maintained throughout the years. The back deck granted you sweeping views of the valley and mountain ranges. These were the kind of views you undertake this type of hike for, they were breathtaking, and all you really had to do was drive up to the lodge. Shows how dumb we are. There was more to Big Meadows than just the lodge. The big meadow, so to speak, had cabins on one side and a campground on the other.

We chose to camp beside the lodge in the campground. We still had access to good food, drinks, and comfort the lodge offered, and we didn't have to pay for beds. Well, really, I didn't have to pay. Matthew wasn't too happy about my decision, but he doesn't pay for anything, so tough shit. He argued "why sleep on the ground when there were beds a hundred yards away?"

There was a smattering of tents about, but there were mostly massive motor homes. You don't quite realize until you put your tent up next to something that size, just how small your tents are. We both came to the same conclusion, anyone driving an RV in during the night might not see our tents, which we would be in. Seeing as all these sites were "pull through" sites we found it prudent to take safety measures. Matt and I grabbed some nearby picnic tables and moved them to block the entrance/exit to our site so as not to be crushed by a motor home in our sleep.

After our normal housekeeping chores were done I asked Matt, "Want to grab a cold beer?"

How the lad can perk up at times, "Sure," he was already ten yards ahead of me.

We made our way up to the lodge to partake in their cultural activities, i.e. a few cold ones and a nice meal. We sat in the Tap Room for a while enjoying a nice frosty beverage, but after spending the day hiking, dinner was at the forefront of our minds. We liked any place with a menu since ours was normally pop tarts (breakfast), followed by tuna with mayo (lunch) followed by a Mountain House freeze-dried meal (dinner).

The dining room in the lodge was huge, as I said, maybe sixty by one-hundred feet, or so it seemed to us. We took our seats in this cavernous hall and looked around at the staff. It would seem that all the original staff from the sixties were still working here. Not one person waiting on the tables look to us to be under seventy years old. It also appeared they carried everything to the table one piece at a time, one plate, one cup, etc. Although they seemed old they did their best to get the meals out and to serve the tables furthest from the kitchen, which by the way, is where we were sitting. Matt bet me our food would be cold by the time it reached us.

At the table next to us were two mid-twenty something year old Germans. I couldn't tell if they were a couple or not, the fashion styling of Europeans is lost on me, they all looked feminine if you ask me, but who am I to judge? I asked Matt, "So you think these two are, you know, together?"

"Being a bit homophobic, perhaps they are merely metrosexuals."

I didn't disagree but I quoted the Seinfeld episode, "Not that there's anything wrong with that."

Unfortunately, these two Germans were loud and obnoxious going back and forth with each other speaking mostly in German. They would speak in very loud broken English whenever the waitress came to their table, which was annoying, but may have been warranted since I believe the old gal turned her hearing aid down when she approached their table. Every time she came by they complained about something else, "Excuse me, zis chicken, how do you call them, fingers? Zey are cold."

"Yah, zey are cold," chimed in the other, "and zey are much too expensive. We did not come all the way to America for zis."

"I thought zis was the land of the free, isn't the customer always right? We could have made zes meals ourselves."

I could see the waitress was a bit flustered at their complaining. I've never really been one to hold my tongue and that remained true here, so I offered them some advice.

"Zen maybe you should have," I said in a German accent, "spent a few more bucks and gone with the prime rib," which was conveniently being delivered at that moment. I don't think that counts as racist if you use a false accent, right? I was tired of hearing them bitch, they were at a tourist trap in Appalachia for God's sake.

They started spraying German back and forth which each other and occasionally pointing at me. I guess they were deciding which one would be chivalrous and confront me for the other.

I interrupted, "Ich weil was du sagsts." That should roughly translate to, "I know what you are saying." I didn't really have a clue, but two years of high school German had to be good for something.

They looked a little shocked to hear that. "You Americans eat whatever is put in front of you," Klaus said with his German accent.

"Well apparently you do too, you ate the shit food put in front of you and you have been complaining about it for the past fifteen minutes. You trying to get it for free?" Well that's certainly got them going. They started yelling at me in a mixture of broken accented English and the unmistakably angry language of German. They may have even been some civil rights violations thrown in there.

Matt pointed out that I may not have been politically correct, as he continued to carve his prime rib. His astute liberal college mind picked up on the culturally insensitive joke I made at the German's expense, but that's what happens when you lose a war. Matt thought I should be more sensitive to their feelings. I never listen to him, so why start now?

"Hey! Adolph! Speaking ze English will you? No one here except your comrade Hans Gruber understands you." I was hoping he would get up and kick my butt so I could have a legit reason to get off the trail, but no such luck. I guess they were a couple, not that there's anything wrong with that. Von Braun threw some cash on the table and stormed they both off.

We finished our prime rib which was amazing, and I had an epiphany in that moment that perhaps I was a bit brash. I wonder how many times I came across that way to others on this hike. Perhaps this was learned behavior from Psycho. Maybe Psycho was channeling through me. I realized that I had to reinvent myself, it was time to become a kinder, gentler Bob, a Bob who isolates those negative emotions, almost a planet unto himself. And so, I would become Planet Bob once again.

Of course, that wouldn't last, but sleep did come easy that night. I had dreamed all night of storming the beaches of Normandy while and Hans and Franz were throwing chicken fingers at me.

The next morning we packed our things knowing it was a short easy hike to Skyland, the next lodge in the Shenandoah's. I decided this time I would rent a cabin for the night to avoid the prospect of being stabbed to death by any murderous Germans along the trail. When you realize there are likely multiple persons on the trail that would relish the chance to stab you, you know it's time to be a softer, gentler, Bob. I figured a lock on my door might do me some good.

There was a group of twenty kids ahead of us going to the next shelter where we had planned on staying. Nope, that was not for us. We decided to let them get well clear of us by indulging in a night with soft beds, a few more beers, and most importantly, no Germans. We've seen what large groups of kids can do to a shelter, we'd rather be comfortable and make up the mileage later.

We unloaded our gear in the room and shower-boy wasted no time getting into the shower while I organized all our things. I then cleaned up and with both of us fresh we headed over to the Tap Room. Now even though we had changed our clothes there was still no mistaking us for anything but thru hikers. We had on long sleeve shirts and were wearing hiking shorts and Crocs. We were unkept and unshaven, but at least we were smelling fresh while in public. Well, to the best of our abilities anyway. The room was pretty full when two guys came in that were staying in the lodge and slack packing the area. Matt engaged them in witless conversation, it's what he's best at.

"So, you guys thru hikers?" Matt asked the pair who were sitting next to us while wiping the foam mustache from the beer off his mouth. He knew damn well they were not.

"No way man, we blue-blazed it on the so and so trail. Blue blazing is really tough dude." For those of you who may not know blue blazes are usually for loop trails and side trails for beginning and sightseers.

"You don't say," began Matt, "how many miles did you cover today?"

"We had a ten miler today, but tomorrow we're looking at pushing for twelve."

Matt rolled his eyes and chuckled, he looked over to me and started grinning. "Yeah that sounds really tough, you may even lose sight of the lodge pushing out that far. That does sound much harder than walking from Springer Mountain. How did you manage all those five-hundred-foot climbs with those heavy slack packs?" I figured I'd let the boy sow his oats; besides I was now Planet Bob. He was becoming a man, soon he will grow pubic hair. I am so proud.

The two friends gave each other blustered looks. "You guys are full of crap. If you're saying you hiked here from Georgia then prove it."

I don't understand people with such bravado, especially when it's for nothing, but then again, I am sure I am a psychiatrist's dream patient. I was going to chime in, but I figured my answer may inadvertently come out in German since that debacle was still fresh in my mind, so I stayed out of it while sipping my beer bemusedly.

"How would you like me to prove it? Should I name all the shelters we stayed in? Would you like to see my journal, but perhaps I should get it notarized first as proof? Should I print out some pictures for you? Better yet, would you like to see my blisters?" I guess Matt had enough as he turned his back to them and got back to the most important issue at hand, his beer.

The two beside us went back to congratulating each other for being "Masters of the Outdoors" with their cumulative twenty miles under their belts. Normally I would never disparage other hikers, but to say blue blazing is harder than hiking the AT is just nuts. They were laughing and joking with each other about how bad they smelled, each one taking turns sniffing the other's armpits.

Matt overhearing that and said, "Yeah, that's another thing, why don't you try being considerate of those around you and shower before coming into a public bar?" Shower King can never leave well enough alone.

The short one was about to reply and I'm sure it would have been a great response when the bartender approached, "You guys are right," the bartender exclaimed, "you do smell and you are cut off until you shower and change into something proper." The bartender glanced over at Matt at myself and gave us a nod, I guess he had overheard our conversation. Then he continued, "I'm sure experienced hikers like yourselves understand we mostly cater to tourists and your scent is offensive to those around you. Thank you for your cooperation, I hope to see you soon."

With that the two left to prepare themselves for their backbreaking stroll through the woods the following day. As they were walking out Matt stood up and mimicked the action of "dropping the mic," which they did not find nearly as funny as he did. I think he watches too many movies, I don't know where he gets this shit.

After a few beers and a decent meal we went back to our cabin to call it a night. The cabins on this property were like row housing, each one was attached to the one next to it. We settled down for the night, but sleep did not come easy, apparently we were next to the what was the Honeymoon Suite and I was haunted by the sounds of passion for hours on end. Normally I ask myself who the hell honeymoons in the Shenandoah's, but considering I've stayed in the Jungle Room at the Road Kill Grill, I know that would be a pointless question to ask. I had an extra cup of coffee the next morning for good measure and we were back into the woods.

1,253.7 miles to go.

Chapter 33
The Roller Coaster

God, this state never ends. Matt and I headed into town to restock. We got lucky and we were picked up by a guy in an RV that said he had once thru hiked the trail. I don't know if I would have taken this ride if I was by myself, if you catch my drift. There was just something off about him. He had two tiny little French poodles. He dropped us off at a motel where we had prearranged a food drop, only Patti forgot she sent the first one, so we had two drops, over twenty pounds of food, with no hiker box there. The owners of this motel were wonderful to Matt and I and took us into town for dinner. There was a bluegrass festival going on down the road and they dropped us off telling us they would be back in two hours.

"Dad, why do we have to be here? This is all country backwoods shit ass music. Who listens to this crap?"

The kid does hate country music. "Son this all part of your cultural education."

"Yeah right. It's a muddy freaking field and they're playing banjo music."

"Matt, look out in the field. See all the young girls with no shoes on covered in mud dancing away to the music? Go get 'em Tiger."

"Dad, all those young girls probably have three or four kids, looking for a husband if they are not already married to their cousin or uncle. That's the life you want to doom me to?" The kid did make a good argument.

We sat and listened to the music, and Matt may have been right about the girls. The problem was after a few beers they were starting to look good to both of us. Time to go. We didn't need a shotgun wedding anywhere down the road. The guy with the RV had said he would pick us up at eight the next morning and take us back to the trail, and he did. Trail magic.

On our way to Harpers Ferry, the only real obstacle left is the section of the trail they call the "Roller Coaster." What was interesting for us on this section of trail, we passed our first SOBO. A SOBO is a south bounder, having started in Maine and was heading to Georgia. We chatted about the trail, each of us explaining what the other faced. Besides the SOBO, we also encountered our first rattlesnake, a four-footer, and it rattled.

It was also caterpillar season, if that's a season. They are little green buggers. Some hang from trees, dropping a few inches at a time. You constantly walked into them or swatted them to the side with your sticks. And when they were in the trees eating the leaves, they constantly crap and it sounds almost like rain when it hits the dry leaves on the ground.

Okay, now into the Roller Coaster. It is fourteen miles of trail with no switchbacks that go up and down and over ten significant climbs. The climbs are three hundred to five hundred footers, mostly loose rock or boulders. It was physically challenging to say the least. Lots of ankle rolling, more than I can remember. We didn't get through the whole section but hit a shelter not far from the end. We were exhausted and just wanted to sleep. We always hung our food bags like the guidebook said, and our near empty packs were hung in the shelter in such a way that the mice could not get into them. At two in the morning, even with my earplugs in, I could hear what sounded like a child crying.

I took my plugs out, looked around, it was pitch black out, but I could see the shape of Matt cuddled to the side of me. "What is it little fellow, the darkness has you scared?"

"What are you talking about, you dreaming again?" he responded.

"I heard you crying. You must be dreaming, not me. What are you dreaming about to make you cry? Doing the trail a second time?

We both laid back down. Minutes later we both heard crying. "What the hell is that that? Sounds like whimpering?"

Whatever it was it was close. I felt around for my headlamp and lit up the front of the shelter. There it was, a black bear, a small one, maybe four feet high, reaching for my backpack hanging from the front of the shelter. In couldn't quite reach it so it was crying. There was no smell of wet dog, so I guess that shoots down that theory. We chased the stupid critter off and went back to sleep only to hear crying about thirty minutes later. Enough was enough. Matt and I got up, grabbed our backpacks, and armed with our pocketknives, we walked down the trail and hoisted them up into the tree with our food bags. We headed back to the shelter, but we were able to make out the silhouette of the bear standing under our packs, still crying. We both agreed that if the bear gets them and takes them into the woods, we would go home. No such luck again, they were still there in the morning.

The next day we went into Bears Den Hostel. One of the nicest hostels to date and has some history to it. We got bunks with a mattress, a shower, laundry, Internet, free long distance, ice cream and pizza. It was heaven. Nice after the Roller Coaster hike.

There were some slack packers in the hostel, section hikers, out for a few days. At night while sitting around we listened to their comments about the Coaster.

"Oh, wasn't it challenging? What a great trail, I wonder if the whole AT is like this?"

Our favorite was, "isn't it fun climbing all these rocks and hills." We bit our tongues, probably because we were still eating pizza. Our final opinion of the Coaster was that it sucked. The only good thing about the Coaster, we would have a nice two day walk into Harpers Ferry from here. Tonight, we would stop at David Lesser Shelter, it is just about at the thousand-mile mark on the trail north.

Gin rummy is 85,367 two 84,998, I am still in the lead.

And now 1,176.2 miles to go.

Chapter 34
Harper's Ferry

It was eight miles into Harpers Ferry and mostly downhill as you hike to the Shenandoah River. These were Matt's favorite hiking days, short days that took us into a town. He was practically skipping and hopping down the trail. We would learn too late that some hikers grabbed a canoe way upstream and paddled down into Harpers Ferry, saving themselves quite a bit of walking. I didn't mind though, we were "purists" who only hiked the blazed trail. Besides, after Matt's near-death experience whitewater rafting on the Nantahala, I doubted he had the sea legs or the gumption to tackle another waterway.

On the march into Harpers Ferry we finally hit the thousand-mile mark. We had hiked one-thousand miles. Think about that. One-thousand miles. Perhaps the most important fact was that neither of us had intentionally tried to kill the other yet. We were both plotting all the time of course, but we were both still alive. It wasn't quite the halfway point, but it was pretty damn close and in our minds, it was a major accomplishment.

Now as luck would have it there was a festival going on in Harpers Ferry. It was a celebration of the Niagara Movement, which was founded over a century ago, it is an organization for equal rights based originally out of New York. It was about one-hundred years ago the movement met in Harpers Ferry and it is believed to be one of the first civil rights movements in America.

Due to the celebration in town the sidewalks were blocked and packed with people because of the parade. There was no way Matt and I could push our way through those people with our packs on without causing a commotion. We did the only reasonable thing we could do; we jumped into the street and fell in line with the parade. We waved and smiled for the people, but I'm certain they knew we were just two idiot hikers. We weren't with them for long, just long enough to march into the historic district.

If you haven't been to Harpers Ferry, it is absolutely worth a visit. The history alone is worth the trip. We weren't so much interested in the history as we were in the bars and restaurants in the historic district. We stopped at the "Secret Six Tavern," which sadly has closed since then, but it did have the coolest name, which was enough to earn our business. We sat there and had a few beers while waiting for the hubbub to die down before going off in search of some lodging.

We were attempting to make our way to the Appalachian Trail Conservancy building, which was headquartered in Harpers Ferry. They have a ton of information on the trail for hikers heading both north and south. On our way there we came across a KKK booth, right in the middle of a civil rights festival. Down a bit further was a booth filled with what we believed to be White Supremacists dressed in full Nazi uniforms. None of them spoke German as well as I did. Most people were steering well clear of these booths. I guess that's freedom of speech for you, your First Amendment rights in action. This naturally drew law enforcement, as I counted badges from at least three different states.

At the AT Conservancy we were told there were no rooms anywhere in town. All the motels were full, as well as the campgrounds. Thanks, civil rights. Matt and I were planning on taking an extended "zero" for two days here since we were waiting for another hiker to join us. We were being told that basically our only options were to either hike an additional six miles to the nearest shelter outside of town, or we could take a chance stealth camping. Neither sounded very promising. There were too many cops around to chance stealth camping and we had two days to kill anyway. The prospect of hiking twelve miles round trip, back and forth, from town to shelter was unthinkable. Matt made his feelings on this abundantly clear.

"There is no way on God's green earth I am walking to and from that shelter for the next two days. I would sooner throw myself into that river and end it all." It was all rather dramatic for someone who had just walked one-thousand miles, but he was right, this was less than an ideal situation to be in. In fact, it sucked.

We sat around for a couple of hours at the AT Conservancy while wasting daylight and trying to decide what our best play would be, none of it looked good. We'd debated taxis and motels in nearby towns, but in reality it wasn't much of a debate since I'm the only one who ever paid for anything, so again when I say "we," I mean I was trying to decide our next move. Sitting at a shelter for more than a night was torture, the boredom is too much to handle. We had no idea about the festival, so much for planning ahead.

That's when the skies parted and an Angel, a "Trail Angel Supreme," descended from the heavens. We were hanging around the Conservancy mulling over which suck plan would suck the least, when a gentleman approached us. "You boys thru hiking?"

"Yes sir," I responded, "my son and I are headed to Maine."

"That's incredible. I did the whole thing back in '85. You two are very lucky to be able to do this together." I wasn't so sure of that at the moment, but I guess in retrospect he was right.

We chatted for a while and entertained him with some stories of the trail and he entertained us with a few of his own, which were mostly how empty the trail was back then. He asked if we were heading to the next shelter and we described the predicament that we found ourselves in. His eyes lit up a bit when we told him we were essentially homeless for the next few days.

"You boys wait here an hour or so and I'll be back, I may have a solution." What was another hour to us? We stayed put.

True to his word he returned roughly an hour later. "I think it may be your lucky day." It sure didn't feel that way, but it would.

"I am part of a larger group here," he said, "we rented out an entire B&B and one of the couples couldn't make it, so we have an extra room if you are interested."

To say we were interested was an understatement. "That's awfully kind of you, I told him. How much are these rooms going for? We are grateful but as someone who has done this, I'm sure you understand we are operating under certain budgetary restrictions."

"Of course, I understand. Well, truth be told, the other couple already pay for the room and there's no refunds, so it's yours if you want it."

"God bless you sir!" I said and Matthew added, "and your family too. I love you." Matt hugged him.

People can talk about trail magic all they want, but this was magic unsurpassed. The kindness of a stranger can at times be quite remarkable. When Matt heard the news he almost jumped out of his skin and started doing the "Thriller" dance with intermittent bouts of moonwalking.

271

"I'm Peterman, and this dancing fool is my son, Firestarter."

"My trail name was Rain Man. Seemed like the rain always followed me." I could understand that. Rain Man could almost be anyone's trail name out here.

Matt said, "It should be Guardian Angel." The boy was still dancing

We followed him over to the B&B he was staying at. It was a beautiful large Victorian house that seemed to fill these towns along the AT. The owner was a wonderful woman who showed us to our room. We should have figured since we were taking a couple's room there was only one queen size bed to be had, but the thought did not occur to us. Queen beds are big, not big enough. We both looked at the single bed then at each other. The hostess could sense our distress and informed us that there was a cot in the garage that we were welcomed to carry in ourselves and use.

"Look son, in the spirits of fairness we can rock paper, scissors for the bed and the loser gets the cot, how's that sound?"

"Really Dad? that sounds great, I figured you would just make me take the cot."

"You're right, I was only kidding. What kind of idiot do you think I am, now go drag that cot inside." Man, it's so much fun to mess with him sometimes.

"Well jokes on you," he replied, "I would have gladly given up the bed for my aging father."

I could see the defeat in his eyes, and he accepted his fate. "Would you rather we hiked to the next shelter? It's not too late."

"Absolutely not. Cot's fine."

"Yeah, that's what I thought."

Our kind hostess told us dinner was at six and breakfast was at eight, both were included with the room. Holy shit, we were in seventh heaven and even high fived each other at the prospect of free home cooked meals. Before she left the room I asked her, "If you don't mind me asking, what do you normally charge for this room per night?"

"No trouble at all. The going rate is one hundred fifty per night."

I was floored. These people were beyond generous, they were truly incredible. On her way out she left us with some subtle advice. "Towels are behind your door for the shower and the washing machine is down the hall, feel free to join us downstairs after you have used both."

Matt and I chuckled, I'm sure she was more than used to hikers coming through. "Yes ma'am," I assured her. "You can count on that."

"Dad I'll jump in the shower while you get the laundry started, sound good?"

"I don't know, maybe you want to rock, paper, scissors for it?" I could tell by the exasperated look on his face that he most definitely did not. "Don't worry Matt, it seems this is our routine, you relax, and I work."

With our clothes in the dryer and both of us thoroughly washed we decided to bounce around town for a bit since we still had a few hours to kill before dinner.

The town was still abuzz from the festival and the KKK and Supremacists were still in their booths. Now Matt being the token college liberal in the family, thanks to his university education, could not come to grips with this. "How do these people still exist? How are they even allowed to be out here?" Matt asked.

They were not unreasonable questions. "This is supposed to be a celebration of civil rights," he continued, "and these clowns are allowed to set up here. It seems wrong."

"You know Matt, that was a well thought out, intelligent, and timely question once again. Sometimes you surprise me."

"Well then?"

"Unlike your college professors who think anyone who doesn't think like them should be eradicated or imprisoned, these people also have rights, no matter how much you may disagree with them."

"But they espouse hatred and violence."

"And so do I, but I do it equally. I don't think we should talk politics, we will never agree on anything until you graduate and start paying taxes."

After a while we got tired of meandering through the crowd, we stopped and listen to a great jazz band that played for a bit. When their set was done we made our way back to the B&B. The owner was in the kitchen preparing dinner for the group. She allowed us to keep a few beers in the refrigerator but only if we drank them in the kitchen since the group renting the place were not drinkers. This turned out to play to her advantage which leads me to believe she made the whole thing up. Matt and I were going to sit out back and drink a beer or two and I had scored a cigar in town, but she promptly put us to work in the kitchen helping her prepare dinner for the group. Fair enough by us.

We met the whole group at dinner, we couldn't thank them enough. I pledged that upon my return to civilization I would donate to their group to repay them for their kindness. Dinner was lovely but the conversation was rather drab, it turned to religion and we both kept our mouth shut lest we insult those who have been so benevolent to us. Matt looked as though he wanted to jump into the conversation at a few points but a quick jab with my fork reminded him to zip it. Last time he was asked if he believed in God his response was something to the effect, "Do you believe in the Easter Bunny or Santa, come on, a guy that walks on water?" Matt was obviously a non-believer.

After dinner we walked back into town for a night of partying which meant the two of us sitting at a bar, I was a proud father that night as my son, previously known as "Four Brew," grew up and became "Six Brew."

Holding at 1,167.4 miles to go.

Chapter 36
Hiker Babe

I t was here in Harper's Ferry we met Hiker Babe, a self-imposed trail name. Hiker Babe was my older sister. She wanted to hike a few weeks with us, and Harpers Ferry was an easy spot to meet, the train from Washington DC ran right into Harpers Ferry. Our stay at the B&B had expired, we could not afford to stay there another night if we had to pay. We moved to a campground that was accessible by taking the parks bus, which ran from town to a historic site next to the campground, and best of all was free to ride. I rented a little cabin that had four bunk beds. Matt and I dumped our stuff and headed back into town to wait for the afternoon train. We were well positioned to observe the arrival of hiker Babe, sitting on an outdoor patio at one of the bars overlooking the station, tipping back a few of the ales that were available.

The train pulled in after a short while, Matt and I waiting with anticipation for Hiker Babe. Of course, she was the last one off, this should have been a sign in retrospect, struggling with an obviously overweight backpack in some hideous color. I guess she thought that the rescue teams would be able to spot her from miles away. Sunglasses, oversized straw hat, shorts and shirt that would have made any fashion model proud. Definitely runway material. After our laughter and remarks subsided between one another, we made our way down to the platform.

"Hey Hiker Babe, what's up. You bring any hiking clothes?" I thought the apparel she was wearing might be traveling clothes.

"These are my hiking clothes, what's wrong with them?"

"Where did you get them, the hiking section in Victoria's Secret?" I wanted to set the tone for this adventure with her right away. I knew her wit to be just as biting as mine and Matt's.

"Well, I see you two have been in the bars already. Where can I dump this bag?"

"Matt, grab her bag, we'll head back to the campground."

Matt hoisted the bag up. "Holy crap, what's in here? It weighs twice what mine does."

I knew we would have to go through her bag and see what she had brought, and that's exactly what we did when we hit the cabin at the campground. I know I mentioned the two hundred feet of kite string earlier in the story, that went. The full set of silverware went. Pots and pans went except one. Extra water bottles went. A second pair of shoes went. Paperback books, a small battery powered fan, a Bowie knife, electric toothbrush (we bought a regular one at the campground store), a shovel, make up, the list went on and on. We packed it all up and shipped it home. Hiker Babe was reborn, a lighter, sleeker version. Hiker Babe 2.0

We crashed early that night after a nice dinner. In the morning Hiker Babe made her way to the general store again, and her only purchase this time was earplugs. Welcome to sleeping with Matt. We grabbed our gear and we were off. There was mention by Hiker Babe about how light her pack was now. You're welcome.

We took the parks bus back downtown to the Winchester and Potomac Railroad Bridge. Crossing the river now put Matt and I in Maryland. Five states down and nine to go and 1,163 miles. When you cross into

Maryland you are now on the flattest consecutive three miles of the trail as it travels along the C&O canal, a biking and walking path.

Fun Fact: The C&O Canal Trail is 185 miles long running from Cumberland, MD to Washington, DC. It is a bike and hiking trail that is well traveled.

Hiker Babe was in her glory, how easy can this be? Well, after three miles you start up the mountain ridge which climbs nine-hundred feet in two miles and had numerous switchbacks. We could look back through the switchbacks and see her tooling up the trail at a snail's pace. Hiker Babe was promptly renamed "Turtle." Matt and I simply could not believe how slow she was, it looked as if she was taking baby steps. At the top of this mountainous climb was a nice clean shelter. Turtle thought we were done for the day.

When she reached the shelter Matt and I were sitting at the picnic table waiting for her. "Welcome Turtle," Matt called to her.

"That wasn't so bad. What's up with the Turtle thing?"

Matt smiled, "You've been renamed." She was not pleased with her new moniker. She gave me a hateful look.

"Don't look at me, your favorite nephew came up with it. Trail names are earned out here. It's your new one till you shake it. Thank Matt."

"We in for the night?" Turtle, aka Hiker Babe, asked seriously.

"We're just breaking for lunch, so drop your pack and let's eat, get your tuna fish from your food bag, squirt some mayo out of the package into the tuna pack, mix and eat," I told her.

"We're not staying here?" It was almost a whine, Turtle and Matt were obviously from the same cut.

"No, we've only done five miles. We need to do at least fifteen or more a day. I don't want to be hiking in December." Now I had that evil Joker smile on my face. She was not pleased with this turn of events.

We continued hiking into the late afternoon, Turtle was affecting our pace. We passed through a Civil War battlefield with museums and finally ended up at Crampton Gap Shelter. It was a nice shelter, we were the only three there. It had a big platform deck and cooking area and a nice view. It was starting to turn dark, Matt and I were not used to getting into shelters this late.

"Well, let's set up before it's pitch black." Matt and I started to lay out our sleeping bags.

"There's no front here, couldn't we stay at one with four walls?" Turtle was a chronic complainer it seemed.

"There are only a handful of shelters like that on the entire trail, and none within walking distance right now," I told her.

"But there are bears and snakes. I can't sleep out in the open like this."

"What did you think the trail was? Lodge to lodge?" I was getting impatient. I am not a fan of needy people.

"Dad, I'll set up my tent for her," Matt was acting the peacemaker, obviously looking for a bigger Christmas present. "Will that be okay Turtle?"

"I guess so, but a bear can still get through the tent, and I don't like the name Turtle."

"I'll have Matt sleep in front of your tent, that way the bear will take him. Is that better Turtle?" I threw in Turtle for the hell of it.

A dirty look and then, "What if I taste better than Matt?"

279

"It's doubtful, you're too bitter. Goodnight." With that I turned in.

Matt and Turtle continued talking for a short time, she was already questioning why she was out here, telling Matt that some type of creature was going to drag her off into the night. She woke up at two in the morning and could not get back to sleep.

We were only going to do eight miles the next day, at that point you hit a state-run campground with flush toilets, hot showers, water, it sounded nice, or so the guidebook said. But as is Bob's world, when we got there it was a shithole. The bathrooms were a pigsty. I would rather crap in the woods any day. I was sick just walking into them. The tent sites had two burned to the ground tents on them. There was trash scattered all over the place. This was on a Monday, so its possible kids had camped here over the weekend, but it looked like this place was just never maintained. The state should just demolish it rather than "maintain" it.

Turtle was now lost to us. You could see it in her face, she was done. We were going to push on to the next shelter, we didn't really have a choice. I knew about half a mile up was a road was a restaurant. I stopped there and Matt and I had a long talk with Turtle, they say you can see defeat in a person's face, and I truly believe I saw it in her. Why be out here if you are miserable on the second day? It just gets worse. I got her a ride back to Harpers Ferry from a shuttle listed in the guide and off she went. The Turtle was to be no more, or so we thought. She would make another appearance.

Matt and I pushed on and two days later in the early morning we were standing on the Mason Dixon Line at the Pennsylvania State border.

1,126 miles to go.

Chapter 39
The Keystone State

We entered Pennsylvania kind of unwillingly, because let's face it, we didn't have a choice. There are no bypasses on the AT. We had been told horror stories concerning Pennsylvania, with the rocks being the culprit of our impending dread. I was under the assumption that Pennsylvania, being the Keystone State, was due to the inordinate amount of rocks and boulders scattered on the trail. That seemed perfectly reasonable to me.

I came to find a keystone is the bigger stone you see in the middle of an arch over a door or window locking the smaller stones in place. I figured it was because these rocks would lock me in place on this hike. Apparently, Pennsylvania, being one of the thirteen original colonies, was in the middle, there-by locking the colonies in place. That also seemed perfectly reasonable, but my theory was more plausible at the time. History is amazing. That being said, back to the story.

We were heading toward Waynesboro in Pennsylvania and decided to stay at a hostel the day before, which appeared to us was run by hippies. We tried to keep to ourselves, they served dinner for a price, but Matt and I were going to eat Mountain House meals since the menu was not to our liking. Before anyone got to eat, the owners wanted us to all hold hands in a big circle and say what we were thankful for. We tried to hide, but they found this, into the circle we went. There were about twenty of us, and they started far from me, going around in a circle.

Most statements were along the lines of being thankful for God, good friends, the hike, weather, all that happy horse shit.

It was Matt's turn, who was to the right of me. "I'm thankful for spending all this time with my Dad and getting to know him better after he abandoned me when I was a kid." He smiled at me thinking he got me on that one. Everyone was now looking at me in anticipation. I guess waiting for some type of reason why I would abandon my son.

"I'm thankful for the court system that made me pay child support for years. I am also thankful for DNA tests that proved the bastard is not my son, but since I supported him my whole life and I can't get my money back, I have accepted, by the grace of the good Lord, praise Jesus, him as my son."

The hush that fell over the crowd was amazing. The stares, the whispers. It was frightening. I looked across at the two owners who had disgust written on their faces.

"We're just screwing with you guys. Thought we needed some laughter."

No one came near us the rest of the night, and our leaving in the morning was welcomed. We headed into town the next day. They were probably a cult anyway.

We were coming out of the Waynesboro area now and had been hiking on and off with two other young hikers. These two were also college students, Golden Child and Flip, they were spending their summer break hiking and they were a real two-person comedy team. They had carried a Nerf Football with them since Georgia to play with, but it had developed a crack in it. These guys were partiers too, we tried for a few days to get and stay ahead of them, but they kept showing up at the end of the day, much like Psycho. Flip and Golden Child would sit down and smoke a joint and discuss the best course of action to fix their football which was in disrepair. We were all sitting around the campfire when a solution was decided upon. They were going to heat up some pine tar and spread it on the football with a stick. That would seal and strengthen the crack forming in it. They spent the following evening repairing it in just that manner. Unfortunately, the pine tar did not harden the way they had intended. The pine tar was sticking and smearing all over them as they threw it back and forth. It seems that college education was well worth the price. I'm sure their parents are very proud.

The next shelter we reached had a unique design to it, it was rather unusual compared to its counterparts. There were two shelters with a pavilion in the middle, which had an eating area with a roof which connected the two shelters to each other. Matt and I knew Flip and Golden Child were headed here for the night, but we also knew they had stopped in town with another older hiker. On top of that we knew they were intent on bringing a case of beer to the shelter for the night. With great foresight Matt and I spread all our gear out across one side of the dual shelter, doing our best to make it seem crowded and uninviting. They could have the other side all to themselves.

Our plan worked without a hitch, well almost. Golden Child and Flip, along with their new companion came strolling into camp about an hour later. They had brought their case of beer with them. I won't lie, the sound of beer cans cracking open did induce a twinge of envy. As they drank the sun began to set. They stumbled through the woods collecting firewood and after about an hour they had enough for a bonfire, and that's exactly what they started.

When the sun had fully set, they began drinking in earnest. They were dancing around the fire and beating their chest's like cavemen. At the same time I noticed two lights bobbing in the night, coming up the trail, heading our way. A woman appearing around thirty-five years of age came in with her son who appeared to be about nine or ten. She took a good look around the shelter area and at our festive friends enjoying libations by the fire. She came over and asked if they could stay on our side of the shelter, and frankly I didn't blame her, we seemed the safest bet. I don't think she liked the looks of the young ruffians drinking by the fire. I knew they were harmless, but they made Matt and I look like upstanding citizens. Had we been in town we would have been drinking with them, but as the saying goes "pack in, pack out," and a case of beer was a lot of trash to carry to the next town. I told her she was more than welcome to share the shelter with us.

As mother and son got settled our genius friends decided it was dinner time. I guess their plan was to save their fuel and cook on the open flame of the bonfire. They must have been architecture students or engineers, something of that nature. They were always trying to rig something up, new and inventive. One of them built a little wooden shelf to put their pot on over the fire. The Nerf Football plan may have failed but the alcohol coursing through their veins left them determined in this new task. Now, you may have thought, like I did, that the constructed shelf would just burn up and the pot would fall into the fire. Nope, that wouldn't to be a problem here. As the shelf started to burn up, Golden Child reached down and grabbed the pot by its handle before it collapsed. Matt and I sat there, jaws wide open, in pure amazement as he dropped the hot pot, spilling its contents, as it fell into the fire.

Matt, never passing up a chance to relish in someone else's misery, was laughing hysterically next to me. That did not please Golden Child.

"Hey man, that's not funny, that really hurt." He was shaking his burnt hand vigorously.

Matt, for his part took it easy on him, "You don't say. Almost as if fire is hot." I chuckled, it was funny after all. The sheer stupidity of it seemed lost on Golden Child.

"You wouldn't like it if you were burned," he responded.

"You got me there Goldie, but I don't think I would have reached into a blaze to grab a hot metal object." Matt conceded, letting it die, while chuckling to himself. I think the whole thing was a boost to his ego, he does some dumb shit, but knowing he was smarter than they were was good enough for him.

Matt and I sat silently now watching Flip and Golden Child playing out the "pot rescue mission." I don't think this was the only "pot" that day that had been lit on fire for them, if you know what I mean. They finally managed to use two sticks as tongs and fished out their now charred cooking tool. Matt stood up and clapped when the whole ordeal was concluded. Flip found it amusing but I think Golden Child was still a bit "burned."

We settled in for the night, ready to catch what shuteye we could while these idiots were drinking by the fire. Matt managed to weasel himself next to the wall of the shelter. That left mom next to me and her son Todd on the other side of our shelter by the other wall. The boys outside finally quieted down and peace fell over the shelter, probably because they ran out of beer.

Somewhere in the middle of the night that peace was broken for Bob. I awoke to mom curled up next to me and her arm across my chest, pulling me in tighter. What if she is awake and doing this on purpose? You cannot imagine the thoughts that the raced through my mind, on the one hand this was the best kind of trail magic, if you will, but on the other hand I pictured Patti holding a pistol to my crotch and slowly pulling back the hammer.

We've already established that's not how I want to die. I gently cleared my throat with an "hmm, ahem," but nothing. Damn it, she was asleep, it wasn't intentional. I wanted to gently rouse her, hoping not to frighten her, but rather she'd just roll over and we both avoid an awkward situation. Once again that would not be the case for Bob. I nudged her. Her eyes opened slowly adjusting to the dark. I heard her whisper questioning, "Todd?"

Well who am I to pass up such an opportunity, besides I did try to wake her. I looked her right in the eyes and said, "Mommy?"

"Oh my God," she said flustered, "you're not Todd."

"I could be though, if you wanted me to." It was time for Bob to have some fun with this situation.

"That's not funny."

I wasn't sure if she was fully awake yet. "Your arm is still around me."

She quickly yanked it away. "I am so sorry, I've never done anything like this before."

"Oh, that's too bad, but I believe you, but you're still sort of cuddling with me," now she pushed a good foot away from me.

"You're not making this easy on me." She was clearly embarrassed and slid even further away.

"Shh, listen, it was a moment shared and I know that its best for both of us if we end it this way. You have Todd, I have Matt, but will always have Paris."

She rolled her eyes, "I think I would have been better off with the drunks."

She flipped over and muttered a goodnight, and as I rolled over all I heard was Todd say "Mommy?" I burst out laughing.

The next morning as we packed up, I threw mommy a wink and thanked her for last night and the memories. I had not told Matt what happened yet so the expression on his face was almost as funny as the events from the previous night. She smiled at me as they left, or flipped me off, I'm not sure, it's all a bit blurry.

The next day brought us to the most earth-shattering moment to date. We officially hit the halfway mark on the Appalachian Trail. There were high fives, hugs, and plenty of self-congratulations. I did a little dance, we took some pictures, all in all it was a magical moment.

"We did it Dad, halfway," Matt was beaming.

"You know what this means?" I didn't want his joy to last too long, "we have just as far to go to finish."

Matt's smile diminished, "God damnit to hell," is all he squeaked out.

"But," I interjected, "we can cruise through New York to New Hampshire, we have family and friends all up in that area. We'll be slack packing and eating home cooked meals as often as it allows, soft beds, showers. The best is yet to come my son."

"Yeah, whatever, let's get this over with." I could not get a read on him at that moment.

1,091.4 miles to Katahdin. It was getting closer, we might finish.

Chapter 37
Pennsylvania Rocks

The title of this chapter about Pennsylvania is misleading. It doesn't rock in the sense that it is amazing or cool, it is about the rocks themselves in Pennsylvania. Ninety-five percent of thru hikers will tell you that this state is by far the worst because of the rocks on the trail. Someone said it was due to the glaciers that these rocks were dumped here. The northern part of the trail in this state is the worst, it is in this section that the rocks on the trail are some type of pointy shale or quartz. What do I know, I'm not a geologist. Your shoes will be destroyed. As you hike this part of the trail it seems as though there are no rocks anywhere else in the woods or surrounding area, just on the trail where you are hiking. It would seem as if they were placed here, sharp ends up.

It was in this northern section that I snapped my poles twice in three days. The first time we made it into town and they were repaired for free, as is the policy with the sticks I had purchased. I called the guy who fixed my poles two days later telling him they snapped again. He met me at the trailhead the next day in his van and repaired them again. The tips tend to get caught in the rocks, and if you are not careful the lower portion will snap before it gives. Getting through this part of Pennsylvania is like escaping Alcatraz, or Kathy Bates in Misery.

After the midway marker we got into Pine Grove Furnace State Park, home of the half gallon challenge. As a thru hiker if you ate half a gallon of ice cream you are part of the club. Matt jumped on this challenge for several reasons, he thought it was cool, I was paying, and he loves ice cream. I secretly was hoping he would puke, but no such luck. We stayed at the Iron Masters Mansion in the park, it's now used as a hostel, and we got a tour of the place by the keeper. It is a place with history dating back to the Civil War.

It was here in this hostel that we met some "Aussies" who were going to be there for a few days and were section hiking part of the trail. A husband and wife. Nice people. Matt named the husband "Platypus" and the wife was named "Koala." Matt has got a thing for weird animal names. They loved their new trail names, go figure. I asked Platypus how he liked being over here in the States.

"Great mate, a lovely country, just don't bonker the tipping thing." I loved that accent.

"I can help, what do you want to know?" I truly am a nice guy and I thought I knew what he was talking about. I didn't realize you need an interpreter with Australians sometimes.

"Well mate, here's how it blows." Matt giggled when he heard blows. Immaturity. "I tipped the cabbie from the airport to the hotel, the bloke that opened the door for us, the bellman, the lassie that cleans the room and the bloke at the front desk."

Koala interjected, "There were a few others."

Matt answered, as only he can, "Crikey!"

I, on the other hand, was thinking what would happen if Koala and Panda mated, what would they have? A Kanda? A Panola?

"For sure mate. And your bloody toll roads. In the outback, a toll road in American money is about twenty bloody dollars. I pull into a toll with my twenty ready and the laddie told me it was eighty cents. I nearly cracked a fat. Told him keep it as a tip. Fair dinkum."

"Well, let me help you out." I was really thinking what the hell did he just say? "Cabbies okay, never more than twenty percent. Maids, two bucks a day maybe. Wait staff also. Pretty much no one else, especially toll people."

"Bonza, that's good oil."

Good oil, what was that? "No trouble. By the way I also know all the words to Waltzing Matilda."

"That earns you and boy a slab of the amber fluid with us."

I understood that. It had something to do with beer, so we were in. We drank and sang Waltzing Matilda about ten times over the next few hours. The next day we continued on, the rocks in this section more like boulders and of course a lot of up and down hills. We were going to head into Boiling Springs but stayed at the shelter three miles short of town instead of an expensive B&B in town. The other option was camping next to the train tracks. That just ain't happening, the trains ran all night long and we even heard them in the shelter.

I got up earlier than Matt and told him I would meet him in town. I started through the forest and once again it hit me. Nirvana. Alone. Peace. Quiet. Soul searching peaceful bliss. It didn't matter all of a sudden how far I had to go, it was the walk that mattered. The woods were quiet, cool and comforting. This is how the trail should be. Then BAM! I walked out of the woods into a blazing hot corn field. Ever smell a hot corn field? Sickening, and the path wound through it and you could see no end. It seemed to last forever, like a maze, get it, maize, but I finally got to town.

Matt found me sitting in a little outdoor restaurant, quaffing a beer, or as the Aussie's called it, amber fluid. Boiling Springs is beautiful. Like Mayberry RFD, everyone seems to know each other. Very friendly town. While waiting for Matt I saw a Golden Child, sans Flip. I asked about Flip, but his answers were short and contrite. Trouble in paradise? Engineering disagreement? Lost the football? I personally think Flip hooked up with little Todd's mom.

After lunch the two of us went the next few miles to an Econo-Lodge. There was no laundry there, the machines, I should say machine, was broke. The Holiday Inn down the street let us use theirs if we ate dinner in the restaurant. That was fine by us. We left hoping to get into Duncannon in two days.

1,054 miles to go.

Chapter 38
The Return of Panda

We booked it to Duncannon, it wasn't particularly far off, but it would take us two days to get there. Panda had done most of the behind the scenes coordinating with Patti before calling us, so he knew where we would be in Pennsylvania and had planned accordingly. He just needed a time and place to meet us

Fun Fact: Duncannon is home of the Doyle Hotel, an original Anheuser-Busch Hotel, originally built in 1770, burned down, and rebuilt in the early 1900s.

Duncannon is home to another must see attraction along the trail. The Doyle. It is an iconic landmark for hikers along the AT. It shared many of the same features as other way points we considered iconic; cheap beer, great burgers, and good company. That was the upside. The rooms left something to be desired, squeaky floors and bedding, peeling paint, electric wiring outside the walls, and only fans to keep us cool. We loved it. For people who spend an average of six nights a week sleeping on the floors of a half built wooden shack in the woods, this was pure luxury. It's one of those places you remember forever.

What was better than the hotel or the town was the fact that Panda was rejoining us for a few weeks. God only knows why he would want to do that. Maybe he gets off on being abused? Who knows? We were glad to have him back either way. He wasn't due to roll into town until six, so Matt and I spent most of the day sitting around, sipping beers and eating food that isn't good for you. We played Rummy and for the first time ever Matt took the lead in the game, 89,654 to 89,534.

We rummaged through town and I picked myself up a Harlequin Romance novel and started reading it. Seriously, who writes this shit? Tragedy leads to finding love, which then in turn leads to more tragedy, which then begets love again. I was rooting against them the whole time, hoping the main characters would be siblings or something to that effect. Happily ever after would never come. Never let your wife read this shit, it can't be good for your married life, unless you already happen to be a Prince.

Panda rolled in a little after six like we predicted and was ready to party. Matt got up to greet him, "Well if it isn't the Panda. I guess you just couldn't get enough of us, eh?"

"Well, I've got some time off, I figured why not?"

"Oh yeah, we heard," Matt continued, "what did you do? Get fired? Couldn't you earn enough selling Girl Scout cookies or whatever it is you were doing?"

"Actually, I've taken a new job in Colorado selling carpets commercially."

"Is that some euphemism for selling weed?" I asked him.

"No, but it doesn't hurt that the job happens to be in Colorado," Panda was smiling. "Well, anyway I don't start for another month and all the moving plans have been arranged, plus SLiF gets some time alone." SLiF, as you may remember, is Pandas special lady friend.

"I'm eager to get back out into the woods with you guys, but I hear the beer here is pretty cheap, so the first round is on me."

"That's good oil," Matt said to him, and all Panda did was stare at him like he was an idiot then walked away. The beer prices were as cheap as promised; Panda was like a fish to water. He kept throwing them back like

293

he had the world by the balls. Matt and I were bit more cautious, we knew what it was like to hike hungover and did our best to avoid being in that situation. However, we did encourage Panda to drink his fill, after all his misery would give us a lot of ammo the next day. We eventually called it a night and followed a jolly stumbling Panda back to his room to make sure he wasn't taken by any exotic animal dealers.

He was a sad Panda the next morning, that's for sure. There were more than a few factors that may have made Panda miserable his first day back out. Some were the good old familiar ones, like smelling my breakfast and the occasional spider web, the other was unfortunate for us all, our lucky streak of sunny days had ironically run dry. We were smashed by one thunderstorm after another for most of the duration of the day. I doubt the thunder helped his hangover headache.

We stopped and huddled under some trees trying to stay as dry as we could while eating our lunches. The only thing worse than plain tuna was plain tuna soup, so we ate fast and kept moving. It was about an hour later that my lunch had probably worked its way through me, transformed into a gas, left my ass, and found its way to Panda's face. For the most part this had become an accepted part of Panda's hike, however due to the mixing of the thunderstorms, a hangover, and tuna, this particular fart was too much for our poor sad Panda.

Panda stopped dead in his tracks and began gagging. "Jesus fucking Christ Bob!"

"Actually, it's Planet Bob these days, but I can understand the confusion."

"That's awful... ugh... ugh," Panda was about to pop, he was white as a ghost and trying to hold it down.

"Ah, just pull the trigger," Matt offered, "you'll feel much better afterwards, that's what I do sometimes if I drink too much. Just let it out man, no judgments here."

"Yeah, no judgment from you two, right," and with that Panda gave his lunch back to Mother Earth two-thousand feet above sea level on the side of a mountain. It's too bad Psycho wasn't here to trail behind Panda and lecture him once again on the evils of drinking.

The sun came back the next morning, but the effects of the storms can be felt for a day or two afterwards. Everything was wet and Pennsylvania being the bitch she is essentially became one big slippery rock. The animals are also more active when the sun comes out, especially the cold-blooded ones that like to warm themselves on these rocks. The hot sun was high in the sky and it was beating down. Matt was buzzing along ahead of me, head down and focusing on his next step, I was a good dozen yards behind him, and Panda was still gagging on the cloud trailing behind me. I noticed the note taped to the rock first as it was easy to miss and not something you expect to see this far up on a ridgeline. Panda stopped as soon as I did because Pandas can't think for themselves. I read the note and shouted for Matt to stop immediately.

"Hey Firestarter, you may want to hold up a second."

"What's the matter old man, can't keep up?" The little bastard was trying to shame me and here I am trying to save his life again. "Well, did you read the note taped to the rock back here?"

"No, who put it there? Psycho?"

"Oh, I didn't know Matt could read," Panda joked.

"Good one Panda, took a lot of thought, did it? Anyway son, had you stopped to read the note you'd see it says danger, rattlers sunning on rocks ahead. Proceed with caution." The last person through must have left the note after encountering the snakes. It was an incredibly thoughtful thing to do.

I do love my son, but I'm not sure my love runs deep enough to suck rattlesnake venom from him. I guess it would depend where he got bit. I would probably help him if it were his arm, but then he could do that on his own. Maybe Panda would do it, he's been told he sucks so many times that maybe he believes it's his purpose. Otherwise, as the saying goes, Matt's a dead man walking.

"See those big brown things coiled up on the rocks about four feet from you? They are called rattlers." I had a bit of air of arrogance about me as Matt jumped back. "Careful where you jump, there may be more."

As I approached Matt, I could see the two coiled snakes we're only about two feet long. Not that it doesn't make them less dangerous, they can strike about two-thirds of their body length. We backed up a few steps and snapped a few pictures. A larger snake appeared out of a crevice on one of the rocks and began to rattle, that would normally be a good time to leave for a sane person, but instead it was Matt and me.

"What, you're not going to poke this one with your sticks?" Matt sounded as if he was daring me.

"Real funny, but I'm thinking, ever had rattler for dinner? I hear they are good to eat."

"It's always something with you two," Panda shouted at us. "Can we please just hurry along past the part with the killer rattlesnake please?" I guess Pandas are afraid of snakes, they may be natural enemies.

As Panda sped off, I took a moment to appreciate the rattlers. They were beautiful creatures, but deadly, in a lot of ways like my wife. Panda was right, time to move on, from the snakes, not my wife, not yet. I may need her to suck out some venom.

Survival Note: Read notes taped to rocks. They are there for a reason.

940.2 miles to go.

Chapter 39
Scouts and Religion on the Trail

That night brought us more rain. We had booked it to the closest shelter where we had planned on staying anyway. As I've described many times throughout this story, these shelters are not very big, most of them only having the capacity for six to eight. This was one such shelter, eight was its max. Well, this would be another poor experience with the Boy Scouts. A troop of twelve boys and their scout leader came plodding into the shelter. The three of us had already staked out our claim, but it became evident that all these boys were trying to cram into the shelter with us, and there was no room at the proverbial inn for all of them.

Matt and I had the spots closest to the wall meaning Panda was right up next to these boys, who all appeared to be about ten to thirteen years of age. As more and more of them hopped onto the platform Panda's fur for began to rise. He was now a mad Panda. Matt and I were not faring much better as we were being pressed closer and closer together. This was another one of those times you wish Psycho was around. Just as I was getting ready to tell the troop leader and his kids to fuck off Panda channeled his inner Psycho and took the reins.

"Okay, enough of this," he said loud enough to get everyone's attention. Looking at the troop leader he said, "Okay guy, the shelter sleeps eight, so eight can be in here."

"You can't make room for the boys? It's raining outside," the troop leader replied. I was ready to say, "screw the boys," but Panda was taking over.

"Look, there are twelve of you. Like I said this place sleeps eight, there are three of us here already," Panda said pointing at us, "so five of you can stay in here, you could always sleep on the ground and set a good example for the boys."

The troop leader was starting to get upset. Meanwhile Matt and I sat there enjoying the showdown, wishing we had some popcorn for the event. It seems Panda had grown a pair of balls since he was gone. Tired of getting bossed around by SLiF?

"Look, they are small boys, we can fit more of them in here." The troop leader was being adamant.

"No," Panda said firmly. "As scout's they and their leader should adhere to the rules. Isn't that one of the values you teach? Besides I'm sure that some of them need their tenting badge or whatever." Score one for Panda. We looked at him in a brand-new light, at least until he did his next dumb thing on the trail.

"And," I chimed in just for good measure, "if more thru hikers come in, they are given rights to the shelter over you."

"I'm not aware of any such rule," the troop leader retorted. It was one of those unspoken rules of the trail, or at least that's what I've been telling people this whole time.

"You'll learn real quick if another thru hiker comes in," Panda said, "besides I didn't walk all the way here from Georgia to argue with Boy Scouts, I find it a bit strange that a grown man would devote so much of his time to young boys." He was embellishing a bit, but he made his point.

"I am shaping the youth of today, clearly nobody did that for you," the leader said, slamming the Panda.

"I'll save you some time pal, ditch the kids, get a hooker, you'll be happier." Conversation over. After that remark the leader gathered all the kids at the opposite side of the shelter, they decided they would all pitch their tents that night. Badges were earned, we think. We were grateful for the extra space, Matt even applauded Panda, saying something like "the force is strong with that Panda."

Panda woke up refreshed the next morning and was sure to make as much noise as possible as we got ready to head out toward Leigh High Gap. We grabbed a motel that night, as Panda says, "never pass up a chance to shit over water." No fancy dinners or anything of the sort this time, just an early dinner and early to bed. The climb coming out of the gap was one of the most difficult climbs to date. It's nothing but loose rocks at a forty-five-degree angle for about a thousand feet out of the Lehigh. The one smart thing we did was arrange a ride to pick us up about twenty miles up the road so we could slack pack through this difficult climb. I couldn't be happier that we did, it was a bitch of a climb and when you have three people slacking you only need to bring one bag, especially when you're taking turns carrying it. This was probably the toughest climb before you reached the White Mountains.

At the top of the climb out of Lehigh Gap you pass into the Palmerton PA Superfund. The site was used as a zinc smelting zone and was in production for nearly a century. The next few miles were shock and awe. We had not encountered an area like this one before. The landscape looked as though it were a nuclear blast testing site. There was hardly anything living or green to be seen. It was haunting, to say the least. It gave hikers a firsthand experience of what environmental devastation looks like. I've seen the remnants of forest fires before, but this was far worse, all the trees were still standing but they were dead. Everything was dead. We were told by locals that trucks come up to spray fertilizer once a week to encourage growth, someone even told us it was human waste. Either way it wasn't working. We were glad to put those miles behind us.

Not So Fun Fact: For nearly 70 years, the New Jersey Zinc Company deposited 33 million tons of slag at the site, creating a cinder bank that extends for 2 1/2 miles long and measured over 100 feet high and 500 to 1000 feet wide.

Time had no meaning in Pennsylvania, all you do is walk on rock after rock, all the while completely destroying your shoes. This time Panda was taking the brunt of the blistering feet. He had gone soft in his time off. We did come across a bit of trail magic while hiking so we stopped for lunch at the same time. A gentleman had set up at a crossroad handing out power bars and cold apples. Panda popped off his shoes and began to rub his sore paws while we rested. Just a few minutes behind us another hiker appeared. His name was "Lizard King" and he was from Texas, and we had met him days before at one shelter. We never did find out why that was his trail name, but we did end up shadowing each other for a few days.

It turns our Trail Angel fancied himself an actual angel. He was out here to proselytize to hikers as they passed by. Once he had the four of us sitting there he seized his chance, "Well gentlemen, I hope you all know this nature and these gifts I've brought you today were made possible by Jesus Christ, our Lord and savior. Are you boys familiar with Jesus?"

My son, ever the smart ass asked, "Hey dad isn't that the guy who does your lawn?" We all got a good chuckle out of that except for our holy host.

"How about you young man?" He was looking at Lizard King. "Have you accepted Christ? You have the look of a sinner about you."

"Well, it's funny you should mention that. I'm actually Jewish, so yeah, no Christ here." Our would-be preacher looked as though he'd seen a ghost. I guess Jews were not exactly abundant in these rural areas.

"Young man, you need Christ now. The Jews are walking in darkness, my son. It was the serpent that lied about the apple."

Our hiker friend strongly replied, "I am the Lizard King."

Matt being half Jewish from his mother's side was getting ready to throw down the religious gauntlet on this guy, but Lizard King has already started with his rebuttal. I pushed Matt ahead of me down the trail so we would not get sucked into an argument with religious zealots.

"Thanks again for the snacks, you two have fun debating," I yelled.

"Go with God my friends, for the end is near." He blessed us with the sign of the cross.

Matt being unhappy about not getting his chance to go talk with the guy simply said, "I assure you the end is not near, we've still got about nine-hundred miles to go to get to Katahdin."

We were heading into Port Clinton that afternoon and seeing as it was Sunday, we knew everything would be closed except the hotel. The Port Clinton Hotel isn't very big, and we knew there were a few hikers coming in behind us. If you couldn't get a room then you had to camp at the town pavilion. Given this information, I told Matt and Panda I would book it to town and make sure we were shitting over water that night.

The trail into town is entirely downhill, somewhere about one thousand feet in elevation lost on the descent. It was, of course, a particularly rocky area. I used a technique that Psycho had taught me some time back, he called it rock dancing. He'd say, "Yo Peterman, you got to dance with them, one fluid motion, like ballroom dancing."

It was rather insightful for a guy like him. So, I danced. Unfortunately, I did not dance long, this section going into town was known as "The Slide," and for good reason. The boulders ended and it began to become a big slab of rock, no steps, nothing. So, I slid, we all did as Matt and Panda told me later. Each of us took some ass bumps on the way down. At the end of the day we were all sore and walking like sumo wrestlers.

I got us rooms, it was a self-check in, first come, first served. We found Port Clinton did not have much in the way of food, and what little there was happened to be shut down on this God-fearing Sunday. You find yourself in a town and the last thing you want to do is eat Ramen noodles or some other trail food. It might be PFG out there but in a town we wanted something with substance. We had cell phone reception so I called Patti to see if she could find something around town via the magical internet. Lo and behold she found a Pizza Hut that was not too far from us and they delivered. She phoned in our order for us and we got a pepperoni pizza with extra cheese delivered to our door. God bless Patti, I wanted to have her children at this point. Panda would not like walking behind me after this.

"Panda, is there something special between you and SLiF?" I asked curiously.

"Yeah," Matt threw in, "getting a little? Need some help? Pandas do need help mating."

303

"Hey, she's a nice girl." Panda was trying to end the conversation.

"What's a nice girl doing with a furball like you?" I questioned.

"Well at least you're with a girl." Matt was breaking Panda's balls again. "How did you meet?"

"Through a match site online." Panda seemed proud to have found a match.

"What site? Zooanimalslookingforlove.com?" Matthew was on a roll.

"No sense ever talking to you. I don't see you with any lady friends."

"Panda, I have a harem back at school. You think the girls want to pass all this up?" Matt said as he displayed his body in some perverse style. Girls always seemed to be a constant conversation with Matt and Panda.

The water at the next shelter was about half a mile south so we filled up before getting there. Two hours later three nerds came wandering into camp. They asked us about the water source and where we got ours. Maybe they had been pranked before because they refused to believe us when we told them. They spent the next forty minutes searching all around the nearby side trails before finally accepting their fate.

The funniest part of the group was that they could not get Panda's name right. They kept calling him Penguin all night, which led to some funny jokes about him being a Batman villain.

The shelter filled up and it began to rain again. Naturally more hikers showed up, Jed and Jethro Clampett are what I called the next two. They were some good ole' boys and they wanted to squeeze into the shelter. Luckily this time around it fell to the nerds to be the bad guys. We pretended to be as accommodating as we could saying things like, "Shucks, I'm so sure we can make room for them if we tried."

Jed and Jethro were no fools though, they had a plan to stay dry. Their idea was to set up their tents under the shelters overhang and then walk it outside, thereby not getting themselves soaking wet. It was sound logic on paper, but you need to lay down a footprint first for your tent so it is not on wet ground. In their haste they didn't bother to set up their rain fly either. The scene was hysterical. To make things better they started telling us how they are practicing nudists, often playing tennis in the buff, eating, and so on. I think Panda was getting into it. Out in nature in just his fur, that would make him happy I'm sure.

It rained and thundered all night, by the next morning everything the naked Clampetts had was soaking wet. I guess they will spend the next day hiking in the nude.

When we left that day, we had to pass over Knife's Edge, it's about a thousand yards of upheaved shale that looked like a knife blade. Steep drops on both sides. We had to hike, actually knee slide along it until we reached the end.

That night I had a dream I was moving to Pennsylvania and the only thing I was packing were boxes and boxes of rocks. This shit is seriously ingrained in my subconscious. We'd soon head into the Delaware Water Gap and then on to New Jersey. Familiar territory.

895.8 miles to go.

Chapter 40
The Garden State

Garden State my ass. I never saw one garden the whole time we were in the state. There were, however, lots of mountains and hills, so a real nice change of pace there. We pulled out of the Water Gap where Panda must have been feeling a touch of homesickness, he had called his special lady friend five times and she had not answered. Matt and I wondered if it is mating season, he's very fidgety and tense.

"I wouldn't worry," Matt offered, "she's probably just cheating on you with someone better looking and more financially stable."

"Yeah, well that's the kind of shit that I'm afraid of, she wasn't too thrilled I was coming back out here."

I jumped into the conversation hoping to cheer the Panda up. "Whomever she is with is probably much more sexually satisfying to her as well. So at least now she's fulfilled. I hope that helps."

"You guys should do children's parties, you know that." Panda gave up and put his phone away.

Jersey started easily enough but turned into another nightmare. Water was becoming harder to find, with further distances to go in between. We never had a problem before in the South and we were especially hoping this didn't become the new normal. We were also in the sun much more often than before. The trees thinned out a bit and there were more open spaces.

It must be noted that New Jersey, it is said, has the highest ratio of bears per square mile on the trail, so it's not really a matter of if you see a bear, but when you see a bear.

You would think that nothing much could happen in New Jersey, after all it's only seventy something miles through the state. Compared to the southern states, especially Virginia, this was a blip on the map. However, our ragtag group of merry travelers always seem to run into something.

We were into our second day hiking in our normal order with Matt out front, myself behind him, and Panda quite literally on the ass end, breathing in my breakfast once again. As we're marching along Matt came to a dead stop.

"What's up Firestarter?" He loved being called Firestarter, his face would become aglow every time he was addressed that way.

"Look Dad, isn't that cute? Two little bear cubs in the middle of the trail." Survival is not the child's strong suit.

"Hey Panda, you see the mother anywhere?" I spoke in a low, calm, and authoritative voice. "Matt, do not move." More than likely he was thinking of petting the cubs or feeding them.

One of the first things you learn is that, like most animals, never come between a mother bear and her cubs. A mother will tear you to shreds to defend her cubs, and no, we were not yet torn to shreds yet, but we were faced with a mother bear and her cubs.

"Why what's up?" Matt asked. It weighs on me sometimes that my son is destined to die in some completely survivable scenario.

"The mother has to be around and we're in trouble if she's already behind us." The level of my concern could now be seen in Matt's face as I spoke.

"What do we do? Can we sacrifice Panda?"

"Panda will live. Pandas sleep twenty hours a day, so he'll have no problem playing dead." There was always time for a panda joke, besides I was just hoping I could outrun the kid, Panda be damned.

"Thanks guys, just once would it would be nice if we came up with a plan that doesn't involve somehow killing or maiming me so you two can escape. I feel like it's not much to ask, besides I'll remind you both pandas are endangered so if anyone needs to survive its me." Shit, he had a good point.

"So, what do we do?" Matt asked again.

"We are staying put," I was now taking control, my training from years on the force kicked in again. "Nothing has happened yet so let's sit still, let it play out, don't do anything that might escalate the situation. Panda, don't start playing dead just yet."

"Well Dad, what if we just rush past where the cubs are and just get away from this area." He lost the whole meaning of my last speech, fear does that to children.

"Not a good idea son." As soon as I finished that sentence momma bear came bursting out of the woods onto the trail. She was about twenty yards in front of us, which looks like a much further distance when you're watching football on TV. She was a five-footer and still no wet dog smell. Whoever said that is going to get punched in the face when I remember who it was. She saw us and stood up on her hind legs sniffing the air. I became more concerned when I heard whimpering behind me, I thought somehow a cub had gotten behind us and that momma would be readying her charge. Instead I turned to see Panda clutching the back of Matt's backpack hiding behind the lad. The bear dropped onto all fours, gave a little grunt, and meandered back into the woods behind her cubs. We never moved.

"I just saved your lives, you both owe me big." They knew that deep down inside anyway.

"Oh please, you did not. All you did was say don't move." Pandas, it seems, are not appreciative animals.

"Okay, the boys plan would have had him actually running right into the mother bear and as appealing as your plan of whimpering and shitting ourselves was, hoping the bear would laugh and take pity on us, I think I made the right call." That shut him up.

This far north the hikers began to really thin out. It's really no different here than it is in Neels Gap two or three days into the hike. Everybody has their reasons, exhaustion, illness, injury, homesickness, the list goes on. Every now and then you catch up to someone and you will ask each other about other hikers you've been with along the way. It's not uncommon to hear so and so got sick or twisted their knee. It's equally not uncommon to hear so and so went home, they had enough. Some of those names surprise you, you never know who will make it the distance. It's hard to imagine someone making it as far as New Jersey and then throwing in the towel, but it happens. It's hard to believe but we've passed people never to see them again, but I think the majority of people are now well in front of us. With each passing day it seems like there are less interactions, less stories being told, and not to mention we've seen no sign of Psycho in weeks.

There was a little town on the New Jersey/ New York border that we decided to stop in before crossing into the home state. I'm pretty sure it was Unionville. I think I remember that the main reason we decided to stop there was the tavern. It was time for beers and burgers. There wasn't much to make this place remarkable except that the two places to stay in town were either the tavern or the Mayor's yard. For us this was a no brainer, we would eat and drink and sleep in the tavern, or so we thought.

"Hey barkeep," I asked as we ordered our burgers and beers, "the hikers guide say we can bunk here for three dollars a night. Is that right?"

"To a degree," the bartender replied. "You don't bunk here in the tavern, we have a storeroom attached to the bar, it's out the door to the right. Leave your money on the bar and the door is unlocked."

We were beat already and half in the bag. We were ready to sleep. New York was coming up fast and that meant easier hiking once we got close enough to our family and friends. I led us all into the storeroom expecting to find bunks. There were no actual bunks, only storeroom shelves they called bunks. We actually slept on shelves, like we were produce. I suppose we've slept in worse places. I grabbed the big bottom shelf, leaving Matt and Panda to fight over the two middle unused shelves. Matt grabbed the one in the corner, away from the lights coming in through the window. Alas, poor Panda was stuck on the shelf that was window high, lying there while the lights of passing cars danced across his face. Matt and I eventually fell asleep leaving Panda to fend for himself.

Matt and I were rudely awoken by Panda giggling about two in the morning. "Hey guys, you gotta see this. "Come look out the window."

I didn't want to get up. It's a real pain in the ass getting out of a sleeping bag while you're playing Elf on the Shelf. However, at this point I know well enough that the trail always holds something unusual and mysterious. Panda was standing there at the window with his eyes wide and grinning ear to ear. Matt popped up to see what was afoot and started blushing immediately as he got to his feet. Okay, now I had to see what was happening. I stood up and peered out the window and sure enough parked right in front of the storeroom was a car with two people going at it furiously, and loudly. They must have met in the bar. We began to hear them as their session went on, their moments of ecstasy and impassioned praise to God flowing out their open car windows. There was a bare ass pressed against the windshield like a canned ham and heaving breasts in the throes of carnal desire. This was a quarter a minute porn show.

I tried to shield the lad's eyes so I wouldn't have to explain to him what was taking place, but he kept pushing my hands aside. I was hoping this would not last much longer, but with those little blue pills out there, who knows? I banged on the window as loud as I could without breaking the glass. It didn't slow them down at all, other than a brief pause when they both stopped to flip us off and then they went right back at it. Welcome to the Tri-State area. I was home.

845.1 miles to go.

Chapter 41
New York, New York

We crossed the New York/New Jersey border officially the following day and for the first time ever, we ran out of water. Water was scarce, but the main reason we ran out of water was because of the big stupid animal we call Panda lost his water bottle. Being the humanitarian's that we are, Matt and I shared ours with him. It's always something with pandas.

With the shortage of water, we decided to abandon the trail in favor of a side trail down into a small hamlet. The trail down was steep, and not as well maintained as the AT, but it was also better than dying of dehydration, so we chanced it. We stayed in the only motel in town, I do not recall its name, but it was more like a freak show at a carnival rather than a motel. Every time we opened the door, for whatever reason, every person staying there would open their door and stand in the doorway and watch us. The people were all oddities, hence the carnival descriptor. I think these people may have been left behind when the last circus pulled out of town. It was spooky, very spooky. We grabbed Subway sandwiches, there's a plug for you Subway, because there was nothing else in town. We took them back to our room and locked ourselves in until sunrise. This was one of the few times I think Matt was happy to leave a motel and get back into the woods.

After a few hours we crossed a road where a Trail Angel had left several jugs of water. The cop in me is naturally suspicious of things like this even though I know it's commonplace along the trail in this area. I was eager to slake my thirst, but I graciously allowed Panda to sample the product first. After a minute passed without Panda dying, I gulped down as much as I could handle.

Later that day we came across another pair of hikers, who we thought were mother and son. Both were older and they had set up camp right on the side of the trail. They were sitting there smoking weed, passing a doobie back and forth between them as we hiked by. I was beginning to think there is a lot of pot smoking on the trail. We hadn't seen them before, but I doubt they were thru hikers, they didn't seem the type. Panda wanted to stop and set up camp next to them for the night, but I didn't want to hike with a stoned Panda the next day. We found a campsite a few miles down the trail and pitched our tents for the night.

I would love to tell you all was well, that it was going to be just another peaceful night camping under the stars, but by now it should be obvious that our restful nights are few and far between. This night would be Panda's first experience with a bear in the campsite. Matt and I were not much better prepared to deal with it as we've only had one confirmed encounter with a bear while in a shelter. Again, the shelter only offers an illusion of safety. This time we were in our tents, essentially already divided and conquered for the bear. About midnight we were all awoken by a heavy breathing and snorting noise. After listening for a minute and making sure it wasn't just Matt snoring, I heard Panda call out, "Uh, guys, anyone awake and hearing this?"

"I hear it," Matt said. That rules him out as the culprit. I saw his headlamp flick on and I did the same.

"I'm gonna check it out," Panda exclaimed. We heard him start to unzip his tent and he let out a shriek as he was face to face with a black bear. "Shit, it's a bear!" We then heard him quickly zip his tent shut again.

"Good thinking Panda," Matt said, "that zipper will certainly keep a four-hundred-pound bear out."

"What do we do?" Panda asked. Pandas are by nature lazy and timid creatures.

"Well Panda, Dad and I could just make a run for it. He seems to recognize you as one of its kind. You better hope it's not a male looking to mate. Just sit tight and let the men handle this. We've been through this before."

"Tell it the Bambi story!" I shouted from the relative safety of my tent. "I love the Bambi story." It was true. I love the way the kid told the story, and like most of his stories it got better each time.

Matt started making noises, not as loud as Panda's initial yelp, but loud enough and threatening enough to scare the bear out of our campground. We all slipped back to sleep eventually, but the stillness of the night only lasted so long. Our visitor came back. "Psst. Guys. I think I hear the bear back outside my tent."

"Ugh, I guess I shouldn't have left those Snicker wrappers on your rain fly," Matt joked. "Unzip very quietly and snap a picture with your camera. It would be a cool live action shot to send home to SLiF."

To the surprise of Matt and myself, that's exactly what he did. We could hear the bear rustling around on the edge of our campsite, coming closer and then moving away again. It had to hear us, but I guess it didn't think of us as much of a risk. If only Frog Croaker were here. We had all zipped our flies down a bit to try a catch a glimpse of this beast. That's when we saw Panda's arm slowly slip out from behind the tent screen, camera in hand. Click.

Survival Note: Black bears, as I'm sure it goes with all bears, do not like flashes in the middle of the night.

The bruin stood and roared; I don't think Panda got the shot he wanted as the bear was by Matt's tent at the time. Panda popped back into his tent like a turtle into its shell, safe and sound with that miniscule layer of nylon protecting him from the apex predator outside his tent.

It's really amazing how the human brain is able to process things, especially danger. What had just seconds before been a relatively safe encounter was now on the verge of becoming an extremely perilous situation. All because a stupid Panda took a joke literally. I pointed my headlamp at the creature hoping to distract it since it was now facing the boy's tent. I could see him clearly and how wide open his eyes were looking up at that bear.

I unzipped my tent all the way, my fatherly instincts had kicked in. I would tackle the beast if it moved toward Matt's tent. My seed must live on. I would give him enough time to escape, live, and tell my story. The bear was rubbing his eyes with his paws, still blinded by Panda's sneak attack. I was getting up into a sprinter's stance, ready to pounce, but by the grace of Mother Nature the bear dropped down to all fours and went crashing into the woods. From the sounds of things, it ran off straight into a tree, but we couldn't convince Panda to go check it out.

That was it for the night, no more bears, and no more pictures. I went back to sleep knowing I basically saved their lives yet again.

We rolled into another shelter the following day. It was nice to have solid walls on three sides again. It's all about living that illusion. Thank God for Trail Angels though, if it weren't for them leaving water out along the trail on the way into and through New York, it would have been much less pleasant.

We set up everything we needed for the night as it began to rain. Shortly after the rain started a group of four young guys came in. I sized two of them up as terrorists and the other two as a Canadian and an Oriental. Matt quickly reminded me that everything about that was completely racist except perhaps the Canadian part, and even that was because I meant it to be derogatory. He was right, boy did his liberal professors get their hooks in him.

The two terrorists, I dubbed them Mohammed and Abdul, were determined to set up and sleep in their tent. There was room in the shelter, but they wanted to rough it I guess. Either way it was fine by me. The two of them were getting soaked, as was their tent. When they finally finished setting it up, they came back into the shelter triumphantly. I had to remind them that they had not put up their rain fly and the inside of the tent was going to get soaked. Out they ran back into the storm.

After interacting with these four for the evening, I was convinced they also did not belong in the woods. Tragedy will befall them sooner or later. Panda quickly became best friends with all four of them and spent the night partying with them, if you catch my "scent." Matt and I were asleep at eight after another rousing round of Rummy, 97,998 to 97,904, I was back in the lead but I'm still worried.

796.6 miles to go.

Chapter 42
The Night of the Grizzlies

The following day we pulled into our next shelter and we were surprised to see the pot smoking mother/son combo had somehow leap frogged us. We could not figure out how they got ahead of us unless they hiked by moonlight or yellow blazed. They rolled their eyes when they saw Panda coming in behind us. I guess they remembered him. They mostly ignored us and retreated into their tent, which was pitched about ten yards from the shelter. It wasn't long before Panda's eyes went wide when his powerful bear nose detected a familiar scent wafting on the breeze.

We would frequently stumble across people smoking pot along the trail. It really isn't that big of a deal but it's always amusing to see people's reactions when they find out I was a police officer. It's like they think I could somehow still call in SWAT in the middle of nowhere and have them extracted and jailed.

Matt could see Panda eyeing Ben and Jerry's tent and was having some fun with him, "Hey Panda, I smell a doobie. I bet you wish you had a doobie."

"Be a lot cooler if I did," Panda mumbled. "Hey, do you think I should ask them if they'd share?" He was raising his nose sniffing around as if he might lose the scent and be unable to find them again.

"I think that's exactly what you should do," Matt told him with a grin.

"Not a good idea Panda. What if they are not mother and son and are doing the deed? You really want to interrupt that? Besides, I don't think they like you." I was trying to be the voice of reason once again, Matt being the instigator.

Over the next few minutes Panda began walking closer and closer to their tent, until it seemed like he was circling them. From our vantage point it looked like he was trying to get a contact high from any smoke rolling out of the tent's vent. Matt and I were laughing at this desperate act from reefer deprived Panda, that is until we heard someone shout.

"Hey what the fuck are you doing walking around outside our tent asshole?" a male voice said.

Panda jump back startled, "Nothing, what are you doing inside the tent?"

With that remark from Panda Matt and I started to laugh even harder. We both thought, what a stupid question.

"What we are doing is none of your fucking business." The response came from the mother and it was far more frightening than the male's voice had been.

"Well I smell something coming from your tent, if you know what I mean." Panda had changed the tone in his voice trying his hardest to sound friendly.

"Are you a God damn cop?"

Matt yelled over, "No, he's just a sad Panda."

"No, no, you don't..." Panda was cut off immediately.

"I don't want to hear it," she snapped from behind the nylon pop up. "Get lost you fucking pervert."

Panda turned back to us red faced and sulking. Matt stood and applauded as Panda made his way back to the shelter. I stood and joined him, 'cause why not.

"Well, I don't think that went quite as planned," I said patting him on the back as he approached.

"I think it went brilliantly," Matt countered.

"Well they certainly weren't too hospitable, were they?" Panda was a defeated panda.

"You were circling the tent like a vulture, breathing in the fumes. That's some psycho level shit right there. All that for a little smoke? For shame Panda, for shame."

The Odd Couple did not come out of the tent for the rest of the night. In fact, we never saw them again. We would later hear from other hikers that there was a rumor going around of a guy stalking people in their tents.

As we are now safely in New York, we were headed into the Bear Mountain area. We hit the summit and hung out for a while enjoying the view and guzzling some frosty cokes, smiling like the assholes you see in the commercials. I think I had four in an hour while sitting at the visitor center.

Fun Fact: Bear Mountain is famous for being able to see New York City on a clear day some 70 miles away.

We may have stayed a bit too long since the sky was beginning to turn to dusk. We still had a way to go before we hit the next shelter. We realized that we weren't going to make it to the next shelter before dark and the decision was made to stealth camp down a gravel road we crossed. This was completely illegal to do on Bear Mountain, but we figured who would be going around checking in the middle of the night.

We managed to get dinner cooked just before dark and settled in for the night. We cleaned up our campsite and hung up our bags down the road a bit. We climbed into tents, Matt and I were side by side while Panda was set up facing us. I put in my earplugs and drifted off to sleep. It wasn't long before I woke up. Even with my earplugs I could hear the crunching of gravel nearing our tents.

It persisted for a minute or two, so I called out to Panda in a low voice, "Panda," I said almost whispering. "You awake?"

"Yeah, I'm up now."

"Something is walking around outside my tent, I hear the gravel crunching. Zip down your flap and take a look, will ya?"

"Why, you think it's a bear? Look yourself, been there, done that pal."

"I can't, I'd have to crawl halfway out of my tent to see what it is. Just take a look and reassure me so I can go to sleep. I'm not asking you to take another picture."

It took a lot of back and forth conversation until finally Panda unzipped his flap grumbling to himself. I saw the headlamp flick on casting shadows outside my tent, "Fine, hang on, I'm checking."

I heard some shuffling around and then Panda responded, "It's a tiny little deer." Panda's tone was very condescending.

"I've had my fair share of run-ins with deer, they are not as meek and mild as you may think. Goodnight Panda."

"Yeah, yeah, it's headed up the road now so you should be safe." We both lowered ourselves back into our sleeping bags and tried to get back to sleep. It wasn't ten minutes later we heard this tiny deer come running back down the road and past our tents.

"Psst. Panda. Did you hear that?"

"It's hard to hear anything over Matt snoring, but yeah, I heard it run by."

"Wouldn't it be funny if a bear scared it off? This is Bear Mountain after all." The words had no sooner left my mouth when the silence of the night was shattered by a chilling roar.

Enter Matt. "What the hell was that?"

I couldn't see him, but I could tell he was sitting straight up in his sleeping bag.

"Got to be a bear," I answered him. "He's come back for revenge on Panda for trying to blind him. We need to get out of our tents now." I said the last sentence with concern in my voice. It also had a touch of authority; command is my life.

We were out of our tents in a matter of seconds after the collective unzipping of our tent flap's. Matt was standing there in his underwear with his pocketknife in hand, as if that would stop a bear. I didn't have the heart to tell him I got him a plastic toy one with the rubber blade so we wouldn't hurt himself.

The roar had come from the direction the deer had run from. The three of us stood there focusing the light from our headlamps in that direction. The silhouette was unmistakable, it was a bear and from the looks of things a big one. It was on its hind legs about twenty yards from us at the top of the ridgeline. It was under our food bags, reaching up for them, swatting at them. With any luck it would just take Panda's food and leave mine and Matt's alone. We had grouped together attempting to make ourselves look like one big animal, but bears in this area are probably so used to humans that the bear was thinking "what are these assholes doing?"

We shouted and stomped, the bear dropped to all fours and scurried up the road. This went on for the rest of the night. Seemingly, every time we got into our sleeping bags and began to get comfortable, we would hear another growl or roar snapping us right back to reality and out of our tents. Eventually dawn broke and the "Night of the Grizzlies" ended, so we packed up quietly and left. I guess that's why it's illegal to camp in non-designated sites on Bear Mountain.

Regardless, we were alive to tell the tale. Once again, it was thanks to my natural leadership ability and survival skills. The size of the bear varied depending who in our party you asked, I claimed the bear at five feet, Panda at six, and Matt had it at eight feet and walking upright like Sasquatch. It was a slight exaggeration, but it made for entertaining reading in his diary that he had sent home. The shelters were looking better and better all the time, it seems whenever we stealth camp something happens.

785.8 miles to go.

Chapter 43
Panda's Special Lady Friend

We had a fairly easy day ahead of us, we were hiking to the other side of Bear Mountain Bridge which was only six miles or so. There was no rush since we were being picked up in the afternoon by a friend of mine, Michele.

Michele and I have history, and no, it's not that kind of history. I used to be her boss. She used to think of herself as quite the practical Joker, of course that was until she began working for me. I would love to say it was a battle of wits, but she lacked the balls and creativeness to outdo me. I destroyed her with my pranks. I sent nudist colony reservations to all her neighbors addresses but with the reservations in her name. She got some looks at the annual block party that year. I filled her car with packing peanuts, and I sent her kids an explosive prank kit to use on her at home. In the middle of the night when she went to use the toilet, it exploded. The list goes on and on. It could be a book in itself.

Panda and I would spend the next few nights at Michele's home slack packing on the trail. While we were there, Panda's special lady friend would be coming to meet us as well. Matt would be coming with us but the following day he would keep going without us, he has family on his mother's side that would be picking him up for a few days at the next trailhead.

We got to the pickup point well ahead of schedule. Normally, this just meant sitting by the side of the road for a few hours waiting for a ride, but I decided to call Michele and let her know we arrived early. It turns out that in preparation for my arrival she had taken the day off. She came to pick us up, we didn't have to bake in the sun on the roadside. It was probably the first time I was happy to see her, I'm not so sure she was happy to see me, bad memories and all that.

Michele had been on the "newsletter" Patti had been sending out to friends and family, so she knew we'd be hungry. We showered up, this time making Matt go last so we'd have some hot water. We kicked back and had a few beers on the deck and then the dinner to end all dinners. It was practically a gourmet buffet. I assume this was all a front because Matt and Panda were around, otherwise I'd probably be served gruel with ghost peppers or laxatives in it.

She laid out a smorgasbord of food, bringing first out appetizers, chips and salsa, cheese, pepperoni, and mini pizzas. After that we moved onto the main course, roast chicken, roast beef, gravy, stuffing, mashed potatoes, and some venison. All the fixings were included. She truly outdid herself. Matt, Panda, and I were like kids in the Willy Wonka Factory, the Gene Wilder version of course.

Panda had set it up beforehand that SLiF would be in New York City while we were in upstate New York at Michele's. Being the lovely woman that she is, she rented a car and drove up to see us, meaning Panda. She just couldn't bear the idea of being so close to her big furry love toy and not seeing him. She's from Kansas, so that explains a lot about her right there.

Matt and I could not wait to meet the woman who would want to breed with Panda. It's a good thing she came too. Panda was facing a wardrobe crisis, his boots had been crumbling beneath him as each day went by and he had asked her to bring his second pair, which were wisely broken in. He also needed a new t-shirt and shorts for around town. SLiF tossed him a bag with clothes in it and told him to change out of his hiking clothes. We were going to wash all our clothes at Michele's. We could hear Panda knocking about in the other room and he let out an audible, "Oh for fucks sake!" As he opened the door. "God damn it Laura, what the hell is this outfit?"

"Love Bunny," Laura cooed at him, that phrase and tone alone making me sick. He was a Panda, not a bunny. "You said shorts and a t-shirt."

Well that's what she brought him. They looked like the gym shorts you wore in high school fifty years ago. They were too small to say the least, bright red, and slits running up the sides which barely covered his ass cheeks. He essentially looked like a Hooters waitress. Naturally Matt and I were jubilant, this was a gift from God. The laughter started in earnest.

"With all the shorts I have, this is what you bring me? Especially in front of these two," Panda said with a squeak in his voice, "I told you about these two."

"I know Boo Boo bear, but I have to be conscious of the travel weight limit of my luggage. There are limits you know, and these are small and light."

I believe she knew damn well what she was doing. She enjoyed doing this to Panda and we would not let her down. Matt and I were having a field day hurling insults at Panda. To make things better, Panda held up the hiking boots she brought.

"Okay, Cupcake," Panda said with bitter emphasis on the word cupcake, "why did you bring these then? They are your hiking boots."

This was clearly the case as the boots he held up we're about as large as his hands and there was no earthly way Panda was squeezing those onto his paws.

"I don't know Love Muffin, I guess I thought they were yours. I should have double checked." This could not be real. Does everyone just love screwing with the Panda?

"Laura these are a size six, I wear an eleven."

"I'm sorry Pumpkin," SLif said softly as the evil Joker smile that apparently all women possess crept across her face.

"ATS Panda," I said.

"And what the hell does that mean?" Panda retorted.

"All the same. Women are all the same, they do these things to men on purpose." Michele was nodding her head vigorously in agreement.

"I hope that's not the case Laura, don't forget, we're a match, ninety-three out of a hundred."

"Coochy-coo, of course that's not the case, you are my little panda bear." Matt spit his drink across the room when he heard her say that.

Survival Note: Never ask your special lady friend to bring your gear.

I couldn't believe all the nicknames Laura had for the Panda. SLiF took her little Boo Bear into Michele's son's room where they spent the night. I imagine there was a lot of crazy panda love going on. I told her son to strip the bed, burn the sheets, steam the carpets, scrub the walls, and take a blue light to the ceiling. The next morning SLiF left to go back to the city and the second she left Panda's cheerleading shorts went straight into the trash.

We were "zeroing" for the day with Michele and her family, but we did drop Matt off at the trail where he

326

would continue along until being picked up by his uncle, then meeting us further up the trail. It was with a heavy heart that I let the lad continue on alone, I figured for sure it would be the last time I saw him since he cannot survive without my guidance. Luckily, he wasn't going far. Just two nights alone and half a day's hike to meet his mother's family.

Panda and I were slack packing and moving on without the Firestarter. We were staying in Michele's house so we would not freeze to death at night without his services. This far north this time of year it gets into the low seventies, so he thought he was essential to our survival.

The plan was for us to slack this day and another friend of mine, Jeannie, Patti's best friend, would pick us up after work. That night we would get our backpacks from Michele's since we are only talking about a twenty-mile difference. As is my luck it started to thunderstorm with four miles to go. We didn't carry any rain gear in our day bags, so we got soaked. To make things better we got caught on a ridgeline with cloud to ground lightning. It was strange not having Matt in front of me, but I found plenty of comfort in Panda's fear in Matt's absence.

We got down from the ridge line to the trailhead, soaking wet and chilled to the bone. Once you stop moving there's no staying warm when you're that wet. We were concerned because we were running a bit late, but none of that mattered when hearing from Jeannie that she wasn't there. She couldn't find us. These back roads can be confusing, and it was a bad time for us to have to wait on a ride. She finally found us after an hour of waiting in the cold. We dove into the car and blasted the car's vents, the heat warming our hands and faces.

There was another incredible home cooked meal at Jeannie's. I don't know if these women were truly good cooks or if just the idea of having a home cooked meal tricked our brains into assuming it was amazing, either way it was "PFG." To add, another nice perk for Panda and myself was being able to take steaming hot showers, separately of course, and not have to worry about running out of hot water.

The following day is when I came across the man and his flock of flamingos mentioned earlier in the story. That was an interesting sight. Panda and I had really been covering ground since we were unencumbered, we managed another twenty miles under our belts, however we would slow things down again in a few days while we waited for Matt to catch up. We slacked another day from Jeannie's, ate another great meal, and got ready to dive back in full steam ahead.

It was always a bitch putting your pack on each and every morning. It was the part of the day you dreaded the most, conversely taking off your pack at the end of the day is a close second to taking off your boots. Putting your pack on after a full restock, after several days of slack packing, was like wearing concrete shoes, it was heavy and more difficult to move in. That's what we had now. Jeannie dropped us off at the trailhead and we headed off for Connecticut.

An interesting side note, we passed the smallest train station on the trail. It's on the Metro-North line. There is a platform that is twenty feet by ten feet with a small bench. It will drop hikers off in Manhattan and bring them back to the trail. Just be sure to tell the conductor you want to get dropped off there on the way back because they are used to just blowing past it. You don't want to wake up in Wassaic, wherever the hell that is.

734 miles to go.

Chapter 43
Matt's Very Own Chapter

First let me say what an honor and privilege it is to get my very own chapter in this compendium of true stories, which are not exaggerated in the least. I'm sure all accounting up to this point has portrayed me in a fair and impartial manner, including all my heroics and contributions to our survival to this point.

It was a strange feeling leaving my father and Panda behind at the end of the day and continuing without them. They were being picked up again for another night at Michele's and I forged on alone. They spent most of the day deciding in which fashion I would meet my demise. Panda was putting his money on my falling off a cliff, if that we're going to happen it would have happened by now. Then on the other hand, my father went with a more plausible death scenario of ruination by rattlesnake bite. Needless to say, it was a tearful goodbye when we split at the trailhead.

I didn't stick around to see them get picked up. I had ground to cover and daylight was wasting. It wasn't far to the next shelter, but it was my first time hiking alone. You quickly become aware of the quiet. It fills you with an eerie feeling knowing that there is truly no one around for miles. If something were to happen, you are alone, and on your own.

I pushed those thoughts from my mind and put myself back on track. I would only be spending two nights alone before getting picked up, which was entirely manageable for a pro like myself. After putting another six miles or so behind me, I came into a shelter. I went about my normal routines, setting up my sleeping bag, getting water, cooking dinner, and so on. Again, the silence is jarring. With no one to talk to and no Panda to make fun of what do you do with your time? I didn't mind being alone, but the boredom is real. No conversation, no card games, no jokes, so Firestarter did with the Firestarter does best, started a fire.

As the last log on the fire smoldered into ash and coal, I found myself alone and at this point in the night it was unlikely any stragglers would be coming in. I decided to pitch my tent inside the shelter, deluding myself into thinking that would stop a bear or a thru hiking serial killer.

I awoke in the middle of night to relieve myself and it was another surreal experience. Heavy fog had settled in over the shelter area taking visibly visibility down to almost nothing. I'm not ashamed to say I pissed a foot in front of the shelter. There was no way I was wandering into that fog, that's how people go missing. Momma didn't raise no fool. It felt like a dead zone, there was no noise to be heard at all, it was so quiet it made it difficult to fall back asleep.

The next day was uneventful. My goal was to make it to Native Landscapes in Pawling, there my uncle would pick me up and I would spend two days with him and his family in nearby Poughkeepsie.

Native Landscapes was a cool and unique stop along the trail. It is a garden nursery, however its owner is an avid AT enthusiast and offers certain amenities to hikers passing through. There was a shower available in the back of the shop which I used before I was due to be picked up. It's just considered polite not to smell like a dumpster if you can help it. After showering I powered up my phone and I had a message waiting from my uncle. I won't get into the details but basically he could not pick me up until the morning. No big deal, the nursery had a small piece of land that they allowed people to camp on. What I didn't know at the time was that it was about three feet from the Metro-North tracks, which came speeding by every thirty minutes.

I had planned for an event just like this, where the sleeping situation would be impossible for someone like me. Dad and I had been taking Tylenol PM on occasions, like in an overcrowded shelter or real stormy nights. I had something a bit stronger. After dinner I climbed into my tent as it shook violently from the passing southbound train. I had my headlamp on and was reading my book waiting for an acceptable hour to go to sleep. Around eight o'clock I pulled out my Ambien, it was still light out but that would change in the next twenty minutes or so and I figured it was as good a time as any. I thought at least I might sleep through the rumbling of a chugging locomotive.

I slid into my sleeping bag and arranged everything the way I like it inside my tent. I had my headlamp in a hanging pocket by my head, some water in the corner, and my book to my side. Right before I was putting my phone away it started ringing. My uncle was calling, he said he was in the area after all and was coming to pick me up.

This was great news, aside from the fact that I had already taken an Ambien, the affects were starting to kick in, but it was better than sleeping three feet from an active railroad. By this point it was completely dark outside and now I had to take down my tent, pack up my bag, and wait for my uncle. The problem being, and those who have taken Ambien before can back me up here, is that when you try to fight it's affects things get weird.

It's like your body is drunk and your mind is on a mild trip. Now compound that with being in the dark and attempting to disassemble a tent and get everything to fit into your bag. My brain was firing on the proper cylinders, but my effort was sloppy at best. I got my bag ready and rather than pack up my tent, I carried it crumpled up under my arms. I walked to the parking lot and waited.

After thirty minutes my phone rang. My uncle was on the other end telling me he was waiting in the parking lot, but I was nowhere to be seen. At this point I could barely keep my eyes open. It felt like I had drunk ten beers. I assured him I was in the parking lot leaning against the only light pole there. Well it turns out my uncle looked up the wrong nursery. He was thirty minutes away in a different town.

His answer to the whole thing was, "Oh, bummer. Well I guess I can pick you up in the morning then." That was not going to work for me.

I explained to him, slurring most of my words at this point, that I had taken this pill and setting up my tent back up in the dark was no longer an option. After a good round of laughter coming from the other end of the line, he agreed to come get me. And so, I waited.

It's hard to say how much time went by but I was eventually shaken awake. I was obviously groggy and bleary eyed but after a minute I realized my uncle had found me, asleep under the parking lot light. Everything after that was a haze.

I spent the next two days relaxing at my uncle's and visiting with family. It was the usual overindulgence of food, hot showers, and sleeping in. Nice, but rather uneventful and after the past few days that was fine by me. The plan moving forward was to meet Dad and Panda, but I had two long days ahead to catch up with them. I would be spending another night in the woods alone, something I was not really enjoying.

The only issue I had was that there was no supply drop for me. Dad had our next supply drop scheduled for our first day or two into Connecticut. I had enough to make it, but I noticed I was dangerously low on toilet paper. Not out, just low. Naturally, I blew it off, my constitutionals had not exactly been daily anyway.

The great part about hiking New York was that you are always in a relatively populated place, you are never as far from civilization as you are in other states. This means you have the option to walk to a deli or order pizza to shelters, which I planned on taking advantage of.

My uncle dropped me off at the trailhead to much fanfare. My family stood there teary eyed wishing me Godspeed on my journey. I plunged back into the woods once more, though in reality this was mostly people's back yards I was walking through. Well, I'm sure it could be inferred but soon after I went back into the woods my stomach began to percolate from the excess of my family visit. This presented an awkward situation for me as this was the least private stretch of trail on the AT. With no choice but to relieve myself I stepped off the trail to do my business. Not a minute went by before a local jogger came running up the trail. There was no hiding my shame. Needless to say, I was shot a look of disgust and he picked up his pace. After that bit of unpleasantness, I was grateful for the small bits of toilet paper I had.

Now that I was feeling a bit lighter I picked up the pace again. There was a crossroad a few miles ahead that had a deli nearby, and nearby means a half mile, but at this point that distance is nothing. When I came to the crossroad there was a cache left behind by some anonymous Trail Angel. There were jugs of water laid out and several coolers filled with ice, Snicker bars, sodas, beers, and perhaps most importantly, Twinkies. I chugged an ice-cold Coke on the spot and grabbed a Twinkie and Snickers bar for later. There were a few south bounders hanging around the site eating their deli sandwiches. We exchanged the normal pleasantries and what each of us could expect for the rest of the day in our respective directions. I asked which way to the deli and one of them was kind enough to point me down the road, saying about half a mile further down.

It turns out he was a no good dirty rotten liar. Having walked a half mile and then some, I realized that I was getting further into the country rather than the town I had sought. So, I headed back to the trailhead having done the full round trip a mile or so out of my way. My southbound friends were still sitting there enjoying the beer left by the Angel. I politely thanked him for his guidance, flipped him the bird, and continued in the right direction.

I did get to the small corner deli as a light rain settled in. I ordered myself a giant turkey sandwich so I could have half now and half later at the shelter for dinner. The rest of the day was intermittent with drizzle and sun and all in all rather uneventful.

It was nice not eating tuna for lunch and knowing I didn't have to eat another freeze-dried meal for dinner. I set up all my gear at the shelter and prepared for the night. I would be meeting with Dad and Panda the following night and we would resume as our happy trio once again.

That's when this disaster struck. Turns out cokes, Snickers, Twinkies, and giant turkey sandwiches may not rest so well in one's stomach. I left the confines of my sleeping bag, grabbed my backpack and dashed into the woods. After sharing the contents of my innards with Mother Earth the realization dawned on me that I had used the last of my trail dollars earlier in the day. This put me in a bit of a tough spot.

I nervously rifled through my bag knowing that all clothing articles were definitely off limit. The only thing I managed to find was a handful of Q-tips. My suggestion to anyone who has not tried "wiping" with Q-tips is don't. I was nowhere near clean and had to resort to finding some nice clean leaves to finish the job. Leaves present another problem. They don't exactly grip, rather they smear. In the end I had to finish myself off with the wrapper from my turkey sandwich, which I then buried deep.

Night finally settled in and I with it. The next day would have me meeting with Dad and Panda once again and we'd all continued north. I'd be lying if I said I didn't miss their company, I still had more Panda jokes that needed to see the light of day. I pulled into the shelter where those two had already set up camp. Both of them were overjoyed at the sight of me, I think my father even teared up a little. I also proved I can survive in the wild by myself.

Chapter 45
Into New England

Connecticut isn't a particularly long state. It's only fifty-two miles through the state, and you can easily get through it in three days, but it marks what I considered to be the beginning of the New England portion of the AT. Being from New York we called everyone in Connecticut "Yuppies." I had filled in Panda on my feelings about these Yuppies and though you would think he'd know better by now, he told me I was exaggerating. We hit the first shelter into the state, lo and behold a Connecticut family was already there. They looked stereotypical too, the dad had boat shoes and a polo shirt on. Mom had on pleated shorts and white blouse. I looked over at Panda, he rolled his eyes and sighed audibly while nodding at me knowingly.

They had set their tent up inside the shelter, typical jerks. I know it stinks of hypocrisy, but we asked them to take it down or move it outside. The footprint of the two of our tents does not compare to the room a tent meant for a family of four takes. Especially since this was not a hiker's tent, this was a leisure tent meant to be spacious. It took up damn near two-thirds of the shelter. Why wouldn't you set it up outside?

Mom and Dad realized this wasn't really a request and disassembled the tent while the two kids ran around rambunctiously.

"Oh, these are our darling little children," Mom said, "Dalton here is four and our girl Virginia is six, aren't they precious little hikers?"

"Dalton and Virginia," I repeated mimicking Mom as though I was impressed but smirking at Panda the whole time. If those aren't Yuppie names, then I don't know what is.

The kids started pounding Panda and I with questions about hiking. But their dense little undeveloped brains couldn't muster much more than, "have you seen any frogs?" and more questions of that ilk.

Mom and Dad told the kids to sit at the picnic table and not move until they got back, they were going to collect some firewood. Mom and Dad disappeared into the woods for about fifteen minutes and didn't come back with any wood, well not firewood. This may have gone unnoticed by the children, but Panda and I definitely picked up on it. Mom was straightening out her shirt and fixing her hair while Dad's doltish smiled betrayed him. They had just got to work on yuppie kid number three, who they would probably name "Buttercup," and they had left Panda and I babysitting their kids. I wish I told them to play hide and seek and watch Mom's panic when she realized the kids were missing.

Dark began to settle in and we sat by the meager wood starved fire. At this point Mom and Dad weren't paying any attention to the kids so rather than have them annoy me, I turned the tables. "Hey kids, if you sit for a while I'll tell you some of the stories from the trail." This was just my paternal side kicking in.

"Yes sir, that would be cool," little Virginia said. Of course, these yuppies would be calling me sir. They had no idea.

"Well, Panda and I were on Bear Mountain with my son. It got dark really quickly, so we set up our campsite on the side of the mountain. My son went out for firewood and came back a short time later saying he found a cave a little way up the mountain which he wanted to explore. I told him to stay away from it, this being Bear Mountain, it could have been a bear den. When we went to bed that night, there was no moon, so it was incredibly dark. At some point during the night I heard a zipper and my son got out of his tent. I asked him where he was going, he said he had to take a piss."

"Sir, what's a piss?" Little Virginia interrupted. I looked at her parents and they just shrugged their shoulders.

"Well what do you call it? A number one, a whiz, pee, take a leak, a squirt, a tinkle, piddle, drain the vein? "

Panda chimed in, "You forgot make the bladder gladder and shake off the dew."

"I think our kids understand what a piss is now, thanks for your illustrious definition," Dad interrupted.

"Just trying to help." Some people have no appreciation for anything anymore. "Anyway, on with the story, my son got up to tinkle, does that work?"

"Fine." I think dad learned a few new terms, the wifey didn't look too pleased. Maybe next time they'll reconsider leaving their kids with strangers so they can screw in the woods. "Anyway, I fell back asleep and the next morning my son wasn't in his tent. I was very worried, I thought maybe he might have gotten lost or fell down a ravine or something and died. Panda and I started looking for him and calling his name. We got to where he had mentioned seeing a cave the day before and outside of the cave was one of his Crocs. Now I was really worried."

The looks on Mom and Dad's faces were telling, they started to realize where I was going with this, but it was too late.

"Someone had to go in and look, and you would think Panda being from the bear family would volunteer, but apparently he's a claustrophobic bear. He told me pandas spend most their time in trees. So kids, I had to go in and boy was I scared. My knees were knocking so bad I think I tinkled a bit. I got deeper into the cave and I saw the bear. It was a huge creature and its face was covered in blood. Then I saw it, a human leg being chewed on by this creature and on the end of it was my son's other Croc."

The kids' faces began to contort into looks of abject horror. They began backing away from me and whimpering as they looked at each other, then at Mom and Dad.

"Okay, I think that's enough, the kids will be up all night thanks to you." Mom was pissed, or was she tinkled?

"You don't want the kids to hear my son's cautionary tale?"

"Yeah," Panda added, "his son died so that we might live."

"Wow Panda, that's a good one, makes Matt sound Christ like, and if he was the son of God then I guess that makes me..."

"Yeah, I'm going to stop you right there," Mom guffawed. "My kids have heard enough from you for one night, we'll not add blasphemy to the list."

Like I said, yuppies. The kids were still backing away from me, looking at each other, then running over to Mom and Dad, holding onto them.

Turns out Mom wasn't wrong. The kids were up all night. They were noisy and tossed and turned incessantly. I guess this was a bit of a self-inflicted wound, perhaps in hindsight the story wasn't a good idea. They kept Panda awake all night as well, which made him one grouchy Panda the next morning. I won't say he did it on purpose but that morning as we packed up to leave camp, he was noisier than I've ever experienced him before.

Our second night in Connecticut we found ourselves hitting another shelter. Matt would be doing a big day to catch up to us, so we expected him to roll in later in the evening. The shelter was filling up quite fast so Panda and I took up as much room as possible so Matt could fit in when he showed up. All in all, seven people pulled in before dusk.

Two of the guys were doing huge days, twenty-five plus miles each day so they could try and finish before the end of August. Three more guys pulled in shortly before the final two guests, who were both cute college girls. If you had a gun to my head I would guess the three guys were following the two girls as they all seemed familiar with each other. One guy cozied up to them in the shelter, the other two, seeming to know better, tented it for the night. I didn't want to pass judgment on them, I loved hiking behind good ole' Buns of Steel.

The two girls were named "Burples" and "Toots," Burples burped a lot and Toots was a farter. I guess that's why two of the three guys chose their tents. After spending a few minutes with them it was easy to see how they got their names, they would just burp or fart then giggle to each other afterwards.

Both girls were hiking in flip flops, which is as crazy as it sounds. Panda was amazed by the sight of their feet, especially their toes. Almost a perfect shade of black.

"So girls," Panda asked, it was easy for him to break the ice and sit with them in the shelter since he was constantly sucking my gas all day, "what do y'all do?"

Burples was first to answer, "We're in college. I major in Art, we thought we'd get some fresh air before school started again." Her answer was followed by a loud burp.

"How 'bout you Farty?" I asked.

"Its Toots, that's way cuter, I major in outdoor leadership," she said followed by a long fart.

"Holy shit," Panda let out a burp. "That one was for you Burples," and he gave her a wink. "Is that even an offered course, let alone a major? Do you just lead people around outside? How do you make money?" These were serious hard-hitting questions from an inquisitive Panda. I quickly came to the opinion that life was going to hit these girls hard.

"Of course, it's an offered course, you study the wilderness, conservation, safe traveling, and things like that."

"I'll bet those seated behind you will love it too," I added. It was a good thing Matt wasn't here for this or I might have to tell the girls of his rafting trip that almost broke his back in Nantahala. The sheer mention of it would have sent shivers down his spine.

Matt finally stumbled into camp just as dark was settling in. I think he had a tear running down his cheek upon seeing me. It was one of the longest days he had done to date so he could catch up with us. Being the benevolent father I am, I prepared dinner for him while he completed his chores to settle in for the night. The sooner we got him finished the sooner I could go to bed.

The next morning we awoke to a Ridge Runner coming into camp. Most Ridge Runners are local volunteers who live nearby. These guys can get up and down these mountains quickly and can be very helpful if you get into a jam out on the trail.

"Hey now," the Ridge Runner said. He looked like the kind of guy that spent most of his time in the woods. He was wiry and had a thick beard, he practically looked like a walking ad for Columbia Outdoor Gear. "I came up here to let you all know there's a water moccasin at the next water source."

"Wow," I replied. "I didn't think they were this far north."

"Well they usually aren't, hence me being out here at seven in the morning before one of you get bit and I got to carry you out." I guess Ridge Runners aren't morning people.

Matt turned to Panda and tried to make a joke. "Well good thing he told us, pandas and water moccasins are natural enemies, we could have been in for a showdown."

The Ridge Runner didn't appear as amused as we were. "Kid, that's about the dumbest thing I've ever heard. Why would pandas and water moccasins fight? They live on different continents." He was dead serious.

"Oh yeah, my mistake," Matt said rolling his eyes as he continued stowing his gear.

"It's okay," he told Matt. "You're not trained in the wilderness like I am."

"Hey, Toots is majoring in the wilderness in school," Panda chortled while tipping his hat to Toots. For her part she also rolled her eyes and continued to pack her bag.

"Well there's more," the Ridge Runner continued, "there have been reports of hikers seeing a Northern Cougar in this area."

"I like cougars," I said. "I believe a woman is like fine wine, they get better with age, like my wife Patti." If only she could have heard me say that.

"Wrong kind of cougar," the Ridge Runner replied. "This kind gets it's jaws around your neck and crushes the life out of you, or if you're lucky she just snaps your neck."

"No, I think we're talking about the same kind," I said while throwing the Ridge Runner a wink. He didn't laugh or smile. Yuppies have no humor, he reminded me a bit of Psycho and that alone was motivation to start moving and put some distance between us.

For the rest of the short time we were in Connecticut there was nothing but storms. This wasn't a particular deviation from the standard. I did learn this time of year putting on rain gear was useless. The sweat from wearing it was just as bad as being rained on. I just tried to think of it as a free shower. Matt loves showers, it should have been no big deal for him, I guess it's a bit different when it's a cold mountain shower.

Our last night spent in the "Yacht Club" state gave us another encounter with what was beginning to become a bit of the norm. This however was the most extreme case. A group of about a half dozen twenty something year old assholes came crashing into the campsite. They also were pushing big days trying to finish before the end of summer. They came into camp late and disturbed everyone as they set themselves up. I found it a good time to attempt an overdose on Tylenol PM.

One of the kids had his water filter break on him. He called the company to send out a replacement part to Salisbury, Connecticut. They agreed to overnight the part, which at this time of day means it'll ship out the next day. Our young friend didn't understand that, and I wasn't about to correct him. He and his buddies decided to get up at six in the morning to hike into the post office for the part. It was eighteen miles. He'll figure it out eventually.

The next morning we had to settle for putting on wet clothes again. There is no feeling more demoralizing than having to put on your wet sweat-soaked shirt. The storms were bad that day which made the decision to stop for lunch at a roadside diner that much easier. I tried to get my brother who lived forty minutes away to come get us, but he couldn't make it. We settled for a cab to the White Hart Inn. The Inn was a beautiful historic place, as most of these places are on the trail, but most importantly it had a tap room too. We had a few beers, a nice dinner, and some more beers before we would catch up on some sweet, sweet, sleep. My sister Sharon would be coming to visit us for a few days so we could slack pack some more, and best of all we were entering into the Great Barrington, Massachusetts area. Four states to go.

682.9 miles to go.

Chapter 49
Red Thread is Best

We had a wonderful dinner that night in Great Barrington, a nice little place called Pearls. Panda wanted to buy dinner, as he said, "to thank you guys for everything." What an idiot, I'm not sure what we had done for him other than make him the butt of every joke, but we still bilked him for three-hundred dollars for food and drinks. Panda and my sister crashed early, not together, he was still mating with SLiF, but the boy and I stayed behind and had a few more beers before retiring for the night.

We took a "zero" day the next day and hung around town with my sister Sharon and Panda. We managed to do all our laundry and pick up another food drop from the Post Office. Panda was washing his clothes as well, which left him walking around town in a plain white t-shirt and nursing scrubs. He looked every bit the part of an escaped psychiatric patient shuffling around with Crocs on with his face unshaven and wild unkept hair. That evening Panda came to dinner smiling ear to ear, he told us unfortunately he would have to leave in the morning.

"That's funny," Matt said, "you don't look like something unfortunate has happened."

"Might this have something to do with SLiF being close by again?" I asked.

"I'm really not at liberty to say, but I will be meeting her in Manhattan tomorrow afternoon." Panda was aglow.

Matt did not take kindly to his buffer leaving, now he would be the butt of my every joke. "Dammit man, you came here to hike, not prance around the city with your special lady friend. You must make a choice, it's either us or her."

"Okay, her." It took less than a second for him to answer Matt.

"Yeah, I kinda saw that coming, but it was worth a shot."

We had a nice final evening with Panda, we laughed while telling my sister Sharon of our exploits, we ate, and we drank. All in all, it was a nice send off and we hated continuing without him, but realistically we would only have been with him another two days before he had to leave anyway. The next morning Sharon dropped us off on the side of the road where we had left off. She was gracious enough to drop Panda at the nearest train station. Matt watch longingly as they pulled away and continued until they were completely out of sight. "I'm going to miss him, or at least I'll miss making fun of him." Panda would be making his way back to SLiF while we plunged back into the woods.

We were hoping to catch up to a few other thru hikers we were familiar with and as luck would have it, we caught up to and kept pace behind Toots and Burples. They were both wearing spandex shorts, God's gift to mankind. So, we kept a nice pace behind them. That was about the only redeeming quality of the day as the rains came in once again. The trail became a mud pit and one misplaced step would sink you up to your calf in mud.

This part of the trail was nothing but a continuous puddle. It was worn in the middle from hikers, animals, and drainage, but in some of the other flatter areas water would start pooling on the trail anyway. This presented you with three options and all of them sucked. You either walked straddling the puddles, making it look like you just crapped yourself, you walk hugging the edge of the trail which was like trying to walk or balancing on a curb, or there was the last option and least appealing, though the result was ultimately the same in the end as the first two, you just say screw it and just power through. We never did that, but our boots always ended up soaked all the same, we should have learned but it's hard to convince yourself to just slosh through the water.

There are low points on the trail that stay muddy in perpetually. We came to one such place and with the pouring rain there was a torrent coming off the mountain side. It was about four feet across, twelve inches deep, and flowing quickly. Like most other places along the trail where this happens, some genius throws a log down so you don't have to slog through the water. I went first, I had to show my son that it was safe to pass, big mistake.

This log was covered in a nice matting of moss, and of course, halfway across I slipped and went headfirst into the water. I was on all fours in the stream and looked up to see my son checking me out to make sure I was okay. Once he did realize I was okay he keeled over in laughter. I had to stop and imagine that if roles were reversed I would be laughing at him. It was hard to be mad about it. I was standing there in knee deep rushing water, sopping wet and looking like an idiot. No sense having the boy fall victim to the same fate, I held his hand while he crossed to keep his balance. I am selfless in all things.

"Hey dad, that cut on your knee looks pretty bad," there was a bit of concern in his voice.

I looked at my knee. I guess due to the shock and adrenaline flowing, I didn't feel it, but once we both across Matt pointed out the pretty gnarly gash in my knee. It was split wide open, was about two inches long, and bleeding profusely.

"Ah shit. That cut is deep." I left out a soft "fuck me." Blood was running down from my knee mixing with the putrid brown mud covering my legs. I hopped over to a small boulder and took a seat. "I think I need to take a break for a few minutes and see what I can do about this."

I rifled through my backpack and grabbed the few first aid supplies we had. I cleaned the wound with some clean drinking water I had and spread some disinfectant on it. I took a clean bandana I had and wrapped it around my leg, then secured it with duct tape. Then I continued hiking with my makeshift bandage in place. Not more than twenty minutes later blood was once again running down my leg.

Survival Note: Always carry more first aid equipment than you think you need. We dumped ours at Neels Gap, another mistake.

"Hey Matt, holdup, I'm bleeding again." I took a seat on a log by the side of the trail and removed my provisional bandage for closer inspection.

"That's pretty deep Dad. How far away from the closest town?" More concern.

"Jeez, at least two days. I'll bleed to death by then. We gotta do something." Matt started digging through his bag and came out with his lighter.

"What are you planning on doing with that?" I asked him.

"Well, I'm Firestarter, I thought maybe we could cauterize the wound."

"For Christ's sake kid, you've been watching way too many movies," I lectured him, "get the sewing kit out of my bag."

Matt came back a few minutes later with the sewing kit I had taken from the Inn we stayed at a few days back. You know those gratuitous little sewing kits that they leave in the bathroom for you.

"Toss me your lighter," I told Matt. He tossed it over and I flicked it on sticking the pointed end of the needle into the flame. Backwoods sterilization. "What color thread should I use? I am partial to red myself."

"No way you're going to do what I think you're going to do. You think you're Rambo or something?"

"You know Matt, a good son would do this for me, but since you have no idea how to sew I'm not letting you anywhere near me with a needle. Sit, watch, and learn." I was going to stitch up the gash myself. This was about survival. Also, I liked Rambo, which would have been a cool trail name.

"I ain't doing it for you, that's for damn sure, but this I gotta see. I need to document for everyone how you went all Kevorkian on yourself. What do I do if you pass out while doing it?"

"I think you're more likely to pass out that I am, but tell the rest of the family that I love them, or at least the ones that count." I had already put the thread through the eyelet and sitting on that log I pinched my skin together and stuck the needle through my skin.

"Man, that looks like it hurts. Scream if you want to, it's okay Dad."

I can say this, it was extremely painful. With teeth clenched tightly I grunted out, "Will... Never... Happen."

The needle was moving through my skin like a hot knife in butter. I finished my first stitch and pulled it tight and tied it off. "Hey hero, do me a favor and cut this thread by the knot."

"How many are you putting in?" He was wincing as he watched me.

349

"Well this would go faster if I had a stapler, but since the needle and thread is all I have I guess I'll do four or five then bandage it. We should have kept that super glue, that wouldn't have hurt as much.

By the end of my third stitch two hikers had come upon us. They greeted us and one blurted out, "Holy shit! Is that guy sewing his knee?"

I looked up at the guys and said, "Neither of you happen to be a doctor by chance?" I asked this knowing full well that they were probably stock boys or dumb ass liberal arts students looking for adventure before joining the workforce. Oh wait, that's Matt.

"Fuck no man, good luck with that." Both of them were chatting about my surgical skills as they walked away.

My knee finally stopped bleeding as I pulled the last stitch tight. I'm not entirely sure if it's because I expertly stitched myself up or because there was just no blood left.

"Well, all done Matt. Bandaged up and ready to go. Let's see what happens. It looks pretty professional if you ask me." I was extremely proud of my work.

"Yeah, you have bright red thread from a sewing kit holding your kneecap on. Real good." He seems to be a very dramatic child.

"Let's go boy, we're losing daylight." I spent the next day and a half limping and walking straight legged so as not to bend my knee and disrupt my artwork as best as possible. The first night my knee was red and somewhat swollen, but it was holding together. I slathered my knee with some more Bacitracin hoping it would help prevent it from becoming gangrenous. I'd prefer it if my leg didn't need to be lopped off.

Upon entering the town of Dalton, we quickly realized there was a lack of medical personnel in this little town. We did find a pharmacy and I showed the pharmacist my artwork. He didn't seem as impressed as I was hoping he would be. He gave me a heavy bacterial ointment to apply and told me to leave it alone for a few days and see what happens. I still carry the scar to this day, a reminder of how death came for me and in a match of survival I prevailed and won.

We used the rest of the day as a "nero" so I could rest my knee and let the ointment do its work. We stayed in a fleabag motel that night and had plans to roll out early the following morning. This motel happened to attract seedy residents. We checked into our room and sitting by the door next to us was what I could only assume was a crackhead with a guitar. He was drinking, smoking, and singing all night to excess. I imagine this was what Psycho was like in his heyday. I cranked the AC up in hopes the fan would drown him out, but to no avail.

I finally asked him, "Hey man, my son and I have to get up pretty early tomorrow, any chance you could move or stop for the night?"

"Sorry Hombre," he responded, "I gotta practice. I'm a paying customer too."

"I realize that, I'm trying to be polite about this, but it's getting late and we need to sleep."

"Yeah, well I'm gonna be up for a while. I can't help it if you can hear me."

"Yes, you can, quite easily actually. You just need to stop or move down. I don't want to involve the front office." At mention of the front office he started laughing.

"I'm not too worried about it. Sweet dreams guy." He turned his back to me and kept playing as I closed the door again. Why are some people such dicks?

After another hour of his howling I decided to go to the office. As I exited my room, I realized the female night clerk was sitting, drinking, and singing, if that is what you would call it, right next to him with two other crackhead residents. Our druggy neighbor saw me look at her and started chuckling, then he tipped his hat to me as I slammed the door shut again. Earplugs did not help. God damn assholes.

Some people may call me a vindictive man, but after my many years in law enforcement, I like to think of myself as a just man, a righteous man. I didn't make a scene that night. I left it alone, for everyone's sake, but the next morning brought a new day. Perhaps I was vindictive, either way I didn't feel one bit of remorse for what I did next.

After Matt and I had packed our bags and we were ready to get back to it, all that was left to do was turn in the key. I stepped outside and it was as though the universe was offering to redeem itself to me. Leaning against the wall outside his room with the dickhead's guitar. Taking a moment to contemplate my next move, thinking that smashing it would be uncivil, I took out my knife and with a quick flick of the wrist, wham, I cut through his guitar strings.

I went into the office to drop off the keys and the girl from the night before was passed out hanging halfway across the counter, like a female version of Dudley Moore's Arthur. I set my key down right in front of her slumbering face and turned to walk out. I happened to notice she left the ring of keys for the motel sitting on the counter. As I passed by I casually palmed them so as to make little or no rattling when I moved them. When I stepped outside I chucked them deep into the bushes. That would teach them some manners.

"Come on Matt, we better get out of here before they figure out what you did and come looking for us."

"What I did? So much for being a new man, huh Planet Bob? I can't believe you used to be a cop. Was that how you handled problems on the city streets while working?"

"Far worse things have been done in the name of sweet lady justice son." The look on his face told me he believed me.

We made good time leaving town. I kept picturing a group of bloodhounds giving us chase with a posse of crack heads in tow. Guessing on the number of empties in the trash outside I should have known they weren't getting up anytime soon.

We kept inching ever closer to Vermont and leaving Dalton put us roughly twenty-five miles from that border. We were eager to get there. It meant only three states left and from what we've been told some beautiful country.

The last town we walked through in Massachusetts was North Adams. Right as you leave town to head back into the woods there is a bridge that crosses a small creek with a pavilion area just before it. It was here that once again Trail Magic took on a whole new meaning. Three previous thru hikers wanted to pay back trail magic they had received when they thru hiked two years prior. They drove over from Boston and set up a portable pizza oven alongside the trail. A shout out to Centipede, Sandman, and Mission. They had lounge chairs, soda, beer, water, candy, and twelve-inch pizzas made to order. It also didn't hurt that Centipede and Mission were eye candy. After an hour, two pizzas each and some beer, we took some candy and up the trail we headed, once again all uphill. It was not smart to drink and eat that much before a climb, a lesson

we learned time and time again, but who are we to pass that up. It would have been just downright plain rude.
Into Vermont. 592 miles to go.

Chapter 47

Vermud

Vermont, the "Green Mountain State" as it's known around the rest of the country, however on the trail it's known by hikers mostly as Vermud. It's not hard to understand why, most of the trails are wet and muddy. It seems they see their fair share of rain in Vermont. Throughout our entire time in this state the trails never dried out. There were several times when walking along the trail you would step down and the suction from the mud would pull your boots right off regardless of how tight you tied them.

As Matt and I were coming down one particularly steep mountain, we were dodging wet leaves, roots, rocks, mud, the whole shebang. Matt was leading the way and stopped dead in his tracks.

"Do you hear that?" he asked. When I stopped moving I could hear what he was talking about. It was a low muffled sound, like someone who was sobbing, but not really.

"I hear it. Bang your sticks as we 'round the corner in case it's an injured animal or something." That was the last thing we needed, to come upon an injured animal and startle it. He continued around the bend banging his sticks together. I was wondering if it was the Northern Cougar the Ridge Runner had mentioned earlier. When we got close the noise stopped and so did Matt.

"Well you were half right anyway. Looks like the injured animal but not the kind we were expecting," Matt was pointing ahead.

I walked up besides Matt to see what he was talking about. Sitting there in the middle of the muddy trail was a middle-aged woman sobbing. I was right in my mind; it was a northern cougar.

"Oh boy, this ought to be interesting, let's go see what's up," Matt concluded.

"I hope she's okay, looks like she's got a pretty nice rack though," I added.

"Is that all you think about?" Matt asked me.

"No, not really," I answered. If only he knew what I was really thinking about. The woman looked up and saw us coming and started crying even more hysterically. I guess she was embarrassed by us seeing her like this.

"Ma'am, are you okay?" I asked. "We need you to calm down and tell us what happened. Are you hurt?" Sometimes I missed police work, it just comes so natural to me.

"I can't do this," she wailed while gasping for her breath between sobs and pointing down the slick rock and mud trail that lay ahead.

"Sure you can, it's only half a mile to the bottom and my son and I will walk with you."

"I can't, I keep falling in this fucking mud," she cried while slapping her hands into the muddy trail. She was trying to get her crying under control as I stood above her coaching her into slower breathing. I had been a negotiator after all, I was skilled in talking people down.

"You'll walk between us so we can catch you if you fall. Take one of my poles and one of Matt's to keep your traction." We showed her how to straddle the trail and stay on the high ground when it was possible. We went at a snail's pace, but we got her down in one piece.

As we reach the bottom the woman began to straighten up and compose herself. A man was sitting on a rock just below us. When he heard us approach he looked up and stood, saying, "What took you so long?"

"Excuse me?" Matt replied

"Not you, I was talking to my slow poke cry baby wife. It's about time she made it down here. Did she finally stop crying?"

Planet Bob started spinning out of control. I may joke about my wife, but I would never leave her scared and alone atop a mountain, unless it was funny, then I might. I stopped right in front of the guy and it appeared this woman was more than willing to allow me to confront her husband for her.

"Are you shitting me guy? You left your wife up there by herself because she was scared of falling? You're lucky, I'd leave your ass in a second I was her."

"You are free to leave me anytime," the guy said to me with a smug attitude. I wanted to knock the guy out right there and was getting ready to.

"Dad?" Matt had not seen me this upset in a long time.

"You're absolutely right," I said reminding myself that I am Planet Bob. I'm sure he could see in my face that I wanted to choke the living shit out of him. I turned back to his wife, "Your husbands a real dick lady. You can come with us if you want and we'll get you a ride at the next road. Come on Matt, let's keep going."

"Th-thank you," the woman muttered, her eyes lowered to the ground in shame. She handed Matt and I our hiking sticks back and said, "I have to go with him. Maybe hiking isn't for me."

No shit I thought. That put me in a foul mood that did not dissipate quickly even when strolling up and over mountains. I couldn't quell the storm inside of me. Go figure. I carried my sourness into the next campsite, which came in handy considering the following event.

I had set up in a corner of the shelter per my usual routine with Matt setting up beside me. After about an hour or so a group of teenage boys came rolling in, a continuous stream of pre-pubescent juveniles. There appeared to be twenty or so fourteen-year-old urchins with seemingly no supervision. They essentially started taking over the shelter, which was not going to sleep twenty to start with. Matt and I came back from getting our water and found one kid moving all our stuff out of the shelter and onto the picnic table.

"Hey Slick, what do you think you're doing?" I was still pissed about the douche bag and his wife and ready to smack this little shit on the side of his head for moving and touching my stuff.

"Well you weren't here and we need the room," the little snot said with an air of arrogance.

"On what world do you think this is acceptable? We were gone ten minutes to fill our water bottles and you just move our stuff? We were here first and I can assure you we've traveled a lot further than you to get here."

The teen stared at me and started stammering, "I-I-I, er…"

I was perhaps a bit harsh with him and responded back in a mocking stammer, "I-I-I…don't care. How bout I break your fucking hand if you touch one more thing of ours, got that Champ?" I hate teenagers.

"Dad, even if only half of them stay in the shelter do you really want to be part of that?" Christ, I must have been off my game if Matt is the voice of reason. He was usually calm in situations like this, except for when he wasn't.

"But Matt, I was gonna let you kick his scrawny butt, it wouldn't be right if I did it."

358

"As much fun as that sounds, I'll remind you that it would likewise land me in jail, so I'm going to pass. Why don't we set up away from the shelter a bit?" It was more a suggestion than a question. I guess my son didn't want to see me dragged off a mountain in cuffs. The boy was right.

"Okay, I'll grab the rest of my stuff and we'll tent it for the night." I climbed into the shelter and collected my things and recognizing the importance of staying hydrated I started drinking water from my newly filled bottle and wouldn't you know it, I fumbled the bottle and dropped the whole thing on the shelter floor. Accidentally.

A few of the teens began to howl with displeasure. One of them spoke up, "Hey man, you got the floor wet, how are we supposed to put our sleeping bags there?" It was the same little peckerhead as before.

"A thousand apologies Spike, I can be really clumsy sometimes. You guys are smart though, you'll figure it out." I'd be lying if I said I didn't feel good being a prick in that moment.

We set up our tent about fifty yards away from the shelter which was about as far as we could be without being in the woods. Two other hikers we were familiar with came strolling in and headed for the shelter.

Knowing what awaited them Matt gave them a shout, "You guys may want to think about tenting for the night. The shelter looks like a middle school sausage party right now."

The two looked up and saw what Matt was talking about. After a quick chuckle they threw their bags down a few yards from ours. "Good looking out man. I remember middle school and I ain't trying to do that again."

Naturally no good deed goes unpunished. The other two hikers never hung their food bags, so Matt and I figured we would die in the middle of the night by a bear looking for dessert. I am sweet after all.

We could hear those stupid kids all night. To the best of my knowledge no adult supervision ever came in. To make matters worse it rained all night. When we awoke the next morning there were no attempts at being quiet, we gathered our soaked gear, put on wet clothes once again, and trudged out into the heavy fog.

We climbed down out of the clouds and the fog dissipated a bit. We continued along like always, eyes down and breathing heavy, but my knee was on fire. I called to Matt to stop so we could examine it more closely, and much to my dismay there was white pus oozing from the stitched wound. It was painful and I figured that was as good a sign as any to get it looked at by a real doctor.

"I don't know dad that looks pretty bad, they definitely are going to take the leg. Lucky for you prosthetic devices have come a long way."

"You're hilarious. I just don't know what I'm looking at, is this good pus or bad pus?"

"I think all pus is bad pus."

"Thanks for the medical input Doogie. We'll see about hitching a ride at the next road. We're close to Bennington and I can at least get this checked out." We scrounged up a ride with some loop-trail hikers who were packing up their car as we came to the trailhead parking lot. They agreed to drop us off at a hospital, Vermonters seemed to be swell people.

The staff that fixed me up at the Medical Center sat closely like children during story time listening to me regale them with my harrowing tale of survival. Matt wasn't in the room so I may have embellished on the facts a bit. They were quite amazed how I managed to stitch myself up and console my simple wailing child at the same time. They gave me a shot of antibiotics, cleaned it, and bandaged it back up professionally. Matts working theory was that the red dye in the stitches was slowly poisoning me. Like I said before, a simple child at best. We cleaned ourselves up and found a ride back out to the trail.

Days later we were headed over Stratton Mountain, which was a steady four mile climb up and over. It was also a popular ski resort in the winter. Two trail-keepers live in a small hut at the top of the mountain in a completely primitive manner. They forego all the real comforts of home. It's a volunteer job so if selected you are there all summer. They also need to hike down once a week for supplies and then right back up. I talked with Patti about signing up, but she didn't seem too keen on the idea.

It was on the far side of Stratton we had another extraordinary encounter. The trail was descending at a steady clip but at a low flat angle. Matt and I were moving at a fairly quick pace and were deep in a pine barren. Suddenly we heard a loud crashing in the woods to the left of us. Our natural reaction was to stop, bang our sticks together, and yell, "get out of here, go on, get." We were both thinking bear. We were both wrong. The crashing grew louder and closer, it was accompanied by a sound that resembled a bullfrog mixed with a cow mooing. The massive antlers, spread at least five feet across, appeared first, followed by the rest of the bull moose. This thing stood at least a foot taller than me and I'm six-foot. It started toward us and stopped about fifteen feet away. Matt and I kept going, slowly, keeping our eye on this monster the whole time.

"Matt, be ready to jump behind a tree if this thing charges."

"Shit, I'm hiding behind you if this thing comes at us." What a brave lad. The moose matched our pace and shadowed us for less than a minute, which seemed like an hour to us. He broke off his stride and bounded off into the woods again.

In truth, the moose is the most dangerous animal you are likely to encounter on the trail. They don't scare as easily as the bears do and can be just as deadly. I learned much later from a Maine resident that you shouldn't clack your sticks together; it sounds like a mating challenge where moose charge each other for dominance. Lucky for us, no clacking sticks, the boy may not have been a virgin after that encounter.

We took an uneventful "zero" day soon after at Manchester Center. We took in a film at the local cinema and dined at the illustrious Sirloin Saloon. Before we left that fine city we stopped for some pizza, seeing us in our full hiking gear the guys behind the counter gave us a free pizza that someone had never picked up. It wasn't warm but it was "PFG." We ate a few slices on the spot, because you never pass up the chance for calories like that when you can get them, but they were also kind enough to wrap the remaining slices for us so we could have pizza for dinner at our next shelter. The Mountain House meals were good, but any chance to break the cycle of freeze-dried food is welcome.

The humdrum of day to day hiking continued revealing Vermont to be a beautiful yet muddy state. We continue to run across the same handful of thru hikers every few days. There was a group of us each a day or two apart and now and then we overlapped. Most of them were planning to do big pushes in the next few days, but Matt and I were satisfied with our speed for now.

We were approaching the shelter where we would bunk down for the evening. About a quarter of a mile before you hit the shelter is a trailhead with a gravel parking lot for day hikers and loopers. A woman day-hiker had backed her truck up to the trail and was changing behind it. Our timing could not have been more perfect, she was completely naked except for her shoes. I believe it goes without saying she was absolutely mortified when she finally realized we were hiking past. She was sleek, fit, and in excellent shape. I didn't want to embarrass her any further so as I walked by, I complemented her, "nice shoes," and I kept on walking. Matt was chuckling and in awe that he saw a naked woman.

We hit Clarendon Shelter and had ourselves another action-packed evening. The shelter itself was nice enough, clean, and there was a caretaker of sorts. Two other hikers came in and we thought they might be gay, not that there's anything wrong with that, but it pertains to what happened next. I am withholding the trail names as to protect their identities.

We were settled in for the evening when two more hikers came in, an Asian guy and another gentleman. They said their trail names were M&M and Kamikaze. I'll let you figure out which was which. As soon as they dropped their bags, they started drinking whiskey heavily, and that's when the caretaker rolled in on his ATV.

He saw them sitting there getting drunk and intervened, "Hey guys, I can't stop you from drinking, but at least have the decency to do it outside the shelter. It isn't hard to read the room here and see you are disturbing the other guests." He was much more diplomatic about it then I would have been, but I hadn't reached my breaking point yet. I was glad for him speaking up all the same.

M&M and Kamikaze picked up their stuff and moved off into the woods so they could keep drinking without, as M&M put it, "shitting on everyone's parade." After they moved out Matt and I were shooting the shit with the caretaker. He, without any care for the volume of his voice, told us "something ain't right with them boys" as he watched them march into the woods together. I took his meaning, Matt just looked puzzled until the caretaker began using a whole slew of less than colorful verbiage to describe their assumed orientation. The two other hikers, names withheld, were visibly upset with his choice of words, all but confirming Matt and my previous assumption, not that it matters.

This shelter's design was one of Matt's favorites, rather than a flat raised platform that everyone slept on this had bunks built into it. It was the illusion of privacy, but it was nice. A few more hikers had come in and most bunks were full.

We were all awakened in middle of the night as the silence of the darkness was shattered. "Help me! Help me!" It was Kamikaze stumble running into the shelter.

We were all completely startled, but I instinctively began assessing the situation. Was he attacked and hurt, was there a wild animal about, where was the friend, was he okay? Thoughts raced through my mind.

"Okay, slow down there Tojo. What's wrong?" I inquired, ever the cop.

"He tried to make me suck his dick! He crazy! You help me!" He was frantic and given the alcohol they were drinking it was an all too plausible situation.

Matt sat up still half asleep, "Well that's a new one on me." I could see the two names withheld, intrigued and amused.

"What the hell do you mean? M&M wants you to blow him?" It wasn't my most sensitive line of questioning, I was rusty.

"That's right. That's right," he repeated himself. "He grab my penis and say I should suck his."

"Holy crap," Matt said wide awake now. "So, did you? I mean no one would blame you for getting lonely on the trail." I didn't know if Matt was being serious or not.

"Are you for real?" Kamikaze was shaking while listening to Matt's stupid reply. "You must protect me, he might come in here after me."

He wasn't coming in this shelter, either way you chose to read the word. "You can stay in here for the night and we'll go have a talk with him in the morning when everyone is sober. Okay?"

"And you protect me?"

"Sure, why not?" I answered, that was unless it put me or my son in danger.

"What if he breaks my things?" He kept on.

"Again, tomorrow, not now. If he's drunk it'll just escalate the situation and cause more problems. Let's just hope he sleeps it off."

"And besides," Matt insensitively interjected, "if we go over there now, he might want all of us to blow him." I did laugh a bit, it was kind of funny, real or imagined, but it would all wait until the light of day.

The next morning Kamikaze was anxious to get his stuff but needed his protectors. We've been called a lot of things on this journey but never that one.

"Let us clean up our stuff and we'll walk you over to your campsite," I told him. A few minutes later Matt and I walked over with him. All his stuff was still lying on the ground, untouched, and it also appeared M&M was long gone. It was odd because he would have had to come through our camp but instead it appeared he went down stream a bit and crossed there to pick up the trail further down. It doesn't speak well of his innocence.

The caretaker ended up taking a rattled Kamikaze back into town on his ATV, where he said he'd be getting back on a train to New York where his family was. He said he needed to get back to Chinatown where it was safer. Apparently, Chinatown is safer than the woods of Vermont, who knew?

Survival Note: If you're hiking and another guy asks you for a blowjob, get the hell out of there unless you're into that stuff.

505.7 miles to go.

Chapter 48
Bob: Backpack Bandit?

Matt and I left the campsite shaking our heads in disbelief. As we were crossing the stream Matt looked up at me contemplatively, "That was some pretty weird stuff, huh Dad? I mean forget the fact that it was two guys, but Christ who would do that after a day of hiking?"

I couldn't believe he put that much thought into it. "Agreed, we've seen a few screwed-up things out here, but I do believe that takes the cake."

"So far," Matt finished for me.

"Who knows what really went down, you saw how much they were drinking and how fast they drank it. Hell, if we had run into them in town, we probably would have drunk with them. Though seeing M&M's campsite does make me tend to believe Kamikaze's story. Maybe I should start carrying my weapon again." I did carry my mini Glock for a while when we first started hiking but deemed it unnecessary as it was just added weight I had to lug around, and the boy would have shot himself if I had let him carry it. I gave it to Patti to take home with her after the deep tissue massages in Tennessee. I certainly never thought people would get more dangerous the further north we went.

The following day Matt and I were casually strolling along the trail, enjoying a beautiful Vermont summer day, one noticeably and wonderfully devoid of rain. The mud was beginning to dry up, and by that, I mean simply that it no longer sucked the boots right off your feet, but rather just became an oil slick-esque obstacle smattered about the trail. Still, it was an example of the small victories we had no control over.

We came across a small clearing with an outcrop of boulders, sitting there on the rocks, soaking in the sun and eating lunch was another thru hiker we've crossed paths with a dozen times or so, Weatherman. He had the right idea, Matt and I threw our bags down and dug out our plastic spoons and pouched tuna.

"Hey guys," Weatherman greeted us, "just an FYI, there's been reports of a homeless guy stealing backpacks along this section of the trail."

"What next?" Matt chuckled.

"Well just so you know," I too was chuckling, "there is a guy around here asking people to blow him, so you may me want to be on the lookout for that."

Weatherman was good natured but not exactly sure how to respond to that one. I've often been told I can leave people speechless. He just looked at me quizzically and shrugged replying simply with an "Okay, thanks I guess." He finished up eating and got up having absorbed all the sun he could, gave us a polite nod and said, "see you boys up the trail." We bid him farewell and he left.

Several miles up the trail near the shelter there was a trailhead that led down to the designated water source for that shelter. Sure as shit who do you think we run into? We found the homeless guy going through two bags that were left at the trailside while the owners we're fetching water.

"Are you kidding me?" I muttered, but loud enough for Matt to hear me.

"I should be shocked, but at this point I'm not," Matt responded. "Why do we keep running into these things?"

"Hey asshole, get away from the bags, they're not yours." Once again cop mode was activated.

"These are mine," the protest came immediately.

"Do you normally hike with two bags? That's an awful lot of weight," Matt grilled him. What a detective the boy would have made with his astute powers of observation.

"Fine," the homeless guy dropped everything on the ground in front of him and stormed off into the woods.

I walked over to the bags left on the ground, "Hey Matt come help me pick this stuff..." I was cut off before I could finish.

"Hey, put that bag down," a voice shouted from a few yards down the trail. There were two girls coming up the path with full water bottles in hand. "Weatherman warned us earlier about you."

"Do I look like a homeless man to you?" I asked them.

"Yeah Dad, you kinda do." Matt was laughing. I could always count on my son.

"Give us our bags now," the other girl demanded. I dropped everything I was attempting to clean up and let it all fall to the ground.

"For your information," I feigned as much politeness as I could, "we caught a guy going through your stuff, we confronted him, and scared him off. You're welcome. It was a pretty dumb thing leaving your bags here unattended, especially since you say Weatherman warned you."

"Sure, whatever. You two better watch yourselves."

I was being threatened by two twenty-something year old girls, which was quite enough for me. There was no sense in continuing a dialogue with these two malcontents, so we left them behind. They wisely grabbed their packs and brought them down to the water source. Matt and I would later come back after we had set up our campsite for the night and these two were gone.

When we arrived at camp Weatherman was already there along with a husband and wife duo. We filled him in on what had happened, and everyone got a nice laugh out of it.

"Bad timing fellas," Weatherman said, "I don't see how anyone could confuse two upstanding citizens such as yourselves of any wrongdoing."

As if on cue, the two girls came bopping into camp. They saw us and proclaimed to everyone else in camp, "Better watch out for these two, they are bag thieves," the taller of the two let out. Weatherman explained to them what happened and that we were not, in fact, the backpack thieves.

"Oh well, okay then." That was the only answer we got, there was no apology forthcoming. Stuck up college coeds. Our reputations would go untarnished. The homeless man we saw going through their bags walked up into the camping area. I pointed him out to the others and Weatherman agreed he fit the description. He began to walk the outer boundaries, which I noticed is what most of the nut jobs seemed to do, circle their prey. After a minute he made his way toward the shelter.

The look on his face told me this wasn't just a de-escalation situation, it may be a use of force situation. I stepped out in front of him before he could get right up to the shelter and addressed him, "What's up man? I think you had better take off, we went through this before."

He couldn't pretend to be a hiker, which probably had worked for him in the past, after all we were all kind of dirty and smelly, but Matt and I had caught him red handed. He stopped for a second and looked around.

He locked eyes with the other hiker's wife, "Well you sure are pretty," he told her. There was a wild look in his eyes and a belligerence in his voice. My guess is he was on some type of uppers.

"And you need to go, now, and don't come back to this shelter or we will seriously have a problem." I could have not been firmer in my resolve.

"I'll go when I'm ready. Those two are pretty also," he was gesturing toward the two coeds that besmirched my good name. I wanted to tell him to take them, they were a bunch of ingrates anyway, but damn my kind heart.

"No, you'll go now, or we will have a problem here. Matt walk him to the trail and see him on his way. If you come back here today you will have a problem for sure, and far worse than you may have experienced in the past."

He spit on the ground at my feet, Matt walked over and took him by the arm, which of course he shrugged off. Matt walked a bit with him and watched him walk down the trail and well out of sight. We all wondered, some of us out loud, if we would see him again that night. I was by no means itching for a fight, so I was glad when he didn't return.

I turned back to the two girls and said, "You're welcome. Again!" I had some arrogance in my voice which conveyed exactly how I felt about them. "You two might want to hike with Weatherman while that guy's around. I would invite you to tag along with us, but we might go through your packs." There were looks of disdain from the girls, it was expected.

Two nut job encounters in two days. Vermont is a big crazier than I thought it would be. Maybe it's the elevation and lack of oxygen.

The rest of the night was uneventful, our frenzied friend never returned. We awoke happy to have survived another night. We were due to meet Patti again the next day, so we had some unusual pep in our step. We got to Cooper Shelter about lunchtime and decided we'd wait to eat. From Cooper there was a side trail down to the gondola on Killington, another popular ski resort in Vermont. The gondola would take you down to the lodge and that's where we would meet Patti. The trail guide listed it as a steep two-tenths of a mile, what a crock that was. It was practically an expert level rock climb. We should have had ropes and clamps and carabiners. Maybe it was the thought of a hot shower, a hot meal, or maybe it was the thought of seeing my beautiful wife, but we were determined to get down to that lodge. At one point we had to take our packs off and lower them down due to how sheer the rocks were.

It was worth it though. We got to the lodge and were rewarded at the restaurant with cold beer and hot bar food. We sat at a nice table looking over the valley below us. Once we heard from Patti that she had arrived we rode the gondola down to the base of the mountain to meet her. Another Febreze bath and we hopped into her van and we were off to the motel so Matt could drain the state of Vermont of every drop of hot water. We got a suite, so Matt was on a pull-out couch, which was worlds better than any shelter and so it was hard for him to complain, he still did though, gotta admire his perseverance.

Dinner that night was nice, but it was after dinner that was even better. There were fireworks in the bedroom that night. She was my Kamikaze, I her M&M.

We had planned on slack packing the next day but as Patti was taking us to the trail, she realized she didn't have enough gas, so we had to turn around to find a gas station so she would not be left on a roadside alone. By the time we got back to a gas station, filled up, and we were ready to head back out it was already pushing eleven, so we decided our time would be better spent by the pool, and as there were no protests from Matthew, that's exactly what we did.

448 miles to go.

Chapter 49
New Hampshire, Live Free or Die, But Mostly Die

As we moved into New Hampshire our interactions with other hikers became even fewer and fewer. The hardcore hikers have already made their push for Maine, having likely tackled Katahdin and made their way home by now. We however remained. Normalcy was becoming the norm now and for a brief period our days were devoid of the extraordinary and abnormal. We walked with the sun shining on our faces, the boy was singing along with the birds, and his step was spry. It was exactly how I pictured it in the beginning. As it is in life, all good things must come to an end. We caught up to M&M.

We first caught sight of him about half a mile before we got into Hanover. We kept our distance to preserve the boy's virginity and manhood. It's tempting to think that it's no big deal, but there are two of us and one of him, but M&M was a strange duck, he was hiking in his underwear, and only his underwear, not so whitey tighties. Hiking into Hanover takes you partially through a residential neighborhood. Walking along one of these residential streets was a young mother pushing a stroller and looking at him in complete horror. M&M marched right on past her, it's a small wonder hikers can get a bad rap in some places. We got to the main road which takes you into the outskirts of town, and over the Connecticut River into Hanover. It's a busy street, and where we finally caught up to M&M. I wish I could say we didn't, but I couldn't help myself, I stopped and we had some words with him.

"Look man, put on some pants, will you," I told him.

"I was going to, I'm in no rush," he replied brusquely. Just great, he has an attitude.

"Come on dude, you walked right past a young housewife, this makes us all look bad. Use your head for God's sake, we're not in the middle of the woods right now." I admittedly didn't like him due to the incident with Kamikaze days prior. "Don't come into town behind us, I don't want people thinking we're together. You're a mess man. Come on Matt let's keep moving."

We began to walk away, but I could see the wheels turning in my son's head. He was going to do it, he was going to say something. I could just tell. Call it a father's intuition. We got no more than twenty yards ahead of M&M and my brilliant son spun around and shouted, "Hey did you really try to get Kamikaze to suck you off?"

I grabbed a strap hanging from Matt's bag and yanked him along, but if I had doubts before, they were gone now. The look of shock and shame on his face said it all. He disappeared down a side street, out of our view, and we never saw him again. Some say you can still catch sight of him in his underwear roaming the streets, but I don't put too much stock into those tales.

We marched over the bridge on the Connecticut River and right into the Dartmouth College area. My son came alive, he could smell the liberalism in the air, socialism abounded. Not so much for me, I doubled my pace before I became a Bernie supporter.

We were making good time for once and decided upon a more leisurely pace to enjoy our surroundings. We weren't quite getting that homestretch feeling just yet, but we knew that the White Mountains were coming up fast and we'd be putting another milestone behind us. Part of hiking through the Whites is that you get to hike from Hut to Hut, this meant making reservations, another reason for a more relaxed pace. Arriving there ahead of schedule would do us no good, besides we had some special guests joining us for that section and we had to wait for them.

We stopped for a night at Smart Mountain and decided to sleep up in the old Fire Wardens Tower. The views were spectacular, especially at dusk. We settled in and we bedded down for the night. We were alone for the night and we found that to be a stroke of luck as we stretched out as much as two people in sleeping bags can in a small lookout tower. Looking back perhaps it wasn't luck, perhaps other people just knew better. Still the night was wonderous, until the winds picked up.

The fire tower was a forty-one-foot-tall steel structure and although it had a wide base it was narrow enough at the top to sway in the wind. I pictured it from the outside looking like a metronome keeping time. I know it was keeping me awake and making me more nervous by the minute. This damn thing has stood for fifty plus years and this night would be the night it topples over. Not on my watch.

"Yo, Matt, you awake?"

"Yeah Dad, I'm up. It's kinda hard to sleep. I feel like I'm sleeping on one of those bouncy horse spring riders."

"Like the ones at a kid's playground?" I could picture what he was talking about and he wasn't far off.

"Yeah, that's it."

"Okay, well this stupid tower is swaying back and forth a couple of feet and I don't feel like dying up here so let's get the hell out of here." We probably would have been safer staying put rather than climbing down to the Rangers Cabin below in the middle of the night, but we popped open the hatch and began our extremely careful climb down.

The wind was whipping around us and this far north it was starting to carry with it some colder air that we had not grown accustomed to. The tower at forty-one feet tall had steep stairs set up as switchbacks. With all the crap we had in our arms it was impossible to look down at our next step, so we were moving carefully, sort of feeling our way down with our feet. A precarious few minutes later we were back on solid ground. We were nearly three-thousand feet above sea level, so the wind was still blasting us. We threw all our stuff down in the empty cabin, crawled into our bags, and tried to sleep again.

Survival Note: Always sleep at ground level.

The next morning brought us an icy fog, what I called cloud hiking. We'd go down out of the clouds into a dell, then up into another cloud, and so on and so forth until we hit the next shelter. There were two other hikers there, both nature lovers who told us about their time in the wilderness of Alaska and how we should hike there.

"No thanks," Matt said.

"No, no, you don't understand. It's beautiful out there, it's the last pristine wilderness, you have to go," said the unnamed hippie.

"Yeah, I'm sure it's gorgeous, but I've seen the pictures, and out there I'm a whole lot higher on the food chain than I'm comfortable with. Look at me, I look delicious." The other two we met looked Matt up and down and I guess they decided he did look delicious. He would be eaten because they dropped it completely. They turned back to their game of cribbage that they had been playing. Figures. Meanwhile Matt and I played out the world's longest running game of Rummy. I'm up 154,567 to 154,222.

Behind us was a group of preteens and counselors who emerged from the clouds looking miserable. This time luck was on our side and they leaders would not let them in the shelter, a shining example of leadership if you ask me.

The next day we rose a bit more chipper, we were headed to the Happy Hiker Hostel which meant showers and clean clothes. On our way we had our second moose encounter, only this time it was a cow. The conditions from which we saw our first moose were nearly identical, we were in a pine barren, only this time there were not massive antlers and it was standing smack dab in the middle of the trail. Even without antlers these things are huge. I was startled because Matt stopped dead in his tracks, and I walked right into the back of him. As I've said before, we are so busy looking down for roots and rocks that you may not see what's right in front of you. Matt managed to get within thirty feet of it before they noticed each other.

The cow spun in its tracks and faced us. Matt and I slid to the side of the trail and the cow made as though she was going to come at us. My life flashed in front of my eyes. Was I a grandad yet? No. Was Patti taking an oatmeal bath with the neighbor? Don't know, still don't. Was Matthew really my son? Jury's out.

I was brought back to reality when I heard, "That's a big one Dad, huh? What's the plan here?" Matt asked.

"I don't think the Bambi story is going to work here. Don't think this one will care. There's not much cover here but start moving toward a tree to get behind, same routine as always. You handled the little baby man eating dear, I'll take care of this big bitch." I moved toward the middle of the trail and held my poles over my head to make myself look bigger, that's what they say to do anyway. I swear if a moose could laugh, this one would have fell over laughing at me. In a calm but firm voice I started speaking to it, "Look, I know it's not right Rocky got top billing and the cartoons made you look stupid, sound stupid, and act stupid. You were my favorite though, not counting Natasha of course, she was just really hot."

I was ready to dive off the trail if this moose took another step. Matt was hiding behind a tree watching it in awe of his father's bravery. The moose snorted and slipped back into the woods. I once again saved us from the brink of death. I've lost count of how many times this has happened. We do have to learn to keep a camera handy.

We got into the Happy Hiker Hostel, it was a bit of a dive, but we were used to that. The shower was outside, but that wouldn't stop Matt. He went straight for it. We decided since we were ahead of our schedule we'd stop for a "zero" day. Our "zero" was a lazy one and we didn't leave the Happy Hiker, there were NOBO's and SOBO's (north bounders and south bounders) in and out all day. Our focus was speaking with this SOBO's and getting a scouting report on the terrain ahead. The Whites were coming up on us fast and it's one of the most exciting parts of the AT.

The Happy Hiker also brought us back to another acquaintance we met earlier on the trail. Bear Claw, whom we had met back in Tennessee, who was also temporarily running the Happy Hiker while its owner was away. We had helped her paint the giant bear claw on the hood of her car and it was nice to see our handiwork again. It was also nice to learn in these warm days that her trail name was derived from a bear claw tattooed expertly placed on her cleavage.

That night we got a ride into the town of Warren from Phatt Jack, a local who gives Happy Hiker residents a ride when needed. We had been sitting around all day and when you have the option of something besides trail food, you take it. He was going to drop us off to get some wedges, hoagies, grinders, subs, po' boys, whatever this part of the country calls them. As we were driving through town, I noticed a peculiar site and one we had to question Phatt Jack on. There was a rocket, a ballistic missile, again, whatever they call it in this part of the country, standing tall in the middle of town. To say it looks out of place would be an understatement. "Okay Jack, what's up with the rocket," I asked.

"Well, if I recall correctly, I don't do much of that these days anyway, that old thing was put up in the late seventies. Some old army guy brought it up from down south and donated it to the town. Caught us a bit by surprise I guess, but these days it's just an odd claim to fame. At least they had the courtesy to remove the nuclear warhead before dumping it on us. They say it's aimed at the New York Giants stadium."

We had our sandwiches and hung out by the rocket until Phatt Jack was ready to take us back.

402.5 miles to go.

Chapter 50
Above Tree line

We had to be up early the next morning for Moosilauke, our first real climb above the tree line. Moosilauke is technically above the tree line, but it's deceiving. It's not due to its height but rather its latitude. This far north the trees start thinning out at lower elevations. The weather also has its effect making it difficult for trees to mature.

The Guide Book claims Moosilauke is the second hardest climb for north bounders, as well as good training for the Presidential Range. We tackled it without much difficulty If you don't count being sweaty, dehydrated, and out of breath as difficult. It was worth it though; we had the summit to ourselves, and for once we were afforded the views we had dreamed about. It was spectacular. Like we were on top of the world. We could see nothing but majestic mountains in all directions. I'm not going to say it was worth walking eighteen hundred miles to get here, but it was pretty damn good.

We decided to take a prolonged breather at the top and were hanging out in some ruins remaining from an old summit lodge that burned down in the early forties. We laid out our black garbage bags that we used to prevent us from getting covered in dirt and laid back on them and enjoyed the sun. The silence was deafening as they say. The sun felt warm against my face and the cool breeze brought up the scent of the pines from below. I could have laid there forever. However, the silence fell when a massive Pyrenees Mountain dog came trotting into the "Fortress of Solitude" with its owner in tow.

The dog ran up to Matt. "Hey boy, where did you come from?"

"Not another abandoned dog," I said.

"No, he's mine," a male voice said.

I got up and saw a man a little older than I am coming toward us. "How did you get up here?"

"There's a short trail, about two miles to the east," he responded. "How did you get up here?"

"We walked about two-thousand miles. You're smarter than us," I said.

"Ah, thru hikers. Congrats for getting this far. Come on boy," he called to the dog, "let's head home."

We were still running a bit ahead of schedule, I made another one of my executive decisions. "Hey Matt, let's hit the next shelter and call it quits for the day. That should give us a nice relaxing afternoon, plus since the next shelter it is only two miles past that one I bet most people go to the one further on."

"Shit, you don't gotta tell me that twice." An astute response, as always.

"Great, let's do it, it's been a while since I've given you a good beating in Rummy. I'm not going to merely beat you, I'm going to destroy you, I'm gonna make you wish you were dead, not even born."

"Okay Dad. Jesus. I get it. You like winning. Chill." I can get carried away sometimes.

As it has been since day one on this track of dirt, we were not the only two in the shelter. We spent a portion of the afternoon alone, but then the Cribbage Playing Kids came crawling in and went back into their game hardly noticing us at all.

They were followed shortly by another group of camp kids. There were eight this time and two councilors who were nothing but slightly bigger kids pretending to be in charge. They all had a million questions about life on the trail and all attempted to cram into the shelter. Just wonderful.

These kids were different however, they were all from broken homes but also prodigies of different sorts. One kid could solve a Rubik's Cube in fourteen seconds, he could do it in forty seconds with one hand. One girl was a thirteen-year old tennis whiz. One was a talented magician and another a math genius. One kid seemed to be a prodigy in the art of sarcasm, I liked him the best.

The questions and conversations continued. I found these kids to be much better behaved and better company than all the other groups we ran into. They were fascinated by us and really who could blame them. It was like they had never had a conversation with an adult before, if Matt and I could be considered adults.

The funniest part was half of them had never done a crossword puzzle before. They watched for a while over my shoulder while I was doing these word puzzles, until they started annoying me so much, I ripped out a few pages and handed them out. The little bastards finished them before I did.

In preparation for another night spent with the kids, Matt and I overdosed on Tylenol PM and slept. When we woke the next morning it was clear we made the right choice in drugging ourselves. It looked like that Tasmanian Devil had whirled it's way through the camp site spewing backpacks, water bottles, and food bags in its wake. We snuck out quietly to tackle the rest of Moosilauke and put some distance between us and the little savants.

The descent was tough, the toughest to date. The book wasn't kidding. The trail ran down along what is best described as a waterfall. Waterfalls mean wet rocks, and wet rocks means Bob on his ass, which is never a good thing for Bob.

As we stood at the top scouting our way down this glistening precipice I said, "Matt, I'll go down first. We both know I have the predilection for falling on wet surfaces. At least this way I won't take you out with me. I still am a benevolent man after all."

"Fine by me," he replied without thought. "Looks like a ball breaking climb down and I don't want to be crushed to death by my father." We started down slowly and cautiously, everything was slick roots and rocks. I saw my death with every step I took.

There are parts of the trail where steps have been installed into steep climbs to make things a bit easier. The problem is they are never stairs like a person would have at home, that would be too easy, instead each step is two feet apart requiring an awkward step or a painful hop down. This can be even harder on the knees than the trail normally is. To make matters worse the stairs were wet and just as polished as the previous rocks were.

People have accused me, from time to time, of exaggerating. It should be overwhelming abundant at this point in the story that nothing could be further from the truth, so I should be believed when I say this was less of a downhill then it was a cliff. After a few minutes of this wet ladder we were back to sliding on our asses down the glazed rock grabbing onto roots along the way to prevent us from falling to our death. At one point there were rebar handles drilled into the rock, only they were too far apart for normal people, so essentially, we were sliding from one handle to the next. It took me ten minutes to go fifty feet. I can't imagine what a nightmare it would have been had they been hikers coming the other direction. Finally, when I reached the bottom, I was beaming with pride and a sense of accomplishment, until I saw Matt standing there smiling.

"Hey Dad, there's a small trail just to the side of all this, there are plenty of trees to brace yourself against. I did that instead, and from the looks of things it was much easier, but you sure did look cool sliding on your ass the whole way down. You looked like an extra in the movie "Titanic" sliding down the deck as the boat sank. Thanks for that." Matt was wiping some tears from his eyes from laughing and mocking me.

Embarrassment crossed my face, "Well at least I have stayed true to the trail unlike you," I said it as if I thought I could convince myself that it mattered to him.

"Whatever you say DiCaprio." My sons ridicule did not keep me down for long. I looked back up from the bottom and was overcome with a sense of accomplishment. The trail still continues to amaze me even after all this time.

We hit Eliza Brook Shelter early so we could relax after a hard day. The Cribbage Kids came in an hour or two later and told us there was a group of twenty or so kids headed this way. We grabbed a tent pad about one-hundred yards from the shelter and pitched our tents, praying that for at least one night it wouldn't rain on us. The Cribbage Kids followed our lead and grabbed another tenting pad nearby. We were pleased with our decision when the horde closed in on us, they took over the shelter and we were far enough from them to make for a rather pleasant evening.

Then came nightfall. For two people claiming to have hiked in the Alaskan wilderness, the two Cribbage Kids were a couple of real assholes. In the middle of the night I woke to the sound of crunching metal.

"Matt, psst, hey Matt," I whispered.

"Ugh, what. I'm sleeping."

"Do you hear that? Are you making that noise? It sounds like metal crunching." At the same time I could hear the Cribbage Clan talking among themselves.

"No, it's not me," he responded. "At this point I don't care what it is, I'm too tired. I'm just gonna either lay here and die or wait on you to save me."

"I'm tired of saving you." I unzipped my tent and peeked outside. Initially I was shocked at what I saw, but then having learned what happened it was less shocking. There was a sizable black bear chomping on the pot the Cribbage Crew had been using. As I said before, total assholes. The male Cribbage got out of his tent and began shouting and flailing his arms, because he had no pot to bang on. The bear was frightened away but took off with the pot still in its mouth. Someday an advanced civilization will find that pot out in the fossil layer and wonder how it got there.

The next morning Matt and I were cleaning up our site and I couldn't help myself. "How the hell did that bear get your pot?" I asked the Cribbage Kids. "Didn't you guys hang your bags?"

"No man, we stopped hanging out bags about a thousand miles ago. Nothing ever happened so we figured there was no need."

"Until now," Matt stated as a matter of fact.

"Right, well we were told by an older hiker back in Tennessee not to worry about it because he said only brown bears would steal bags. He had hiked in Alaska too, so we believed him. Thinking back on it, the guy was a little bit nuts, I don't see why we listened to him."

"Hey dad, it would be funny if they were talking about Psycho. It sounds like something he would do."

"Yeah, it certainly does. Well best of luck to you two, hopefully you've got some other food that doesn't need to be cooked."

"Yeah man, were going to ditch at the next bail out trail and hitch into town for new gear."

I hope that these two Cribbage Crappers would survive the trail. It seems to me they were becoming a bit complacent and reckless.

The next day we were up and over Kinsman Mountain. We found it to be harder than Moosilauke, but it's all relative I suppose. It was a lot of bare rocks to climb up and down, but I championed the Matt method, staying to the side of the trail and using the trees to navigate my way down. There were times when I'd be at a standstill for what seemed like an eternity planning my route, Matt on the other hand seemed to have an eye for this sort of thing, he could find a path in no time and just go for it. All in all, it was five miles up and over and took five hours, that's back to our turtle days, but at least we had good weather. It took a few days for us to realize, but now New Hampshire officially sucks too.

We spent the night at our first AMC Hut at Lonesome Lake, it was the southernmost Hut along the chain. I buddied up to the cook and got the scoop on the huts and he told us everything we needed to know. We'd soon start up into the White Mountains and from there it's only hut to hut, but for now we'd spend two "zero" days with our family. In hindsight, we might have been better off staying in the woods.

373 miles to go.

Chapter 51
The Mighty White Mountains

The White Mountains should be revered, I'm pretty sure they were by the native people, that sounds like the kind of thing they would revere. They, to me, where the most beautiful and challenging part of the trail. No more 100 bottles of Beer, we were in one-thousand bottle territory.

The scenery is magnificent in the Whites, unlike the rest of the "green tunnel." We got a taste of Alpine hiking in New Hampshire. We were also bringing some guests along for our section through the Presidential Range and that would undoubtedly make things interesting.

Hiker Babe would make her triumphant return to the AT, along with her sidekick, my sister-in-law "Boots." Why did I allow Hiker Babe back on the trail? Well, I couldn't really stop her, but since we would be hiking hut to hut her thinking was such that she wouldn't need to carry as much in her backpack. The huts were buildings maintained by the Appalachian Mountain Club, they weren't free, but for a nominal fee besides getting a bed they served breakfast and dinner, and if you got there early enough in the afternoon, they had free soup as well.

They are stocked with bunk beds, toilets, and a wonderful staff of the highest caliber. Hiker Babe would feel better about sleeping somewhere with four walls, a roof, and a door. I guess she thought it would make it that much harder for a bear to drag her off into the woods as a midnight snack. In short, this would allay her fears. Boots, on the other hand, was a total novice. She earned her trail name from Hiker Babe because she bought a new pair of boots for the hike and then didn't shut up about them for a month prior to the hike. Pride cometh before a fall, as they say. Boots shone with naivete and optimism thinking it would be a leisurely stroll through the mountains going from spa to spa. She prepared for this hike by watching over and over the opening scene from Sound of Music, a dance through the alps. We let her keep thinking that.

Matt and I spent a majority of our two "zero" days watching Boots and Hiker Babe, pack, unpack and repack their bags over and over. They were back and forth from the store a half dozen times getting what they thought they forgot, but whatever it was, it was essential to their survival. Things like mosquito netting and hot chocolate pouches. After they had everything put together and their bags were bursting at the seams. Matt and I went through them, as we did with Hiker Babe the first time out, and got rid of eighty percent of the crap they just bought. They could have hot chocolate when they got home, no need to carry it on the trail.

We watched them repack their bags in the morning and set off from Wolfeboro to Lafayette Campground. We began about seven miles short of Greenleaf Hut on the shoulder of the mountain, which may sound like an easy day, but you gain three-thousand feet of elevation over that stretch. A real treat for the ladies.

The trail was wet heading up to Greenleaf, so Matt and I strode along at our usual pace while Boots skipped ahead of us commenting on how easy this hiking thing was. Hiker Babe had joined her in outpacing us, but she didn't share in Boots enthusiasm. She knew the score, and it was the AT 1, Hiker Babe 0.

We found Boots and Babe waiting for us at a flooded section of the trail. Hikers had placed rocks and logs in the flood zone to make it easier for other hikers, we've seen this dozens of times before, but Boots and Babe had not.

"Okay geniuses, how do we get across?" Boots asked.

Matt studied the layout for a moment and did what Psycho would call "dancing across the rocks." "It's easy," Matt shouted back as he started to cross, "just do what I do." He jumped out to the first rock and river danced his way across.

"Yeah easy," I replied as I crossed in the same manner, but in the back of my mind was the gash on my left knee.

"Those logs are pretty far apart," Hiker Babe was being her cautious self.

"I don't know about this, I don't want to get my new boots dirty," Boots added.

"Well then you chose the wrong outdoor hobby I think. You and Hiker Babe can stand there as long as you'd like trying to figure out a better way across, but Matt and I are gonna continue up to the shelter." I had some reservations about them coming in the first place, and now a little over a mile into the trail, this is what I get, my fears being realized.

"Come on Babe," Boots said gleefully, "it's a snap, follow me."

Boots started across the so-called bridge over the "Puddle Kwai" as Matt had now named it, with the precision of an atomic clock. She floated from rock to log and back to rock again as she neared the halfway point of the flooded trail, but we all make mistakes in life and so it was with Boots. She turned around to Hiker Babe and started to say, "Look it's eas..." and with that her foot slipped off the log and splashed down into nearly ten inches of muddy water.

"Damn it, damn it, damn it, my new boots. These are supposed to be waterproof," she said pulling her boot out of the water and regaining her footing, but this learning experience wasn't done, because a wet boot is not a stable boot. She slipped again and this time both feet went in and she was standing in the shin deep pond. "Shit, shit, shit, shit," she wailed.

Matt answered, "The boots aren't waterproof if the top of them is below water. So, should we call you MB from now on?"

"What's MB?" Boots sneered.

"Muddy Boots, I thought we'd keep it simple."

"Oh, you're a funny kid, is that it?" Boots was shaking off the mud and water after she slogged through the last few feet of this flood zone.

"Muddy boots, cool trail name, makes you sound rugged," Hiker Babe yelled from the other side of the pond.

"Easy Hiker Babe, you haven't gone yet," Boots said turning back to Matt, "and you think you're so damn funny, you and your father. Don't you think for one second I won't remember this come Christmas."

The funny thing was that Boots misfortune was a motivator for Hiker Babe. She jumped right up onto the rocks and made it across, it took forever as she moved about the same pace the continents drift apart, but she made it. She hugged Boots and said, "Well I couldn't look any worse than you, thanks MB, you took the pressure off of me."

Boots wailed again, "Don't call me MB!" Boots was not happy being called MB by Hiker Babe, this was really going to be fun.

Fun Fact: There are eight huts in the White Mountains, and you can hike from hut to hut.

Survival Note: There are eight huts in the White Mountains, and you should hike hut to hut.

The huts are marvels of engineering, with solar panels, lighting, hurricane proof, they are truly amazing. You need to carry your sleeping bag, water, lunch, and not much more, a very light backpack. Hiker Babe thought that since she did not have to sleep outdoors that this was her calling. Boots was another story; she had no clue.

We made it to Greenleaf at about three in the afternoon and laid claim to a bunk. Matt and I were set up in about two minutes, but it took the ladies nearly thirty. It's honestly hard to imagine how that's even possible given they didn't need to get water, pitch tents, cook their own food, or hang backpack's, but they pulled it off. I sat outside for a while enjoying the view and pondering my current situation. If this was an easy day with Boots and Hiker Babe taking this long, I just might be in for the longest week of my life.

Matt and Hiker Babe joined me outside for some conversation while waiting for the dinner bell. Mostly it was an hour spent trying to un-brainwash him from what his liberal professors drilled into his fragile developing mind. When the bell sounded Matt made a mad dash for the dining room, I have the sneaking suspicion that he was no longer interested in being lectured by his father and Aunt. We sat down at the table and Boots came walking in wearing white anklets, black Crocs, and believe it or not, her headlamp, inside at six in the evening in a lit building. What a nerd!

"So, this was basically a breeze," Boots said playfully, elbowing Matt in the ribs. "Can't wait for tomorrow." Boots, unbeknownst to us, spent the afternoon washing her boots to make them look like new again, because surely she had encountered all the mud she would come across on her first day out.

"Well Boots, tomorrow we summit Mount Lafayette and then into Galehead Hut. The guide says it's only eight miles, but..."

"Eight miles!" Boots interjected excitedly, "so only one more mile than today, and like I said, today was a breeze."

"But," Matt continued eyeing her wearily, "there is a lot of elevation change and I don't think it'll be as easy as you think."

Boot was smiling widely, swelling with pride. "I can walk eight miles backwards, Firestarter." She said Firestarter sarcastically, smiling even wider. There is something about the women in my family, when they smile, they all look like the Joker. Hiker Babe, on the other hand, was scratching at her hands nervously. She had flashbacks of her last fight with the AT.

"Famous last words, Boots," I said, "and another thing, ditch the headlamp until it's actually dark."

The conversation between the four of us progressed into the night, Boots continued with confidence, but Hiker Babes words were much more measured. She knew what the trail could throw at you and since it had basically thrown nothing at her, even the slightest challenge could be catastrophic.

The meal prepared by the staff or the "Croo" as they are affectionately known, was delicious. There is something so satisfying about a home cooked meal on top of a mountain you just climbed. It's like breakfast in bed, only the complete opposite.

One of the "Croo" members gave a talk to anyone who wished to listen about a book called "Not Without Peril." It was a book that chronicled all the deaths that had occurred throughout the Presidential Range. She highlighted two skilled hikers that overextended themselves, one in July and the other in August, both during violent cold storms that can pop up in the region. That's all Boots and Hiker Babe needed to hear, so for the rest of the night all I heard was "check the weather" and "we're going to die." I have grown accustomed to these phrases because that was basically Matt's mantra anyway, but with two more parroting it I got to wishing for one of these pop-up storms.

The next morning was beautiful, it was sunny and warm without a cloud in the sky. After another fantastic breakfast meal, we headed out with Lafayette looming before us in all her glory. The mountain was stunning against the backdrop of the Presidential Range, I did feel like Julie Andrews in the Sound of Music in that moment. We told Boots and Hiker Babe to start ahead of us and we'd catch up.

"Oh, so we won't see you again until the next shelter?" Boots said, taking a swipe at us. She would soon learn humility.

"We'll see," I responded, nudging Matt.

We watched Boots and Babe dip down into the woods on the trail before it started to ascend up to the summit. I like to think there is no way they could get lost, but who knows? I told them to follow the white blazes and they would be fine. We gave them about a thirty-minute head start before we plunged into the woods behind them. We caught up to Hiker Babe in about forty minutes and then Boots, who was another ten minutes ahead. She was ignoring the advice of us and not pacing herself.

Matt and I waited for Hiker Babe to catch up, I didn't want to be held responsible for her dying on the

394

mountain, as she is family after all. Boots, however, had summit fever and nothing would slow her down.

She was on the summit when we got there and had been for ten minutes, or so she claimed. She was looking down at us while we approached.

"Where were you guys? You call yourselves hikers?" she yelled, laughing to herself.

"This is going to be entertaining," I said to Matt under my breath. He just nodded in agreement.

On we went starting down the backside of Lafayette after a brief period of rest on the summit. Boots was aglow with merriment while literally skipping down the trail toward the woods on the backside of the mountain, she stopped only to turn and mock us. Neither Matthew nor I were bothered by her demeanor. We could hike circles around her if we wanted to, but we knew better, and we knew the Whites were tough and unforgiving. It wasn't too long until the real climbing began and that's when the skipping stopped and the heavy breathing began. Matt and I stayed with them for quite a while, through lunch and up to the next peak where we sat at an old Ranger station and talked. It was two in the afternoon and at this pace we weren't going to make it for the six o'clock dinner.

"Guys, I couldn't help but notice you're going a great deal slower than before. Everything okay?" I asked compassionately.

"You told us to pace ourselves," Boots replied, "and my feet hurt."

"That's because you have new boots and you didn't break them in first. Any hot spots on your feet? If so, let's get some duct tape on them now."

"Yeah," Matt chimed in, "we can call you Silvertoes."

"No, nothing yet. How much further to the shelter?" She was now whining like Hiker Babe had done on her first trip out. Both Boots and Hiker Babe were red faced and breathing hard.

I pointed to a hut about two peaks over. "That's the next hut there, you can see it from here."

"Oh, that doesn't look too far," Boots said hopefully. "I'll probably still beat you guys there." She was about to learn the fury of the White Mountains. The doubt was easy to read on her face and I didn't tell her about all the elevation changes we'd experience on the way. Matt was grinning but holding his tongue, maybe he is smarter than he lets on.

"The trail is well marked for the rest of the way, we should have about four miles to go from here, like you said it should be a picnic. Matt and I are gonna go ahead, it's hard for us to move this slowly."

"Yeah, yeah, go ahead," Hiker Babe said, "we're right behind you." That was the last we saw of them on the way to Galehead Hut.

The weather had started to turn as the afternoon progressed. The temperature dropped sharply as the sun faded behind the charcoal gray clouds that came rolling in. The cloud cover was low, making visibility along the trail difficult and in these parts that can be dangerous. We knew a storm was brewing, we had seen it a hundred times. I kept thinking back to the lecture at the hut the night before and it was entirely possible Boots and Hiker Babe may be two more names added to that list.

Matt and I reached the hut at Galehead a little before five o'clock. We thought we would see them coming in behind us around six, but six came and went and so did six-thirty, that's when I started to worry a bit. I sat outside diligently focused on the trail waiting for them to pop into view. I kept one eye on the clock knowing that if they did not appear within minutes we have to go looking. When seven o'clock came I told my Matt to grab his pack and empty it except for water and essentials and get his boots back on.

I didn't want to cause a scene among the other hikers, so I pulled one of the "Croo" aside. "Hey man, here's what's going on, we've got two other hikers that are well past due. My son and I are going back down the trail to find them. Please set aside four meals and if you don't see at least one of us back here in two hours call the Rangers and mount a search."

He had an uneasy look on his face as I told him our plan. "Sir, we have protocols in place for situations like this, I should probably radio the Rangers now. We'll have no daylight left here in about an hour."

"I know and I understand, however I don't think that's needed just yet. They're smart and I'm sure they're fine, they're just very slow. I'm more concerned about them missing dinner than missing them." I was trying my best to put him at ease, if I had them mount a full-blown search and these two jerks came waltzing into camp, I'd look pretty dumb, Bob does not like to look dumb.

Matt was waiting for me outside with his pack on, which looked deflated from its contents being spilled out on his bunk. He had plenty of water, head lamps, and our rain gear. "I've always wanted to be part of a search and rescue," Matt joked, but there were lines of concern in his face.

"Been there, done that. It usually doesn't end the way you want it to in my experience." As an officer for all those years that was unfortunately the case, but that's not what I expected here. We weren't going to find Hiker Babe and Boots dead on the trail, more than likely we'd find them dehydrated and hungry somewhere along the way, still crawling along at a snail's pace. The winds were picking up and the sky was looking ominous, we wanted to get them to the shelter before the bottom fell out, and from the smell of the air that was likely to be any minute.

Matt and I were about ten minutes down the trail when we first heard the faint sounds of feet shuffling and heavy breathing. I gave a shout and Boots responded in kind. Everything I guessed was exactly what happened. They were "bonking." They were so far behind they decided to skip their afternoon snack and were entirely out of water, as a result they could barely move. We hurried over to them, Matt handed each of them a water bottle which they chugged. Both Matt and I each took one of their backpacks and carried it the rest of the way for them.

"Well," I said, "the good news is the hut is only about ten minutes up the trail." Neither responded with words but merely nodded. These were defeated hikers. I've been in their shoes before, I know it's tough to recover from.

We went up to the hut in silence. It started to pour as we entered the shelter. There wasn't any real conversation until after dinner was eaten. Thankfully the "Croo" set aside some food for us and there was no need to radio for help. There was a welcome look of relief when the "Croo" member I had spoken to saw all of us walk in, but somehow I think he relished the idea of an all-out search and rescue.

Matt pushed his empty plate away after dinner, let out a satisfied burp, and asked the million-dollar question, "So," he started "you guys decided to take a nap on the way or..."

Man, if looks could kill Matt would have been double tapped right then and there. "You said it wasn't far, that was like twenty miles," Hiker Babe said with a sneer on her face.

"No, you had eight total and only four from where we had that conversation," I reminded her.

"My feet are killing me, my boots don't look new anymore, and my calves are sore." Matt was right, Boots would need to be renamed. We'd have to discuss that later.

Hiker Babe added, "That was ridiculous, nobody should have to ever have to hike that far. Is tomorrow any easier? "

I laughed at her question. "We normally average fourteen to sixteen miles a day."

Matt, ever the walking AT Guide chimed in, "Well, tomorrow is only about seven miles. There isn't as much elevation change either, it should be easier on you, but you still may want to consider leaving at sun-up. It's only up and over two peaks on the way to Zealand Hut." Matt was studying the guide.

Matt was getting the "if looks could kill stares" again from his two aunts, a look he had become accustomed to lately.

"You know, dear nephew, you're not as nearly funny as you think you are," Hiker Babe said to him. "You are no longer my favorite nephew."

"I have an idea," I offered, "why don't Matthew and I take half of your gear. We can carry your sleeping bags and mattresses and you guys take your water, food, and other essentials. It'll cut the weight of your bags down and help you move things along at a better pace."

"You guys can carry all that stuff?" Boots asked. "Not a problem, dearest aunt, so long as I'm back on the Christmas gift list."

"Your mother is Jewish," Babe said massaging her feet.

"Oh, right," Matt answered, "so I get a gift every night for seven nights. Yeah that'll work."

"Yeah," Boots snickered, "wait for them at the door."

374.4 miles to go.

Chapter 52
Go West, Young Man?

We went bed at nine that night, which was a late night for us. They were no horror stories that night and we all slept soundly in our bunks. The huts were warm and cozy compared to what we were used

to, and they came with breakfast the next morning. It was nice waking up and not being covered in dew or immediately freezing.

We had Boots and Hiker Babe leave earlier than us again, but it was no use as we caught up to them within thirty minutes. We tried hanging back but their snail like pace was too much for us, we'd pass them, sit for a while playing Rummy, they'd catch up, rinse and repeat.

There was one point on the trail where a young man in a hiking kilt was keeping pace with us between huts. His name was "Piper" and we'd come to know him a bit over the last few days. He was familiar with our family dynamic as well as the legendary pace of Boots and Hiker Babe.

"Hey Babe," he came dancing up next to her, "bet I can hike circles around you at the pace you're going."

"My pace is fine, thank you, it isn't that far to the next hut." Her answer, however, was not good enough for Piper. He began to literally hike circles around her. He circled her like an annoying fly circles Matt. It was amusing to watch, but Hiker Babe didn't find it as funny as the rest of us.

He eventually stopped and said, "Well, now I feel stupid. That was tiring. See you guys at Zealand, I guess." Then off he went.

I'd be lying if I said hiking with our two extra companions didn't make me a bit nervous. We started letting them get well ahead of us, but every time we passed a side trail, I couldn't help but wonder if they wandered down it by accident. They gave me no reason to believe that scenario wasn't a possibility. We did eventually catch up to them and once again slowed to their pace, determined to prevent a repeat of yesterday, and the possibility of them wandering off the trail. We tried speeding them up, but Hiker Babe made it very clear that she was not to be herded along like cattle.

We reached the summit of one of the peaks before reaching Zealand, and you had to cross one-hundred yards of open loose granite on the windward side of the mountain, which also had a radically steep slope to it. Of course, to make matters worse, there was an accompanying stiff breeze blowing across. Naturally Babe was panicking.

"This is crazy, I'll be blown off this mountain, or worse, I might slip on the loose granite and fall to my death. How do we go around this?" I had seen this before. Hiker Babe was breaking down like she had several hundred miles ago.

"There is no going around," Matt offered as he stepped out onto the loose rock and began crossing.

"See," I pointed. "You can't be blown off the mountain. Now slipping and breaking a bone is a realistic possibility, so try not to do that, besides with your pack on you you're more anchored down.

"So that's why you and Matt offered to carry all that weight, to anchor yourselves down!" I thought she was kidding but she was dead serious. "You probably read in that stupid guidebook of yours that this is the spot on the AT where most people are blown off the mountain to die."

"My boots are getting scratched up." Boots, I almost forgot about Boots. She was more concerned about how her footwear was looking than getting blown off a mountain, which I suppose is easier to deal with. For the life of me I can't remember why I ever agreed to this venture.

"Look, Matt is almost across. I'll be right behind you, so let's get across this so we can head into the tree line on the other side and get out of the wind." I was getting tired of all the whining, I get enough of that at home, I have two kids and a wife, I don't need it out here.

"Sure, you just want to be behind us to record our deaths." Babe was not joking.

For some reason an incredible thought hit me, and I wondered what Buns of Steel would look like crossing here, with her muscles rippling and her taut legs, that perfectly formed tight ass, but no, instead I had Boots and Babe who's next move shocked even me. They got down on all fours and crawled across the granite field. It took nearly thirty minutes, time just wasted. Matt was on the other side staring with mouth agape. I was walking leisurely behind them, shouting what I like to think of as encouragement. I'm not sure they took it that way.

As they got closer to the other side Matt was waiting for them. When Boots was about ten feet from him he leaned over and began to beckon her like a dog, "Here girl, come on, good girl, who's a good girl, you are, that's right," and he scratched her behind the ear as she got up, unamused by the whole thing.

Babe, when she got up, just looked at him and said, "Try it and you die."

Matt and I kept pace with them for the rest of the day. We assumed it would be better for us to move a bit slower and act as shepherds rather than get too far ahead and leave them to their own pacing. At least this way we could keep an eye on them.

We finally caught a glimpse of Zealand a little before dusk. It is a beautiful place, with a nearby waterfall that drives a generator for electricity. It was a welcome sight to all of us but for different reasons. Matt and I were happy to be done for the day, Hiker Babe and Boots were happy to have a wall around them and a place to sit. We let the ladies claim their bunks first and then we set up on the empty bunks.

Boots started the conversation from there. "So, what's tomorrow looking like?"

Both Boots and Hiker Babe had looks of anxiety on their faces and exhaustion in their voices. "Matt you can answer this one, you've got the guidebook with you, besides my answer would likely be sarcastic."

"Gee thanks." Matt quipped. "Okay girls, here's what you're looking at," Matt began speaking to them with an airline captains voice, "the trip from Zealand to Mitzpah Springs Hut is...... approximate fourteen miles. It's...... the longest of the hut to hut hikes. We will be cruising at altitudes of...... approximately four-thousand feet with three severe climbs. Winds and rains are unknown but......uh.... can cause a bumpy hike if encountered. We estimate a travel time departing at eight AM and arriving at five PM, averaging one and a half miles per hour."

Matt's theatrics were world class, but unfortunately lost on the audience. Hiker Babe had that look on her face, I'd seen it before. It was the defeat, it was easy to see she was ready to quit. I looked over to her normally more cheerful counterpart but Boots simply fell back onto her bunk and mumbled, "You've got to be shitting me."

The air was getting heavy in the room and I could tell emotions were running a bit high. "Let's all go get some dinner and we can talk about this in the morning. We'll all feel a little better with some hot food in our stomachs."

Once again Bob was the calming presence and voice of reason. I already knew what they wanted to do but I figured I could shower them with praise at dinner and maybe recommit them before they called it quits.

Dinner was a solemn event for Hiker Babe and Boots. Matt and I went about our normal routine of Rummy and socializing with other hikers. It was an early night for all of us and at least half of us had a big day coming up.

When we woke the next morning, the sky was grey. It set the tone. We sat and ate breakfast and I asked the inevitable question, "So ladies, what's it gonna be? What do you want to do?"

It's hard to admit defeat, especially in our family, but it was written clear as day on their faces. There was no joking or smiling and their eyes were sullen.

"Well what are our options if we want to get off the trail? Boots and I talked last night and even though we can do it, we're just holding you two back." It was a bullshit statement, but everyone gets to save face a bit, in psychiatry they'd call it denial.

Matt was prepared for the question, the boy was maturing and learning compassion for others. "Well, I looked at the maps last night and there is a side trail. It goes down to a parking lot with shuttle buses that run to several locations. If you hike down that trail you can take a bus to Highland Center and Nana and Gramps can pick you up there."

"And," I added, "it's all downhill and about three miles."

"So, you should be able to make it before the buses stop running," Matt joked. It was perhaps a bit premature for jokes as neither looked amused.

We decided we would hike with them until the trail split, left for them to the shuttles and civilization, right for us to continuing misery. Matt and I would push on and meet them at Highland Center, it was a bit out of the way but not enough to deter us from the idea of hot food for lunch. With everything decided it was remarkable to see how their spirits rebounded. They had spring again in their steps. If only I felt that way.

It's almost hard to imagine but we beat them to the Center. My mother and father were already there, I guess the buses up here aren't always on time, but the two of them eventually showed up. We had a hot lunch and pulled out our maps, we were only mere inches from Maine on the map! We gave each other hugs and said our farewells.

"Are you sure you want to leave? Maybe you can yellow blaze all the way to Maine?" I said to them.

"I'll take my chances with a soft bed, hot food, and hot showers," Hiker Babe replied. "In other words, I'm going home," and with that she slid into the car.

"I'm with her on this one, go west young man!" Boots shouted sliding into her side of the car. The doors slammed shut and off they went.

I looked at Matt and said, "No wonder they couldn't hack it, they don't even know what direction we're going, we're heading east, not west.

353 miles to go.

Chapter 53
Peaks to Bag

Mizpah Hut was up an old bridle trail used by horses way back when. As with all the other huts it was clean, accommodating, and the staff was top shelf. Mitzpah was great, but in truth we were more excited about the next day when we would be heading to Lake of the Clouds, which was just below the summit of Mount Washington.

Washington was not the highest peak on the trail, but it was a close fourth and its northern latitude often tricks people into thinking it's the tallest. We, however, considered it be the Crown Jewel of the AT, the last monster peak to bag before Katahdin, and the most famous, and it was looming ever closer. It was only six short miles so it would be easy for pros like us.

We met Piper and his hiking buddy at Mitzpah Hut. "Hey Peterman, Firestarter, what's up? Where are the slowpokes? Hiker Babe and Boots still taking their sweet time?"

"I think you mean Turtle and Slug," Matt replied.

"Both quit after Zealand," I finished. "They took a side trail down and were picked up."

Piper tried his best to be courteous, but his eye roll was evident. "Well that was quick. I'm sorry to hear it man". Hikers never like hearing about other hikers dropping off the trail. "I hope it wasn't me poking fun at them. I figured they could handle a little ribbing."

"Woman, am I right?" Matt joked.

"You idiot, what do you know about women?" I said to him. I turned to Piper, "If it was you Piper, I suppose I should thank you, their pace was killing us, and they proved early on they couldn't be left unsupervised. However, there is good news for the two of you."

"Oh yeah, I like good news," Piper said.

"Well, yeah, unless you like doing dishes and sleeping on the floors the ladies bequeathed their spots in the huts to you two."

"What? That's amazing, Trail Magic Supreme!" I'm not exactly sure what that phrase means but they both seemed especially grateful. Hikers that are unable to pay the fee to stay in the huts can still spend the night, but they have to work for stay, oftentimes pitching in with the cooking staff and cleaning around the huts. They are welcome to bunks if there are extra, otherwise they must sleep on the floor in the dining room. It was preferable to having to tent a mile or so down the trail, tenting was not allowed above tree line.

"You have to thank them for us." Piper was busy doing a little jig and Matt and I were praying his kilt stayed down, we didn't want to know what was under it, if anything. God forbid he was a true Scotsman!

"Yeah after you did that little circle dance around her and she saw you doing dishes and sweeping, she thought a hiker of your stature deserved a little pampering. Your friend here, on the other hand, just got lucky."

"Let me go tell them I'm a customer now so they can give the bitch work to another chump." Every hut after that he sung Hiker Babe praise.

We ate a hearty breakfast and headed out to Lake of the Clouds early. The lure of hot soup and splendid views motivated us to get moving, we wanted time to relax and enjoy the fruits of our labor. Again, as stated earlier, it was only six miles.

Our ascent had us heading up Mount Pierce in the sunshine with clear skies ahead. It's funny how quickly things can change in the Presidential Range. It was during the descent and subsequent ascent of the following peak that the weather rushed in. The trail wove between the peaks switching from windward side to the leeward side giving us a glimpse of the encroaching weather.

If you are a hiker on the AT, you've heard of Mount Washington and its infamous weather. Its deadly and it can change in the blink of an eye. People have gone up the mountain on the hottest day of the summer only to freeze to death near the summit hours later in a popup storm. It is the deadliest mountain in the continental United States having claimed the lives of over one-hundred-thirty people. Its modest size gives the illusion that it can't be as dangerous as it is, but Washington claims lives a multitude of ways, from drowning, hypothermia, avalanches, and even the freak accident where a Cog Railroad derailed killing eight. The mountain should not be taken lightly regardless of the time of year, especially since windspeeds have been recorded at over two-hundred miles an hour on top of the mountain.

As we approached Mount Washington the weather did change quite a bit, the wind picked up, the temperature dropped, and the clouds started rolling in. I kept thinking back to the lecture about skilled hikers dying on this mountain and picturing a rescue party finding me like Jack Nicholson at the end of The Shining.

For the most part Matt and I had given up on using our rain gear, sure it kept the rain off you, but it also sealed in your own sweat, so you got soaked either way. We found better use in wearing it after the bad weather to warm back up. This was the first time in a long time we suited up due to weather. As the clouds rushed over us we found ourselves wrapped up in a mist which soaked us and sent a chill straight through our bones.

On the windward side we would freeze our nuts off and on the leeward side it was calm and serene, but out on the ridgeline it just plain sucked. I'm not one for exaggerations, but this was the worst weather we had encountered to this point, it was borderline frightening. All those stories just constantly nag you in the back of your mind and I was worried because I was responsible, not only for myself, but for my delicate son as well. No matter how bad this weather got we would tough it out, acting cautiously, I didn't want to explain to the boy's mother that I took him up America's deadliest mountain in bad weather and lost him to the elements. Hell, I wouldn't tell her if it happened unless she missed him, and in that case I would have at least a month to think of an explanation.

It was almost impossible to believe it was summer. The temperature had dropped to what felt like the forties and the wind made it colder still. Though as treacherous as the wind and temperature can be, what truly put us in peril was the mist. When everything is a uniform gray the blazes can be hard to see, especially when painted on gray rocks above the timberline.

"You know Dad, this really blows." It was hard to argue with him or put a positive spin on it just to spite him like I normally would, but I tried anyway.

"Hell, yeah it does, I can't see fifty feet in front of me, but at least it's only six miles." That didn't matter much if six miles took you eight hours to finish. I found myself extremely relieved that Hiker Babe and Boots were not with us. I'm certain they would have died.

We sat down with our backs to a large boulder out of the wind and stopped for a minute. "Well Dad, the good news is if Boots and Hiker Babe were with us we wouldn't be able to hear their bitching over the wind."

"Amen to that."

"Think we can die on a six-mile hike?" Matt said, half joking and shivering badly.

"I hate to break it to you, but people have died on shorter hikes than this. One hiker in the book died fifty feet from the shelter. I saw a movie where the guy cut his horse open and crawled inside it to keep him warm, you look about the right size." I pulled my knife out and smiled at the blade and then at him.

"Hey Matt, I can see there's a small ravine up ahead out of the wind, let's hunker down there. We'll sit and grab a snack."

Matt and I found ourselves in a windbreak in what can best be described as a small ravine, five feet deep and twenty feet long. We sat there and ate a snack. It was a surreal experience as we sat in the calm watching the wind and mist scream past us above. We didn't even feel the slightest breeze. As we ate a figure appeared to be moving in the mist coming from the north. The figure slowly approached us. As cold and wet as we were, he looked like he was colder and wetter. When he saw us sitting in the windbreak, he said nothing, slowly putting down his pack, and plopping down next to me.

"Holy shit, does it feel good to be out of the wind," he said, breaking his silence.

"Hey man, you coming from the Lake?" Matt asked him.

"Yeah, it was nice there this morning but damn, things do change quickly. They were saying winds are reaching eighty miles an hour at the summit." The hiker looked to be about twenty-five and didn't show signs of being out here long.

"How far is it?" Matt asked.

"I'd say you fellas are about halfway."

"You thru hiking?" I asked him.

"No, screw that, just doing the Whites. I don't have the time to do the whole thing, besides I think this would be a bit of a late start. Hey, you guys wanna split a joint?"

Does everyone out here smoke pot? Panda misses out again. "No thanks, you know it's a bit early in the morning for us. We're just gonna hang for a little while and see if the wind dies down. We sat and bullshitted for about another twenty minutes and watched the wind die down to acceptable levels and decided to move on. We suited up. "Good luck dude, enjoy your hike, what's your trail name anyway?"

"People have been calling me "Weed," he replied. No surprise there.

"Well people call me Peterman and he calls himself Firestarter."

"That's who you are man, I was sitting here saying to myself, shit this guy looks familiar, your Elaine's boss on Seinfeld. Cool names."

"Later," and out we headed into the elements once more. The wind did let up a bit and we continued, but the fog just made the hike seem longer, and we kept wondering if we passed the hut. On we went for what seemed like eternity, looking for blazes on the rocks, or at some points rocks that were stacked as blazes. A magical quality of the mist is its ability to shroud landmarks, which leads one to worry about passing the shelter and never knowing it. It's every bit as creepy as it sounds. I saw what looked like another huge boulder in a distance and pointed it out to Matt as well. It slowly began to take shape with each step we took. Much to my relief that boulder's edges began to buffer into the Lake of the Clouds Hut. It was only one o'clock in the afternoon when we made it inside, and we weren't the only ones there. Some of the previous night's guests had not left yet, choosing to wait out the weather where they were. It didn't matter one bit to us, if there was one thing the boy and I could do with precision it was waste time, besides this meant hot soup and putting our feet up. There was no view of Washington, only mist, but it felt good to be inside the hut and out of the crap weather.

As we sat there with our feet up, I turned to Matt, "Well my boy, it's up and over tomorrow. You ready for this. This is basically your Everest, you may not survive."

"Oh, I think I'll be fine old man. What's the matter? You sound like you're scared, you know what Uncle Jim says, "if you're scared say you're scared." Besides I'm part mountain goat, I'll probably do it in record time."

"More like you're one-hundred percent jackass."

"Well there is only you to thank for that."

We sat reading and writing as there weren't really any chores for us to do, and that's when the weather started to clear. The clouds parted as swiftly as they set upon us and the sun brought a much softer warmth and light to the mountaintop retreat. At first we caught only glimpses of the peak and the valley below but soon after it was nothing but blue skies and the views were worth it. It was like a time lapse montage in a film, watching the clouds fly across the sky.

We both knew the next day was only eight miles to Madison Hut, but the trail took us up and over four different peaks, one of them being Mount Washington. Now for the sake of propriety I'll admit the trail did not actually go up to every single peak. We did skirt a lot of them, which was close enough for me. Most peaks had side trails up to the summit though Matt and I would rarely do them unless they were four-thousand feet or more. I believe there somewhere around forty-eight in total. Matt and I would cover twenty-one of them.

Fun Fact: People do try to climb all 48 peaks as a lifetime achievement.

I had been to the peak of Mount Washington before, but last time I had driven up on a scenic road. It was a few miles to drive and filled with perils of its own, namely your brakes giving out on the way down. This time I took a different route. I walked one thousand, eight hundred fifty-eight miles to get there, but on the other hand the day hike up Washington via Tuckerman's Ravine is only nine miles, either way works, so how stupid were we?

"Some Rummy Dad? I want to get back in the lead." He was trying, and it was close, 168,786 to 168,742 I'm leading, barely. We played for a while then shared our stories of our travels with the weekend warriors. Naturally, they were in awe of us, Firestarter with his embellished tales of heroism, and then me telling tales of truth.

We had heard from another hiker that night that it had taken one woman fifteen hours to get to Galehead from Lafayette. She didn't show up till almost eleven that night. We were told the "Croo" had geared up and were walking out to start a search and rescue when she finally showed up. I couldn't wait to tell that story to hiker Babe and Boots.

338 miles to go.

Chapter 54
Never Go Back…..Unless

The next day, W-day as it was known to us, was the day we would summit Washington. The morning did not have a promising start. We woke to a cold overcast forty-five-degree morning with the winds battering the side of our hut at anywhere between thirty to sixty miles an hour. We collected our gear, pulled on our boots, and did what we came to do.

The climb up was mostly loose rock, it was tedious, but not exhausting. We made use of the gift shop near the summit, buying some food and waiting for the weather to pass. It's never did. Yet another mountain top view that Mother Nature robbed us of.

Coming down the other side of the mountain brought us to the Cog Railroad. Our timing worked out well, a Cog was coming up the slope as we approached the tracks. The Cog Railroad is a three-mile-long track that goes up the side of Mount Washington at an average angle of thirty-two degrees. It works with gears that engage slots on the tracks so it does not slide backwards. It is an engineering miracle.

We had to cross the tracks, so we sat for a moment and waited for the train to go by. We could see the people inside looking and pointing at us.

"Get out and walk ya lazy bums," Matt yelled at them as they passed by.

"That's a bit unnecessary, but I agree with you."

Matt looked back up the mountain, "Hey Dad, take a look at Washington."

I turned and looked back, of course the peak was clear without a cloud in sight with a complete three-hundred-sixty-degree view.

"Well that sucks. You want to go back?" I knew the answer before I even asked it. The boy looked at me perplexed for a few seconds and we both bust out laughing.

"Never go back," Matt said still laughing, it may not be a trail rule, but it was ours.

Survival Note: It doesn't matter what you leave behind, never go back.

We were only supposed to have a few miles to go to get to Madison Hut and some hot soup. I noticed that I hadn't seen any blazes in a while and we were headed downward into a steep ravine.

"Um, Matt, have you seen any blazes heading down this way?"

"Come to think of it I haven't," Matt answered back.

"Great, just great." We stopped and pulled out the maps. I traced his screw up back to Thunderstorm Junction where six different trails meet.

"That's what I get for letting you lead up front. We've been going the wrong way." I was astonished he had missed the white blazes for so long a time.

Survival Note: When you are on the wrong trail going the wrong way, it is one of those times when you do go back.

"Yeah, well you should be double checking me, so technically this is your fault too."

"Idiot kid," I mumbled. "I'll lead us back to safety, as always." I did an about face and started doubling back. We could look across and on the other ridge about a mile away and see other hikers we knew to be on the proper trail. I looked back at Matt. "Nice going amigo, you added two miles to our hike."

"Amigo? So, I'm Mexican now?"

"I'm surprised that you didn't get us that far south before I realized your blunder."

"Good, I was so looking forward to another story about you saving my life," Matt threw at me sarcastically.

"You know with the right twist," I pondered, "I could make this into another herculean rescue story."

"It's always about Bob isn't it?" Matt was not happy about his mistake. It is one thing to be the butt of a joke, but it's stings a bit more when it is your fault. We made it to Madison Hut albeit a bit later that initially planned. The dinner was good, and the hut was comfortable. We played a few hands of cards and made it an early night since nothing was going on.

The next morning while we gathered for breakfast, the crew warned us the about the day's weather reports. It was going to be ugly, thunderstorms were expected for most of the day. They told us to use caution and went over some simple safety instructions in the event lightning began to strike nearby. We were already familiar, but we listened again to the refresher course. They suggested everyone use a side trail that avoided this summit all together, however it was a bit longer.

Matt and I were never one for adding time or distance on purpose to our hikes, so we made our way toward the summit. It was thirteen miles to the next hut, we had no interest in adding an extra mile to it. We got about a mile from Madison Hut and about halfway up the summit when the lightning began in earnest. Matt and I separated keeping about twenty yards between us until we made it to an outcrop of boulders.

417

We were crouching there for a minute when I said, "So I'm kind of thinking the side trail right about now. What do you think?"

The lightning was still cracking around us and the summit was still a way off. "Okay, fine, but you have to agree this isn't a lifesaving story. Let's get the hell off this rock."

We waited for the storm to ease a bit, but what we did next was dumb by all accounts. We broke the first rule of hiking, we left the trail. In an effort to save time and not backtrack we cut through the woods to the side trail that went around the summit. We were positive we were going to run across the trail, but still it's a textbook example of how things can go wrong fast. We talked about it afterwards agreeing between each other it was a dumb decision and could have had serious consequences.

On our way around the mountain we caught up to a couple with a young child. The mother had twisted her ankle and it had swollen to the point where she could barely keep her boot on. They were headed off the mountain, taking a bailout trail to Pinkham Center, but obviously it was slow moving and the weather was not cooperating. She had already wrapped her ankle but there is no way to ice it or put pressure on it.

"You guys need some help?" I asked them.

"Thank you for actually stopping to ask. You two are the first ones to offer assistance, most just nod and walk by," the husband said concerned. "There really isn't much you can do, the trail isn't quite wide enough for us to carry her down side by side."

"Hey Dad, we can build one of those litters out of branches and drag her down the trail. It always works in the movies." The husband, the wife, and I all gave Matt a look of disbelief.

"Is he for real," the wife asked wincing in pain both physically and imagined from the thought of being dragged down a mountain.

"I'm afraid he is. Sorry, the educational system failed us all. I guess I can give you my walking sticks and that might make things a bit easier for you. Try it out and let's see." I adjusted them to her height and let her try them.

"This is so much better. I can actually keep some weight off my ankle." She legitimately sounded grateful.

"When you get to Pinkham Notch, leave these with the Ranger there under my name and I'll pick them up in a few days."

They showered us with thanks and made their way inch by inch down the trail. "You know Dad, you are never going to see those sticks again."

"Yeah, that's why you and I are sharing for now, hand one over." I reached out and snatched one of Matts poles from his disbelieving hand. "So we can agree that this was a life saving event? By sharing your sticks, you technically helped."

"I guess we could agree to that. We kinda did save their lives, didn't we?"

Not really, I thought, but I nodded my head in agreement. It would look good in our journal. We finished the rest of our day peacefully. We stop at Carter Notch Hut for the evening and were getting picked up the following day by our family for some much-needed rest.

I stopped by the Ranger station on the way to my family's home, there were no sticks reportedly left behind. Either they took them, which I find upsetting, or they were dead on the side of the mountain, which I find more palatable since that's a pretty good excuse for not leaving them behind after my benevolent act.

281.3 miles to go.

Chapter 55
Maine and Tragedy

We went back to my sister's house, the infamous Hiker Babe, for the evening. She should have been getting off the trail with us instead of picking us up but as I've said before, more than likely she would have died up there. Her house was only about an hour from where we were, so it was nothing to drop in for the night. We got to relax, if that's what you'd like to call it, in the luxury of modern comforts, modern in the sense her home had been built around 1890. Matt and I ate, drank, and joked around with the family. We slept well that night.

The next morning we donned our freshly washed clothes and piled into the car for the ride back to the trailhead. I asked that we stop by Pinkham Notch again, on the off chance my walking sticks were returned, otherwise I'd have to buy a new pair. Sure enough, they were there along with a gift card from Outback Restaurant to say thank you. It was an ironic gift card and a nice gesture, though a gift card doesn't go a long way in the woods.

We stepped back out into the woods and were straddling the New Hampshire/Maine state lines. Maine was last stop of this horror show, our last state with only two-hundred-eighty-one miles left. That would be fifteen to twenty days and then we would etch our names in the history books. Our spirits were high knowing this would be the final push. God they were high, off the charts.

"This is it Silvertoes, or Firestarter, or Turtle Stomper, whatever name you go by these days. This is the last hurrah. We're practically at the goal line. All that's left is Maine and the "one-hundred-mile wilderness.""

421

"Great speech coach," Hiker Babe said. She leaned into Matt, "so, I'll pick you guys up in two days?"

"Hilarious, oh look, see those mountains to the west? Those are the Whites. You see all of them?" Matt responded.

"Yep, that's what Google Earth is for," Hiker Babe replied, but the humor was lost on Matt.

"We've conquered those. I think we can handle Maine. I will make Katahdin, this I vow," Matt answered.

We had added some heavier shirts as the nights were beginning to get a bit cold up this far north. The saying on the trail is, "no pain, no rain, no Maine." Well, we had experienced the first two, and we'd be happy to add Maine to the list.

A few miles into the woods and we were miserable again. There was sweating and cursing aplenty. We learned quite quickly that Maine didn't care much for switchbacks. Every climb seemed like it was straight up and over, and we were sluggish from eating junk at home. It seemed to both of us it was like we had never hiked before, like our first day in Georgia.

"Matt, the pizza and beer are killing me. I'm feeling it big time." I was slow, my blood toxic from the inhumane amount of extra cheese I had on my pizza the night before.

Survival Note: Once again never overeat before an uphill hike, or any hike for that matter.

"Hey," Matt said optimistically, "at least it's not raining."

"Shut up idiot. That's the kiss of death." I looked carefully at the surrounding skies expecting a deluge any second due to his comment, but the skies remained clear.

We continued for hours, much more slowly than anticipated. We were averaging about half the pace we were accustomed to because of extra weight and the steep inclines as we gasped our way up and down. Our day seemed miserably long due to our pace. The normal time we would be stopping for the day left us with yet another five miles to go. It seemed like we were making our way to a shelter that didn't exist.

"Matt, you have the God damn book, where is this stupid shelter?"

Well according to the God damn stupid book it should be a few more miles judging by the up's and downs."

"You mocking me boy?" I gasped.

"Would never think of it, I'm too tired."

It was shortly after this statement we came across a series of bogs. After skirting around a few there was a larger one in our path with a log in the middle. Matt was in the lead and he hopped up on it like it was second nature. As soon as he did, both he and the log sank into the mud. He was standing ankle deep in mud screaming words that cannot be legally written. I skirted around that bog as well, laughing as I did.

"You know what they say son, never jump on a log in a bog." It was funny from my viewpoint.

We didn't get to the shelter until around eight o'clock. This is something that had never happened to us before. We were exhausted and though we knew our bodies needed nourishment, neither one of us were hungry, all we could think about was sleep. Since it was already dark out we shared a Mountain House meal, quickly cleaned up, and both of us passed out cold.

We were heading to Mahoosuc Notch, the bane to so many hikers before us. All in all, it would be a ten-mile day for us from Carlo Col to Speck Pond Shelter, we figured we'd keep the mileage low due to the nature of the day ahead of us. When we got to the Notch, we rested a short while, then strapped on our gear back on and found ourselves at the top of the Notch practically looking straight down.

Fun Fact: This roughly one-mile strip of trail is supposedly the toughest and slowest along the AT. It was formed by glaciers and upheavals that shaped it into sheer cliffs, which over time have collapsed leaving plenty of boulder climbing and an opportunity or two for uncomfortable squeezing between and beneath rocks. There are places in the notch where it is possible to find ice year-round.

We had to go straight down, just to come straight back up. This is where tragedy befell me. The gods are truly cruel. I would love to tell you we powered through that killer mile and comfortably strolled to Speck Pond, but we didn't. I'd gotten about three steps down into the Notch, when stepping down with my left leg and planting it on a rock, my right leg buckled folding my left leg up to my chin. I heard the dreaded pop and immediately knew I was in trouble. My leg was wracked with pain, but due to shock and adrenaline I had not felt the worst of it yet. Despite my injury I must have thought of a sad movie or book because my eyes began to tear up.

I yelled out to Matthew, "Stop!"

Matt had not yet turned around, he was still a good ten yards ahead of me, or below me in this case. "What is it now old man?" Matt replied as he stopped and spun around to see me on my sitting on my ass. He must have known right away things were bad.

"Oh crap," was all he could muster. "You don't look so good. Your face is pretty red."

"No shit," I groaned, "that's what happens when you are literally forcing your body not to explode."

"Well what happened, good old slip and slide? I thought those days were behind you." I could see he was making a joke at my expense, but the concern was written all over his face and pain was apparently written on mine

"My leg buckled and I slipped." It was the sad truth. I've slipped a time or two before but I've never had a leg give out on me. This was different.

"Well can you walk?"

"I honestly don't know. I heard something pop. Let me rest a minute while we're still at the top here and see if I can walk it off." I was lying to myself and I knew it, but I was desperate to be okay, we had come too far to get seriously injured now, not to mention the Notch was a bad place to get hurt.

I climbed back up those first three steps I took, and they were excruciating. I took my backpack off and paced around a bit for the next half hour, but with each passing moment the pain grew worse.

"Get out your map, let's find a bailout trail. I'm fucked." I think uttering those words hurt more than any the pain I had felt so far. "This is bad, I need to get it checked."

"Look, we only have a few weeks left. I can make it from here."

"I'm sure you could."

"Dad, I may never get here again. You're retired, you can come back anytime." He was frustrated and I don't blame him for that. I was as equally upset.

We had found a bail out trail and it would be a challenge in and of itself. We'd have to backtrack to a logging road, then down to a rural road in town. He was suggesting I take the trail.

"I get it, I told him, this is hard for me to, but suppose I can't make it down the logging road. We both know how this must end. What else am I supposed to do?"

"You could always blow your whistle."

I continued, "Funny. Grab your stuff kid and let's go. This hurts like hell. I hate to do this, but we can come back."

"Fine, ruin my life."

"You have your whole life ahead of you to finish, there will be other times when I can actually ruin your life. Tell, you what, we get out of this and I'll give you credit for a life save, how's that?"

"Big whoop," Matt responded half-heartily.

It was a long slow hike down the bailout trail we found, the logging road was thankfully flat but that did nothing to ease the hot searing pain in my knee. After a few hours the logging road spit us out onto the outskirts of the nearby town, if that's what you want to call it. Matt kept walking around in ever larger circles with his cell phone in hand, desperately seeking cell phone service to rescue his injured sire. Eventually he was able to get service and had to call the only person in a position to pick us up, Hiker Babe.

"You know I ought to make you limp over here and call her yourself," Matt yelled over to me. I just pretended I couldn't hear him. It was easier than responding to him, besides he was right, I didn't want to have to make that call. Not after all the hell I had given her.

I couldn't really make out what Matt was saying, but he was standing with his hand on his hip and there was an excessive amount of eye rolling, so I can only imagine what she was saying to him. After about ten minutes he came back over to where I was sitting in the shade.

"Okay, here's the deal," Matt positioned, "she can't come and get us until tomorrow. In the meantime, she's calling us a cab to take us to Berlin. She'll pick us up there tomorrow, so it looks like you're buying me dinner tonight."

"I buy you dinner every night," I said through clenched teeth, the pain was oozing out with every word.

"Semantics," Matt retorted.

"Well, what else did she say?" I asked him.

"You really wanna know? Mostly a lot of "I told you so's" and "not such hot shots now" kind of rhetoric. There was some genuine concern in there as well."

The cab showed up about an hour later and took us to a motel in town. I spent the evening with my knee elevated and iced waiting for Hiker Babe to bring us back to her place the following day. When she arrived she was actually rather polite about the whole thing. I suppose she knew what it felt like.

It would turn out when I got back home to North Carolina that I had a partially torn meniscus. I did not require surgery, but I was told to take it easy for a few months, I would feel pain on and off till the scar tissue broke down. Of course, I did not have this knowledge at the time. We returned to Hikers Babes home in Wolfeboro and plotted our next steps. We still had reservations at Baxter State Park for a private shelter at the base of Katahdin in two weeks' time. We decided to let the knee rest and heal, not knowing the real cause of the injury, and we'd summit Katahdin, then hike backwards to Mahoosuc Notch to complete the trail.

There were still 281.3 miles to go.

Chapter 56
The Never-Ending Story

To continue the tale, since we had some free time we thought we would visit Acadia National Park on the coast of Maine. It's the smallest National Park in the United States and made for an easy day visit for us. We drove through Bar Harbor and enjoyed scenery other than the "green tunnel" we've been in for the past months. The coast was a nice change of pace and neither of us had seen this area before.

It was here that once again I brought my son through another rite of passage. On the ride up the coast there are nothing but lobster shacks along the roads. Matt had never eaten a whole lobster before and as cheap as they were up here there was no reason not to get them.

"Okay Son, today you'll become a man, what do you say to a lobster dinner?

"I've never had one, but I'm certainly not going to say no since you're paying."

"Well, I'll show you how to eat one, and if you don't like it you can get a burger, trust me it won't be wasted."

Out came the lobsters and on went the bibs. I began to mentor my son in the fine art of eating a whole lobster. The boy was like a pig that's been given a truffle. He tore into it, with butter running down his chin, fingers, and elbows. He was a mess, but it was like watching a baby the first time it takes something sweet. He was smiling ear to ear like an idiot.

"This is some good shit! Better than a burger, that's for damn sure." Maybe Maine doesn't suck so much after all. He wanted lobster every meal after that and at these prices I didn't see a problem with that.

We drove through the bowels of Maine to reach Baxter State Park. It is about as remote as you can get on the East Coast. We parked next to our private shelter, which looked the same as all the others along the trail, only it slept four or five people tops. We readied ourselves for the next day's climb. It had been about two weeks since we had done any real hiking so it would be interesting see how our bodies reacted, especially since our bloodstream was about fifty-percent butter now from all the lobster we ingested.

The next morning broke like so many others before it. The air was fresh and clean, this was the zenith of our trip. This is what each step had been bringing us toward since day one. It was an awkward feeling because this was the end of the journey so to speak, even though we had to backtrack two-hundred miles or more. We both had mixed emotions and nerves were extremely high.

Since we were going up and down Katahdin in one day, we didn't need fully packed bags which was nice. We equipped ourselves with only what we would need, stuffed it into borrowed slack packs from the Ranger's Station, and started up the last few miles of trail.

Fun Fact: Climbing Katahdin is only a five-mile hike up from the base campground, and then the same five miles down, unless you choose Razor's Edge after the summit. Then you are just plain nuts.

"You ready old man?" Matt asked clacking his sticks and setting our pace for the climb.

"Yep, we're gonna crush this bitch. See you at the top." The trail to the top is a hell of a climb. It starts off looking like any other stretch of the trail and then quickly moves above the tree line getting increasingly steeper. The weather began to change for the worse, the winds picked up and a constant drizzle started. About a mile into the trail my knee began singing to me again with the increase in elevation, I could not take the chance of making the injury worse.

"Matt, stop."

"Ah, Christ," he responded. "It's the knee, right?"

"Yes, I don't think I can make it." My knee was racked with pain.

"Will you be able to get back to camp?" Concern again.

"Yes, it's not that far, and downhill."

"Then I totally understand. I'll see you in a few hours." He turned and headed back up the mountain.

"Wait, you're going without me? No father and son moment at the top?"

"Well since I'm not carrying you it looks that way. There's no telling when I'll get back here again, so I'll do it now, weather and your knees be damned."

"Okay then, be careful." I understood, roles reversed, he would have been left behind. Matt left and I was truly jealous. He would get to summit Katahdin I wouldn't, it plain old sucked. I turned around and made for the shelter describing Matt to every hiker I saw on my way back down and asked them to keep an eye out for him. He'd come this far without killing himself but who am I to tempt fate? I kept a very leisurely pace walking back, knowing I had a long wait ahead of me.

The shelters, though private, were set up right on the trail itself, so as the afternoon progressed I saw people starting to trickle down the mountain. I recognized a few of the hikers as those I asked to watch out for Matt. All of them as they came down said they had seen him at the summit, but no reports after that. The day was sinking into evening and he still was not back. Weather was still a concern and fewer people were coming down off Katahdin.

Finally, I saw another hiker who recognized me, "Hey man, that kid you told me about isn't too far behind me. I passed him about a quarter mile back. He sure does like to stop and rest."

"Yup, that's him," I replied, "thanks for the update." I was starting to get a bit worried I'd have to go up after him.

A few minutes later Matt came bounding out of the woods with a glow about him. I was relieved to see he survived. Instead of a triumphant greeting I got something different.

"Dad," he shouted at me, "what the hell? Did you ask every single person you saw to check in on me? Twenty people checked on me, I didn't realize I was so popular. Anyway, I did it, I made it to the top, and in keeping with the tradition of this journey it was under cloud cover and there was no view."

"Proud of you son," and I was. "I will be back to finish."

And for me, still 281.3 miles to go.

Chapter 57
Remember the Maine

Every day the specter of that mountain loomed just beyond my horizon. Laughing at me. Taunting me. It was an itch that wouldn't go away, a persistent nagging that wasn't my wife. To have come so far and fail, in the scheme of things, it was depressing, nothing could equate to being just a few miles short. In the meantime, I had decided to hike the Florida Keys from Homestead Florida to Key West with Psycho. Matt, in the meantime, had graduated from college with a degree in liberal bullshit. He generously volunteered to go hiking with me again rather than finding a job. When all was said and done two years came and went before we finally made it back to Maine, and we took her by storm, literally, and there was that two-hundred-eighty-three miles to go.

It was raining when we arrived at Katahdin. A proverbial downpour. That wasn't the worst of it though. Matt and I had flown into Maine intent on hiking backwards, from Katahdin to the Notch. Unfortunately, the shuttle arranged took so long that we were thinking of getting part time jobs as Skycaps at the airport. When the shuttle finally showed up it was another two-hour drive to Baxter State Park.

When we arrived at Kathadin we checked in with beautiful Ranger Julianna who issued us our personal shelter, much like we had the last time. She told us they would be no summitting today, it was too late in the morning. It wasn't that late, but she must have sized us up quickly and knew that they'd have to fly in air rescue if we tried the mountain today. On the other hand, this pretty young Ranger did have some good news for us, there was only a ninety-percent chance of rain the following day. Two years gone by and luck hasn't changed one bit.

The next day fell well within that ninety percentile that Ranger Juliana predicted. I made my way over to the Ranger station to check the daily weather report, but initial indications were clearly not good. However, things were looking up for Bob, I got more good news in the Rangers Station, the probability of rain had dropped to eighty percent for the day. I contemplated waiting a day to see if it cleared up, but what was the point really? I could be waiting a week.

By the time I got back to camp I was soaked and unhappy. To make matters worse, I found Matt back in his sleeping bag.

"Sorry old man, but you're going up alone. Been there and done that with this type of weather. I'll be waiting for you if and when you get back."

Never have kids. I watched as other hikers walked past our shelter and were beginning to ascend the mountain. The Rangers weren't holding anyone back so it must be safe. Yeah, right again.

Now I've done some crazy things in my life and this was easily in the top three. Going up Katahdin in that downpour gaining one-thousand feet of elevation per mile was just nuts. It was raining hard but once I got above the relative safety of the tree line there was no protection from the rain's onslaught. The wind and rain would not let me dance gracefully with the rocks as Psycho would have suggested but slowed things down to a grinding halt. I was slowed even further when I got to the parts of the trail where rebar was once again drilled into the rocks which required actually climbing. About two-thirds the way up this mountain I realized I was not getting off this heap of rocks alive.

The last quarter mile or so when you are close to the top of the mountain is relatively easy, but again, it was encased in clouds. There would be no victorious views for Peterman. I got my picture taken next to the iconic mile marker on the summit, lingered for a moment somewhat expecting something spectacular to happen to me for reaching this milestone. All I received from my efforts was more wind and rain.

The way down was a bit easier since I slid halfway down the mountain on my ass. The weather lightened up on the hike back, but the effects of the climb we're getting to me. My knee was holding up well enough, but I was soaked to the core and jealous of Matt, who was most assuredly dry. I made it to the end of Hunt Spur, the spot where the climb becomes most difficult, and bears my surname as well. I cursed my family's name while I looked behind me up the mountain, I could not see the top of the Spur, let alone the peak. I stepped down into the shelter of the wood line and finished the last mile in calm. I came to the shelter as Matt was throwing some dry wood into the fire pit.

"Hey Dad, jeez, you look awful. So how was it? Everything you've dreamed and more?

"Screw Katahdin. That damn mountain can go straight to hell. It was inhumane. That pile of crap threw everything it had at me and I persevered."

"Oh, do I remember," Matt interrupted.

"Well then have some sympathy and get that damn fire going."

"The wood is wet, but luckily for you I am Firestarter. I'll get dinner rolling, you relax a bit. Let the accomplishment set in."

He was right. It had not yet soaked in, I was still busy cursing the mountain. Matt served dinner while I continuously grumbled pleasantries toward the mountain under my breath, I started to calm down and once I got some dry clothes on and some food in my system. I had climbed into my sleeping bag and was leaning against the back wall of the shelter with my eyes closed and heard chuckling.

I opened one eye and looked at Matt, "What's so funny?"

"You've been smiling nonstop since dinner. I think someone is starting to feel a little proud of himself," Matt said in a mocking baby voice.

"And so, what if I am?" I was proud of myself, but the hike wasn't done yet. Granted, the rest of the way would be easier, but we were out of shape again

The next morning Matt had a good laugh as I limped and hobbled about. "Think this is funny do you? Well guess what jerk-o, this is gonna be you tomorrow so don't laugh too hard." My quads, back, and calves were throbbing in time with each other, pulsating pain throughout my body with each step. It was great to be back on the trail.

It wasn't long before we were reminded that there's a lot of nuts on the trail. A few miles south bound we hit our shelter for the evening and we came across another hiker already setting up. She was fresh out of the military and had the greenest teeth I've ever seen. She introduced herself as "Fatigues."

"How far are y'all going?" She asked as we approached, apparently ready to converse.

"We're just going to the Notch," I told her. "We had to stop there two years ago so we came back to finish what we started. That will be the end of the trail for us."

"That's awesome. I've always wanted to do the trail and since I'm fresh out of the military with no job yet, this is the time, right?" She didn't take a single breath after that, it was just one continuous sentence after another, and she jumped right in with her whole life story. Matt and I set up our camp and she went on about her military career, how she became a born-again Christian, and so on. For two hours she told us about God, Lucifer, their creation, the Angels, heaven, hell, and fire and brimstone. She was clearly serious about her religion. She was hoping that she could use her hike to spread the word. I could not have kept a tally of Matt's eye rolls if I tried.

I was surprised Matt had not engaged her, usually this type of conversation would be right in his wheelhouse. It seemed my son had grown quite a bit in the past two years. Then again, I might have gotten a bit ahead of myself.

"That's quite a great story for kids and teens, but I think your story has some holes in it," Matt said nonchalantly after a while.

"A bit of a skeptic, eh?" Fatigues asked.

"That would be putting it mildly," Matt, the ever-sensitive man that he was growing into told her when she was done, "do you believe in the Easter Bunny? Santa? The Tooth Fairy?"

"No, why? They're fairy tales," Fatigues answered.

"A guy that walks on water? Rises from the dead? Sorry, I just don't buy it."

"Faith," Fatigues replied.

"Same for the others," Matt replied. The hike then became very quiet

About an hour later two other hikers rolled into the campsite. These two guys were also just out of the military and hiking south. Their packs were massive, absurdly so. They both had a hatchet strapped to their bags and one of them had a small chain saw dangling from a carabiner on his pack. Matt and I couldn't help but laugh at the sight of them. These guys reminded us of the couple we met in Georgia when we first started who were carrying gear for the colder months in Maine and refused to mail it forward.

"You guys aren't overseas anymore, there is no need for all the hardware fellas, what are the implements for?" I asked.

"Firewood man, for fires." He looked startled that we were chuckling at him.

"There's plenty on the ground," Matt said, "that's how I got this boy bad boy started." Nodding towards his fire he added, "I'm not sure what else you guys got in there, but we would be happy to help sort you guys out."

These guys were in killer shape, they were used to carrying these large packs and being weighed down, they didn't really think much of carrying all this stuff. We sat with them looking through their gear and explaining why they wouldn't need certain items.

"Man, when you have an M2 Browning hanging off ya, this stuff doesn't seem so bad. Hell, I thought these bags were light already. If I sent all this stuff home like you say I'll be floating down the trail."

"Guys," Matt followed up, "this may seem light, but it's actually bulky and you're carrying canned food, which means carrying a can opener and that's a lot of weight to pack out. Also, I think you can send home the flares, just stick to the trail and you'll be fine."

They didn't have trail names yet, but Matt and I took to calling the one with the hatchet and chain saw "Bunyon" for Paul Bunyon, which through a natural progression turned his buddy into "Babe," the Big Blue ox. He tried to flip it on us and have him and have us call him "Ox," but we found Babe had better ring to it. Both seem to like the names and embraced the trail name culture.

After a few hours of joking around and eating dinner, Fatigues came over and started talking to Babe and Bunyon. At first it was all military talk, where were you stationed, how many times downrange, etc. We just sat and listened.

They shared a few war stories and Fatigues made her move, "So you boys must both be believers in our Lord and savior Jesus Christ," they looked at each other and then at us.

"We went through this already guys, it's your turn," Matt said chuckling.

Fatigues did not seem to appreciate his comments but turned her attention back to the others. Bunyon started to answer, "Well, yes, I suppose, but not really into it."

That was all she needed to hear. She dove headfirst into a monologue about Catholicism. Matt and I took that as I cue to pick up our running game and left the others to her sermon.

During our game, a large group came in and pitched their tents out in the field below the shelter. They kept to themselves, until it got dark. Once the sun set the scent of sativa hit the air. Is everyone on this trail a pothead? After the hopheads were all doped up they decided to play Tag. Tag. In the dark. These idiots were running after each other and falling over everything. We would hear a loud thud as someone would run into a tree followed by an "oh shit." A headlamp would flicker on for a minute and then back off blindly into the night. They were keeping me up, but I couldn't get mad about it, watching these assholes run into trees was somewhat amusing.

The next day Matt and I crossed Rainbow Ledges and we passed two hikers coming up as we were headed down. I looked up to greet the other hikers as all hikers do and instinctively let out a "Hey, I know you." He said the exact same thing at the exact same time. It was a hiker named "Islander" Matt and I had met two years prior on some random mountain somewhere. We had synced up for a few days winding up in the same shelter for a few nights. We stopped and conversed for a while, he was obviously doing better than I was, he was hiking with a twenty-four-year-old version of Buns of Steel while I was hiking with Matt, a religious moderate, and two army kids with one-hundred-pound packs.

That evening Bunyon and Babe rolled into camp looking a bit lighter. "Hey guys, where are your hatchets?" Matt asked them.

"Ah man, what can I say?" Babe answered, "you guys were right. We left them behind at the last shelter, in case someone wants to chop up some firewood."

"That was noble fellas." I replied, nodding in approval, "how considerate of you."

Moments later four "Barbies" came in. All the girls were cute, wearing leggings with short dresses and nice tops, it looked as if they were about to go on a lunch date. One, however, was looking a little worse for wear, she was covered in mud and had fallen off the "old log in the bog trick." From the moment they walked in everything was "OMG" or "Hey girlfriend." On that day the English language died an unceremonious death on the mountain side. Luckily, they decided to set up their tents about thirty yards up the hill. It didn't matter much though since their voices rang shrilly around the campsite all night long.

When the camp was set up "Muddy" came walking down in her sun dress and asked where the swimming hole was.

"Swimming hole? I don't think there's a swimming hole here, not one that we're aware of anyway," I told her, "there's only the stream right here. Planning on taking a swim?"

"Oh no, I just need to wash off the mud and get myself clean." The only way for her to do that would be to lose the dress. I was okay with that and I doubt very much that there would have been any objections from my compatriots.

"That's probably a good idea. Just be sure to go downstream a bit so you don't pollute our water source."

She went ten yards or so downstream and waded into the current which was only knee high on her. She had to know we were all watching since it was out in the open and she was basically right in front of us. In one smooth motion she reached down grabbed the bottom of her dress and pulled it up over her head. Muddy was standing there in her matching bra and panties, took her blemished dress, and used it as a rag to wash the mud off her skin. This type of thing doesn't happen much in the woods.

"Hey, maybe she needs someone to wash her back," Matt said poking Bunyon in the ribs. He didn't say it very loud, but voices do carry on water, she never turned around but just stuck her middle finger up into the air.

"You're real smooth, you must kill it with the ladies," Babe said ripping on Matt.

"Whatever," Matt responded to Babe. "It was only a suggestion.

Muddy came out of the stream dripping wet and sparkling like an Angel in her bra and panties. She walked past us and turned to Matt, "I'm perfectly capable of washing myself asshole," and she walked away.

"Jeez, no sense of humor." We all had a nice long laugh at Matthews expense, it's in these moments' life seems sweetest.

The following day we said our goodbyes to Bunyon and Babe. They were cranking up the heat and starting to do some big mile days. We had no interest in trying to keep up. Matt and I reached our next shelter in the early afternoon and went through our normal progressions. We noticed another father/son duo had come into the area and set up their tent behind the shelter, they being a much younger team then we were. The kid was very young and inexperienced, but they seem to be enjoying themselves.

Matt and I sat in the sun playing Rummy and we observed a guy come into the shelter, look around, and leave. This is not our first time this exact thing has happened and it's weird every time it does. We shrugged it off and went back to our game.

"You know, you sure do attract the crazies," Matt said.

"Me? If anyone is attracting them it's you. I am a purist. I'm also a kick ass Rummy player, "Gin!"

"Right, well they all seem to take a liking to you, they seem to find you a kindred spirit in you. I'm a bit concerned to be honest."

"Yeah, yeah. Well if you so worried about it you can leave anytime. Why don't you go tend your fire?"

"I didn't build a fire, but I do smell smoke."

As soon as Matt said that, the young kid came running around the corner of the shelter yelling for help. We went to the rear of the shelter and could see a tree was on fire. We thought they screwed up, but the father told us the stranger had crapped by the tree and I guess he was doing a Psycho and burning his TP. In doing so he set the hollowed tree remnant ablaze. It acted as its own chimney pulling oxygen in through the holes in the bottom, and now it was fully ablaze.

As luck would have it, there was some buckets for duff left by the shelter. We used those to form a fire brigade passing buckets back and forth. It took half an hour, but we got the fire out. I did notify the closest Ranger Station about the blaze and our shelter location, their response was, "If you think it's out and it's safe, then we're okay." We poured more water on it and watched it till bedtime. There is no out running a forest fire, so it was time well spent.

243.1 miles to go.

Chapter 58
A Female Psycho

Maine presented different challenges, aside from us being out of shape. Instead of mice diving into our bags, it was red squirrels. They were bigger up here and more aggressive. They look like dwarves with razor sharp teeth, always watching and plotting. They were more agile and could chew through the tin cans we used to fend off the mice. Matt and I rigged three different stops to deter the squirrels and it worked for us, but others we saw were not as lucky. Who would have thought squirrels liked tuna and protein bars?

The other, and perhaps more importantly differentiator in Maine were the rivers. Almost everywhere else along the trail there are bridges to cross the rivers, whether man made or otherwise. Maine, however, for the most part required you to ford the rivers you crossed.

We had two ford two rivers on this section of the trail, the first one wasn't too bad, but the second provided much more of a challenge. Everyone has their own methods when it comes to fording a river, some real pros don't bat an eye and just trudge through it, but we considered ourselves semi-pros, so we stopped and took off our boots and socks. Our first crossing was only about a foot deep, but very wide, with a slow current. When you can see the bottom it's easy to walk barefoot across, but still slippery at points. I had a few moments where my bowels questioned my balance, but I stayed up right. It's a pain in the ass to dry your feet and strap socks and shoes back on, but dry feet are happy feet.

The second river we crossed was different. It was about waist deep and flowing fast. As we approached there were a few others attempting to ford the river ahead of us. This was not the type of river where you stopped to take off your shoes and socks. You needed the grip from your shoes. Someone had hung a taut rope from one side of the river to the other, both ends tied off to massive trees. Some people held onto the rope but would still be pulled by the current. We watched two hikers in a row slip, let go of the rope, and fall into the water. They were soaked, but even worse their gear was soaked. We were polite about it and withheld our laughter until they were safely on the other side. Besides, they aren't coming back across to confront us.

"Real funny, huh guys? Let's see you do better," yelled one of our newly soaked friends.

"You know what guys," I yelled across. "I'm gonna let my son show you how it's done."

"Oh sure, I go first so when I fall I'm the one who looks stupid, is that it?"

"It's because I love you," I turned and flipped him an extra carabiner. "How would you use this right now?"

"You want to clip us together and cross so we get swept away together?" I was hoping he was kidding. "Yeah, I got it. Thanks."

Matt took off his pack and clipped it to the rope with the carabiner and he trudged into the river with his boots on, yipping at the cold water contacting his skin. He guided his pack across the line without incident, it was so much easier to ford the river without a pack on.

"Easy peasy guys." Triumph was all over his face. I followed his example, only being the superior thinker I am, I removed my shoes and socks, tied them together and slung them over the guide rope as well. The water was

444

shockingly cold, but since I managed not to fall in I considered it refreshing. There were a few close calls, perhaps losing the shoes wasn't the best idea, but at least I had dry socks.

I was expecting some fanfare when I reached the other side but to my disappointment the others had kept on moving. There was only Matt slow clapping as I approached.

Matt and I reached our shelter for the night and not far behind us a married couple came in looking exhausted and exasperated, and they had a third hiker struggling in behind them. She was a tag along, a female, and looked to be in her early thirties. She had a sour look to her but otherwise nothing out of the ordinary, until she opened her mouth that is.

"These fuckin' hikers. Everyone says they are so damn friendly, well not to me." Matt stopped and gave a sort of sideways skeptical glance. "See that's exactly what I mean, weird looks, hushed insults. Don't think I don't hear it people. These two here are the only nice people I've come across out here." She gestured her head to the two mentally anguished hikers she came in with. She didn't exactly set a friendly tone with her little rant, but Matt and I went about our business.

"You know Matt, she's not bad looking, kinda pretty, but her little diatribe reminded me of Psycho."

"Yeah, well, we're not adopting another stray."

"Agreed, but man I wish Psycho could meet Psycholette. I don't know if they would knock each other out or get married on the spot. I'm not that sure it's a wedding I'd want to attend.

With that Matt laughed, "Psycholette. I like that. Clever."

She began to set the rules for the shelter, "Okay, everyone, you should have dinner finished and cleaned up by six and lights out by eight-thirty. We'll be rising at six-thirty the latest, just to get the day going."

"Dad, she does know we're not part of her group, right? Like I'll go to bed at eight-thirty, but it's because I want to, not because some nut job makes me".

The woman who was hiking with her overheard Matt and leaned in to us, "Look, I'm not telling you guys what to do , but I'll tell you this, life will be much easier for everyone if you just go along with it for the night or two you end up with her, if you think she's sour now, wait until it's noisy after dark."

"Is she holding you two prisoners? We can help," I said jokingly, "we've had one of them ourselves. We'll comply with your request so long as it doesn't interfere with our plans."

Psycholette was true to her word and we were up at six-thirty. We let that little trifecta leave well ahead of us in hopes we would not cross them again. We spent the rest of the day awkwardly stumbling over the roots and rocks that somehow kept these trees up right, though it seemed none of the roots went down, only across the trail. Sometime after lunch we fell in with two more new hikers we hadn't met before. They seemed like decent guys and kept pace with us.

We got to the shelter and our two new friends set up their tents away from the shelter. Psycholette was there sitting by herself on the edge of the shelter because no one apparently likes her. Another hiker came in with his dog and as soon as he let the dog off the leash it ran over to one of the tents that the guys had just set up, lifted its leg, and peed through the netting into his tent.

The dog was just finishing up when Psycholette, who was sitting alone, cause no one likes her, laughed and said, "Hey look at the dog."

The hikers turned and one of the two yelled, "What the hell man? Look at your dog, he peed in my tent." He was pissed about it.

"I'm sorry man, I would have stopped Barky if I saw him." The dog's owner was visibly shaken.

"Well what are you gonna do about it? Being sorry doesn't help me. My bag and tent smell like dog piss man. If you're gonna have your fucking dog out here at least have it under control, and what kind of stupid asshole name for a dog is Barky?"

"I think Barky and I will just be moving on." He put Barky back on the leash and headed out.

"Yeah I think that would be your best move right now. If you stay I'll be pissing all over your stuff while you sleep, even your dog, we'll see how you like it." The guy was extremely upset, he didn't know what he was going to do with his urine covered equipment.

Confrontation is never pleasant, unless of course you're the ones stirring the pot. He turned to Psycholette, "You couldn't stop the dog? No wonder no one likes you."

That hit her hard. She went over to the register and began channeling her feelings into the daily entry. Matt, never one to "let sleeping dogs lie" as our friends say in the south, went over later to see what poetry she had written.

"Hey Dad, you ought to see this. We need to be vigilant 'cause I think she likes us."

"What's that supposed to mean?" I took the register from his hand and read it to myself. She had written "I will kill the ones I like first so they won't have to watch the others bleed to death."

"That's not even something Psycho would write," Matt said.

"Well Matt, I think I'll be killed first, I hope she doesn't bleed you too long. Let's make sure we're on the opposite side of the shelter from her. We could offer up Panda as a buffer if he were here, but we'll be chancing it tonight."

"You know, she would have made Psycho a good wife."

We were both tired and sore and looking to turn in for the night, we wondered if we were allowed to turn in before eight-thirty, would that be okay with Psycholette?

The hiker we now called "Pissed Off" would not stop bitching about his urine-soaked tent. I felt for him on some fundamental level, but when you want to sleep it overrides emotional responses. I was getting frustrated and began to recite Hamlet in my head, "to die, to sleep, to sleep perchance to dream, aye, there's the rub, for in this sleep of death what dreams may come." At this point in the story Hamlet was thinking of killing himself. He must have hiked the AT.

As we headed through Monson we met several out of the ordinary hikers. "Just Charlie" who was finishing the trail this year after thirty-nine years of section hiking. I had a hard time imagining Panda continuing to do this for thirty years. That's perseverance. We also ran into "Disco," a seventeen-year-old girl who had just completed high school. I don't think at that age I would have let my daughter go solo, but then again you will never see my daughter anywhere near the woods. Disco was the youngest solo hiker Matt and I have encountered out here, but she told us there was a fourteen-year-old somewhere out on the trail doing it for some school credits, though she was being shadowed by her parents for support. Where were these options when I was in school?

    148.9 miles to go.

Chapter 59
The Home Stretch

The next morning brought a red dawn, and by that I mean the red squirrels. They were fierce on this section of the trail. They would come out of nowhere and charge at us then break off at the last-minute. It was funny, but a bit nerve wracking at the same time. What if one of these buggers actually decided to attack? And why? It seemed to us they were hunting in packs of five, like velociraptors.

"These little bastards are challenging us," I said to my son.

"Challenge them back, they are significantly smaller than deer, so you should be able to take them." My son is just hilarious sometimes.

They were using ninja tactics, two would run in front of us and block the trail, two would flank us on each side, and one would hang back to cut off our retreat. Another hiker in the area told us they saw these little jerks kick the shit out of a gray squirrel. They have no fear, but I'm sure they can smell it.

Another issue I took with Maine, which to be honest is prevalent everywhere, but I'm going to bitch about it anyway, was the "false summits." A false summit is like a padded bra, you're always disappointed when you get there. You climb, vertically it seems, and just when you think you're at the top because it's nothing but blue skies ahead of you, the trail flattens out for one-hundred yards and you repeat the process. It's happened as many as five times on a single mountain. It's frustrating, exhausting, and downright mean. All one can do is buy into the philosophy that the trail with always go up, no matter what, it just goes up.

We hit the town of Caratunk, better known on the trail as "Caradrunk." We decided not to take a "zero" day but took a "beer-o" day instead. We spent the rest of the day in town, drank our fill, slept it off, and headed back into the mountains the following day, in what we would call a state of semi-sobriety.

"You know Dad, I checked the guidebook and it says if we do seventeen miles today it would be the same as climbing the Empire State Building five times. Pretty cool huh?"

"No, it's not cool, why would you even tell me that? Now all I'm going to be able to think about is all day is me climbing a freaking staircase. I knew I should've smothered you in your sleep with a pillow as a baby, then none of this would be happening." I felt a bit better letting him know I've spared his life so many times.

"Nice, real nice. You're not going to win Father of the Year with statements like that. I should have convinced Psycholette to kill you that night."

"Then you would be out here all alone and I am the bank."

"Yeah, that may be true, enjoy climbing your stairs jerk," Matt finished and picked up his pace, clearly a bit annoyed at me once again. I could live with that.

We were coming up to the Kennebec River Ferry and because of that we had to plan our hike around the ferry's schedule, or so we thought. The ferry turned out to be just a canoe. Hikers used to, and sometimes still do, ford the Kennebec River. It's not really allowed these days because the dam can release up the river without any warning causing the water levels to rise very quickly and flow much faster. It became dangerous for the hikers. The

ATC made the canoe part of the trail since the river is usually two hundred feet wide and a few feet deep in certain spots when flowing regularly. The even painted a white blaze on the canoe for us "purists."

"Dad, want to ford it? Looks pretty low today." My genius son was thinking of wading across.

"No." I climbed into the canoe, and he followed. I may have called his bluff at the beginning of the trail, but we were close to finishing and I was singularly focused. Once safely across the river we went without incident for a few days. It was nice to have some good old-fashioned boring days.

Our mileage count was starting to dwindle, instead of weeks to go we were now getting into days to go. It wasn't sinking in that we were almost finished, because in our minds the damn trail never ended.

We did have our third and last moose encounter. It went pretty much the same as the other two. It still gave me a sinking feeling in my stomach to see an animal that large and dangerous so close to us. We came around a bend and a full-grown bull was in the middle of the trail about fifty yards ahead.

"Okay, Matt, you know the drill, move slowly behind a tree." There were not a lot of them around. "And whatever you do, do not clack your sticks together, you don't want to lose your virginity to a moose. Right?"

I was sliding over toward a tree near me with both sticks above my head in an attempt to make myself look bigger. I was sure not to clack them myself, I've seen what happens when a pony lusted after me, I don't think I can handle a moose.

"Be quiet Matt, I'm busy saving your life again." I loved saying that to him. The moose began walking toward us, we had been told they have bad eyesight, we wondered if it had seen us. "Matt get out the camera."

He began to fumble for his phone so he could snap a picture of this thing. It's stopped twenty yards or so away and stared into my soul. It let out a loud bray and bounded off into the woods. I had won this battle of alphas.

"You get a picture?" I asked Matt.

"Nope, couldn't get it out in time, plus the phone takes too long to turn on, but don't worry, I burned it into my mind."

Two guys walked up behind us, we had been so focused on the moose in front of us that we never heard them coming. "You looked pretty silly there, with your poles up in the air," the younger one said.

I was a bit embarrassed. "Survival skills guys, I saved the little one's life." I was trying to recover whatever I could of my dignity, but it didn't help with Matt standing next to me rolling his eyes, again.

"Well, that was our first moose, at least we got pictures," the older one said.

"Of the moose or of me? I better never see a picture of me on the Internet without explicit written consent." They only had my back I suppose, until I heard the unmistakable click of a camera in front of my face.

"Thanks man, I'm gonna call you "Mooseman" in my journal. I take pics so I don't forget."

Just great I thought, I'm sure he has a well-read blog at Liberal U, but Mooseman was a cool name I thought. "So, where you guys headed?"

They were obviously heading south like we were. "We're just doing a section hike down to the Notch, we got a car waiting there," he said it like it was a stroll in the park. "We'll be there in three days by my count, which means back into my own bed. We've been out here about ten days. What about you guys?"

"Well a bit longer than that," I answered. "Hey, if we keep up with you guys, think we could "Yogi" a ride into town?" I thought it was a reasonable request.

"Sure thing Mooseman, if you can keep up you can catch a ride."

"I think I can keep up. We'll be there. Let's go Matt, we have some ground to cover, and feel free to call me Mooseman for the rest of the hike." We had planned on taking four days to hike through to the Notch, but we could do it in three if it meant a ride back to civilization. Otherwise we will be spending an extra day hiking into town, likely from the same fire road where we bailed out last time. Matt agreed that three days would be a good way to finish, and a ride to town was even a better way to end the trail.

We got up early those last three days and pushed until sundown. There would be no missing our ride. We will prove our doubters wrong. We could smell the finish line, we could taste it, we, for some reason after all we had been through, we began savoring each step. The conversation even began to turn to life after the trail.

As ever before the gods did not see fit to make those an uneventful three days. We almost made it, but on our last day out I had an "encounter." Much like a bear, Peterman, aka Mooseman, had to shit in the words, badly. There wasn't what I would consider a lot of cover around on the sparse ridgeline, so I went a dozen or so yards off the trail and copped a squat. I was getting myself into position three, hoping this would be my last Chapter 5 in the woods. It was almost sad. Almost.

I knew there was no one behind us, but I've never figured someone would be coming the other way. This was one of those times I forgot I was south bounding. I did have some cover, but just as I'm about to open the bomb doors a gentleman strolled by, saw me, and said "hello" while grinning, and kept on walking. Hiker Babe would have died if she was in my shoes, but it's exactly what I would have done if I were him. It was embarrassing but it got worse.

Two minutes later as I'm finishing up, starting my clean up, two young girls came down the trail. I was coming out of my squat and turned to face them as they were snapping pictures of me wiping my ass.

What did I tell hiker Babe? No one wants to see you crap. Well, here were two girls not only watching, but taking pictures. They giggled and shuffled away. I pulled my pants up, not quite sure what to make of what just happened. I reluctantly made my way over to where Matt was waiting for me, sitting on a rock.

"Hey, you see those two girls go past? Not bad eh?"

"Yeah, I saw them, and they saw me." I told Matt what happened and I waited for his laughter to subside, which seemed to take an hour.

"It's not funny, now there's going to be pictures of me crapping on Facebook, Tweeter, Twix, whatever the hell you stupid kids are using. What the hell is wrong with people?"

"Well now it's even funnier when you put it that way," Matt continued laughing.

As much as I hated backtracking I wasn't letting those girls go without deleting those pictures, I want the world to meet the new Planet Bob, not his moon. "Matt, I'm leaving my pack here, I'm gonna catch up to them, they can't be that far down the trail."

"Okay, but I'm sure it would make a great cover for the Backpacker magazine."

I left Matt there and caught up with the girls and the other man who turned out to be one girl's father. I briefly explained to the man what had happened. "I would greatly appreciate it if they would delete those photos."

"Girls, give me your phones," he took their phones and started going through the pictures. He chuckled at the pictures and started deleting them. "You know, next time you can take two hundred yards of string, tie it around a tree and go further into the woods." Now where have I heard that before? Maybe it was a good idea.

"Girls, I've deleted those pictures. You have no need of them and frankly it's a little disturbing, however you'll have fond memories of this moment, I'm sure." Smart man. "Besides, do you really want to share a picture of an old man shitting in the woods with your friends?"

"Old man?" I asked feigning insult. "I appreciate the cooperation ladies," I said to all of them, gave a curt nod and turned back to meet Matt. I could hear them all laughing as I left. It's made me a bit red in the face, but I centered myself in our efforts of the final push.

We had kept up with the two younger guys I've taken to calling "Frick and Frack." We found them about a mile or two from the Notch. They were "cowboy camping" under the stars and we thought it would be an appropriate last night on the trail. We spent our first night out on the trail, not exactly under the stars, but in our tent, roughing it none the least.

It was a good last night. We had our tents assembled in under two minutes, our bedrolls inflated, sleeping bags rolled out across them, all in under five minutes. We were models of efficiency. It was amazing the contrast from the first night. We distilled what initially took us an hour down to ten minutes or so. When it came to cooking, I did everything as usual while Matt built a campfire. I made dinner, our last "PFG" Mountain House meal. After eating our dinner, we cleaned our eating implements and hung our bear bag, and since I was hanging the bags it was also done quickly and efficiently.

We awoke the next morning to a spectacular sunrise from the east of Old Speck Mountain. The kind of sunrise you imagined Alexander the Great saw before winning his most challenging battles. It was a sunrise that had destiny written on it.

"This is it Dad, try to stay in one piece, will ya?"

"Funny kid, but I have to make it, no side trails on this side for me to bail on." My adrenaline was flowing. This was the combination of a lot of hard work, years of my life that went into the planning and preparing.

Approaching the Notch as a SOBO, you start off on a section known as "The Arm." In most parts it's just granite on the trail, with almost no growth. It looked to be about a mile or so downhill, not the best way to start the morning, but again, it was the last mile.

Matt and I got to the top of the notch. "Jesus, it looks like we're climbing down into hell," Matt said softly.

The kid could not have been more right. "Back into the belly of the beast that bit me last time," I proclaimed for no reason as we started descending. We had started out before Frick and Frack were even stirring. I've stated it before, we would be damned if we were missing a ride. We could not see them behind us, so we felt good about our pace.

"Matt, just do me one favor. If you make it out of here and I don't, I want you to cremate me and spread my ashes as far from Maine as possible."

"That's one promise I'd be happy to keep," Matt replied smiling. I think he was imagining killing me in his head and using the insurance money to spread my ashes in Bora Bora, just so he could take the vacation.

"You know if you kill me there is still Patti," I blurted out, letting him know I could read his mind at the moment.

"Oh, I've got that covered," he responded not missing a beat. He was strolling ahead of me whistling "Chopin's Funeral March." He's back out of the will again.

As we spiraled downward into the Notch it was a lot of hand over hand climbing, sliding, scooting, going over boulders, going under boulders, and then the agony of taking our backpacks on and off again to squeeze under and through some rock passages. We kept looking for blazes as some makeshift mile marker was ticking off our progress. It was not hard to understand why this was considered the most difficult mile on the trail. I was holding off patting myself on the back for not slipping on the way down, but now that I was at the bottom I did take a moment to congratulate myself. That's also when Frick and Frack overtook us.

"Come on old man, you can do it... I have nice soft plush seats in my car just waiting for you." Frick waved me on as they passed.

"I'll be there," I countered. "Just don't leave an old man behind." I didn't mind the name calling since he was driving, and I did feel like an old man in the moment.

The climb was difficult. This was bullshit. As horrible as the climb down was, climbing up was much worse. It was the same over under we explained on the way down. It took us an hour longer than we anticipated. Matt and I were going as fast as we could but both of us were nervous about being left for dead.

458

But then it happened. The moment each step had led to since we started several million steps ago. The sun hit our faces, the singing, glistening, bouncing sun with a smile on his face was there, not the evil Joker smile I've encountered with all the women in my life, but Mister Bluebird on my shoulder kind of smile. I stood taller than I had stood in years, or so it seemed.

Frick and Frack were sitting on the trunk of their car where they were parked, slow clapping as Matt and I took those last few steps that have consumed our lives for so long.

"You made it old man," Frick said slapping me on my shoulder. "You finished the trail." Frack high-fived me.

And that was it. No band, no crowd, no fanfare, not even family, just a slight breeze across my face and the sounds of buzzing bugs. I turned around and said it triumphantly aloud to no one in particular, "I finished the trail."

Matt on the other hand still had his pack on and was doing his best Rocky impression, shadow boxing and jogging in place throwing his hands up in the air. He finally threw his pack to the ground and the sense of relief was palpable.

"So, you gonna come back and redo the parts I missed?" he asked me. He didn't miss that much of the trail, and besides, he survived on his own for a night or two, he'd be fine.

"I finished the trail, you're on your own amigo." I still couldn't believe what I was saying.

We changed out of our sweaty clothes in the parking lot, took one last look up at the mountains and loaded into the car. Matt and I sat in the back quietly as we drove out of the mountains into town. This was one of the coolest things I've ever done, I sat there swelling with pride with the sun shining on my face, a massive grin ear to ear. Into town, and obscurity, we went.

Chapter 60
Life After the Trail

I don't know when exactly when the feeling hit, maybe it was the Welcome to North Carolina sign, or maybe when I finally stepped back into the house, either way I was home. It felt good to be home, but the truth is I never really missed it to begin with it. I knew it was there for me. It was nice to see all my family and friends again, especially my darling wife, they greeted me as I had hoped, a champion, a conqueror, but that wore off quickly.

It was easy, too easy to slide back into the old routines. I missed the simplicity of what it was, that crazy outdoor bullshit, the routine, the walking, the whole wilderness thing. God help me, I even missed the time with my son. It was great for a while, people bought me drinks and sat eagerly listening to my stories of survival, but life was noticeably different to me. My bed, for example, is a modern marvel of sleep engineering and yet I would find myself sleeping on the floor when I couldn't sleep at night. I caught myself a time or two getting out of bed half asleep, walking to the edge of the area rug, and whipping it out. I came to realize I'm not standing at the edge of a shelter and would stop myself just before peeing on the floor. At least that was funny.

Food tasted notably different. I suppose my doctor would say it's for the best, but everything tasted salty, unbearably so. I had lost over fifty pounds from my time on the trail. That gave rise to a better sex life, but even that was temporary.

I generally never mind discussing my time on the trail with people and telling my story, it's mostly what inspired me to write it all down, but it gets repetitive answering the same set of questions over and over, who'd you go with? My son. Where did you go? Everywhere the trail went. How'd you do it? With a lot of research. What did you do all day? Hike. Last but not least, why did you do it? Now that's still a damn good question.

Another positive to come from this whole experience is that I no longer mind golfing in the rain. It's just water after all.

Matt and I often discuss what we considered the worst of times, because in hindsight they were the best times. The crazy storms, the crazy people, the crazy run-ins with the wildlife, that's what we remember most, the craziness. I still glow with pride knowing I can bat my eyes at a pony and get results.

As I had said at the start of this story, we didn't do this for any one good reason, but here's the thing I think I took foremost from the trail, it has made a difference in me. I did learn things from the experience. I am even more independent, self-reliant. Nothing that happens seems that bad. It happened, we deal with it and move on. Yesterday can't be changed, so I will move forward. Carpe diem. I am Planet Bob.

I did come out with a new-found respect for the wilderness, the national programs, which I now support, realizing how quickly we are losing our natural resources as they become encroached upon by civilization. Please donate.

Whenever Patti and I drive to visit family and the highway goes over or passes the AT, I make a comment. Patti beats me to the to it these days, "I know, I know, you've been there." But I don't care, I still shout "Hey, I've been there!" and the remembrance of a story that happened nearby pops into my head.

As for the kid, Firestarter nee Turtle Stamper nee Silvertoes, he lives in Nashville now. I'm proud of him and the things he accomplished. I watched him change before my eyes, maturing, turning into an adult. I got to see him change from idiot to man, though he can revert back from time to time. Despite his protestations, I know he enjoyed every minute of it. I truly hope he finishes the parts he missed.

I still keep in touch with Psycho, who now knows his name is Psycho. Panda let it slip one day on a phone call. "Yo Peterman, you been calling me Psycho behind my back this whole time? That's some sick shit." He began laughing, "I knew I liked you guys."

Panda did move to Colorado where weed is legal and made an honest woman of SLiF. We also stay in touch and visit each other from time to time. However, since he learned of this book he has been threatening lawsuits for slander.

I can still picture "Buns of Steel" in my mind, that's forever.

To this day neither Matt nor I would consider ourselves experts in hiking or the outdoors. Everything we learned was mostly by trial and error. After having done this I would definitely not recommend someone to throw themselves into it like we did. Go for a week, see if you like it, otherwise it could be a monumental waste of time and money.

We obviously could not have been successful, if that's what you want to call it, without Patti. She was our lifeline for the entire trip. She understood why I needed to do it in the first place, even if I didn't. She continued to supply us with food drops, which she would prepare herself sometimes. She came in visited us all over nowhere Appalachia, lifting our spirits each time. That had a lot to do with the slack packing more than her, but we'll count it. More importantly though, she took the time, the time to do it all, and she did it for us. She got nothing out of it, well except for a few months of peace and quiet.

We had other friends and family along the way who were vital to us as well, I hope they know who they are. People opening their homes to us and for that we are still grateful. Friends are forever.

Lastly, we wrote the story based on our journals and memories. This is eyewitness account of our story, however in law enforcement we know firsthand witnesses can't always be trusted. All these stories are true, but what is truth really? I believe these accounts to be as they happened. If you ask Matt it might sound a bit different, but whatever happened never asked Psycho, he can't be trusted.

Final Rummy score was me, 187,897 and Matt, 187,546. I win!

Best of all, 0 miles to go.

The God Damn End!

Author's Note

Stories related in this book are all based on true events, and as Matt said earlier, some exaggerated over time, but otherwise true or based on true instances. It should be noted that the hike occurred over a two-year period. The first year we got to Maine and I did get injured, and the second year when we finished Maine.

If you enjoyed reading this book, please go to **Amazon.com** and leave a review.

Made in the USA
Columbia, SC
30 June 2019